Hemingway

AND HIS WORLD

Hemingway

AND HIS WORLD
— by —
A.E. Hotchner

The Vendome Press
New York: Paris

Photo research by Linda Sykes and Joanne Polster
of PhotoSearch, Inc., New York City

Designed by Marc Walter of Arbook, Paris, France

First published in Great Britain by Penguin Books, Ltd
Copyright © The Vendome Press
First published in the United States of America by
The Vendome Press, 515 Madison Avenue, N.Y., N.Y. 10022
Distributed in the United States by
Rizzoli International Publications
300 Park Avenue South, N.Y., N.Y. 10010

Library of Congress Cataloging-in-Publication Data
Hotchner, A.E.
    Hemingway and his world/by A.E. Hotchner.
        p.   cm.
    Bibliography: p
    Includes index.
    ISBN 0-86565-115-9
    1. Hemingway, Ernest, 1899-1961.   2. Authors, American—20th
century—Biography.   I. Title.
PS3515.E37Z634   1989
813′.52—dc20
[B]   89-16444
Printed in Italy   CIP

CONTENTS

FOREWORD

There were two deep currents that ran simultaneously through the tumultuous life of Ernest Hemingway: one was the urge to participate fully in and experience richly the joys and sorrows of existence; the other was the ability to assess these experiences and record them accurately on the printed page. Ernest was an original man. No one else's word was good enough. He had to taste, smell, see, hear for himself. And what he saw and heard and experienced he wrote about in a way that made the reader feel himself a part of it.

Ernest was forty-nine when I met him. He had been married four times, been under fire in three wars, and had restlessly roamed the world—tramping through the northern Michigan woods, fishing for marlin in the Caribbean, hunting for big game in Africa, following the bulls in Spain. He had incorporated these experiences into short stories and such novels as *The Sun Also Rises* (1926) and *A Farewell to Arms* (1929), which had brought to American literature a new style of writing—lyrically simple, direct, realistic—a style that has influenced writers the world over.

"All good books have one thing in common," he once said. "After you've read one of them you will feel that it all happened, happened to you, and that it belongs to you forever: the happiness and unhappiness, good and evil, ecstasy and sorrow. If you can give that to the reader, then you're a writer."

Ernest asked me to adapt some of his work for television, a challenge that involved traveling with him all over the globe, visiting the scenes of his youth and the settings of his stories. We shot birds at his ranch in Idaho, went on the matador circuit in Spain, swam at his place in Key West, Florida, and played the races in Paris. With him I toured the windswept slopes of the Escorial where as a correspondent he had lived with the Loyalist soldiers during the Spanish Civil War, drove along the lovely French roads he had once cycled with Scott Fitzgerald, and walked through the Paris park where as a starving young writer he had caught pigeons for food.

Ernest worked hard when he was writing, and when he was not writing he practiced the art of relaxation with equal dedication. He was never in too much of a hurry to savor the pleasures around him. He had been almost everywhere and had absorbed almost all there was to know about the places he had visited. His knowledge of local terrain, weather, customs, history, orchards, birds, wines, dishes, wild flowers, architecture, and government was prodigious, and he held forth on these topics frequently and cheerfully.

His intense interest in the passing countryside tended to make traveling with him slow, though pleasurable. A stretch which could be covered in one day's driving would take us five. He liked to stop for leisurely picnics or to tarry at street fairs in little towns along the way, mingling with people, testing his skill at the shooting booths, soaking up the impressions that would later appear in his writing.

Once at the races at Auteuil, the gemlike track in Paris' Bois de Boulogne, Ernest stood raptly watching the people crowding to the betting windows. "Listen to their heels on the wet pavement," he said. "It's all so beautiful in this misty light. Mr. Degas could have painted it and gotten the light so that it would be truer on canvas than what we see. This is what an artist must do. On canvas or printed page he must capture the thing so truly that its magnification will endure."

Although his dedication to his writing was a side of Ernest the public never saw, it was the most important aspect of his character. "You need the devotion to your work that a priest of God has for his," he once said. Writing was an arduous ordeal for him, exhilarating, but demanding all of what he called his "juices." When he had a book in progress, he was totally consumed by it, and at the end of each day he would count the number of words he had written and enter them carefully in a log.

"I've seen every sunrise of my life," he said. "I rise at first light, and I start by reading and editing everything I have written to the point where I left off. That way I go through a book several hundred times, honing it until it gets an edge like the bullfighter's sword. I rewrote the ending of *A Farewell to Arms* thirty-two times in manuscript and worked it over thirty times in proof, trying to get it right."

He probably best summed up his feelings about writing in accepting the Nobel Prize. "For a true writer," he said, "each book should be a new beginning, where he tries for something that is beyond attainment. He should always try for something that has never been done or that others have tried and failed. It is because we have had such great writers in the past that a writer is driven far out past where he can go, out to where no one can help him."

To go far past where one can go, to face eternity every day, to try for something that is beyond attainment—these things require courage of the highest order. Ernest's was that. He seemed to court danger. As an eighteen-year-old Red Cross volunteer on the Italian front in World War I, he was in a trench with three infantry-men when an Austrian *Minenwerfer* scored a direct hit on them, killing two of the Italians and mangling his own right leg. Badly wounded as he was, Ernest managed to hoist the Italian who was still alive onto his back and carry him across a field that was being raked by machine-gun fire. The soldier was dead by the time he got him to safety, but for that exploit Ernest was awarded two of Italy's highest medals. A surgeon later removed twenty-eight pieces of metal from his leg.

Papa had similar close calls in the Spanish Civil War. During World War II, he went to France as a war correspondent, but quickly abandoned that role for active combat. Artist John Groth recalls coming upon a French farmhouse being used by Ernest and the band of irregular troops he was leading. They were at dinner when German 88s opened up on them, spraying plaster and shattered glass all over the room. Everyone at the table made a dive to the potato cellar—except for Ernest. He continued calmly sitting at the table, eating cheese and drinking wine.

"How can you just sit there?" the amazed Groth asked.

"Groth," Ernest replied, "if you hit the deck every time you hear a pop, you'll wind up with chronic indigestion."

But, for all his courageous exploits, and his formidable outward appearance, Ernest was a shy and a gentle man. His voice became strained and tense just talking on the telephone. He refused to speak publicly because of his intense shyness; when he won the Nobel Prize for literature his graceful acceptance speech was read at Stockholm by the United States Ambassador to Sweden.

This shy, sensitive side of Ernest was seen only by his friends, towards whom he was boundlessly generous with his money, his possessions, and his time—which to him was more valuable than the other two. There were a half-dozen old pals, down on their luck, who received regular remittances from Ernest. And he responded with dispatch to any cry of emergency from any friend. Ernest had his own test of friendship. "The way to learn whether a person is trustworthy is to trust him," he said.

With his extraordinary good looks, his quiet intensity and animal magnetism, his avid curiosity about everything and everybody, his warmth and wit, the young Hemingway developed a charismatic personality as well as a genius for friendship. Scarcely had he arrived in Paris, at the age of twenty-two, when he forged fruitful relationships with some of the most advanced literary and artistic figures of their time: Ezra Pound, James Joyce, Gertrude Stein, Sylvia Beach, Wyndham Lewis, and Ford Madox Ford; André Masson, Joan Miró, Jules Pascin, and Pablo Picasso. Within his own generation, meanwhile, he virtually dominated a circle made up of such gifted individuals as John Dos Passos, Archibald

MacLeish, Scott Fitzgerald, Gerald and Sara Murphy. Later, in Key West and Cuba, in the Far West, New York, and Spain, there would be lasting bonds with his editor at Scribner's, the great Max Perkins; with celebrities like Marlene Dietrich, Gary Cooper, Toots Shor, and Leonard Lyons; with foreign correspondents Herbert Matthews and Bill Walton; Philip Percival, the white hunter; General "Buck" Lanham; the matador Antonio Ordóñez; Bill Purdy, the Ketchum rancher; sportsman Winston Guest; and Bill Davis, a Málaga expatriate.

Yet, Ernest's standards of friendship were very high and difficult to define. One of those standards was certainly his requirement that his friends be people who "stick together when things are impossible." This unquestioning loyalty was what Ernest prized most highly, to be given and to be received, and it was a trait common to all those with whom he had long and lasting relations. There could be no better demonstration of the principle than the occasion in early 1941 when Hemingway, at the height of his fame following the publication of *For Whom the Bell Tolls*, learned from Solita Solano, the short-story writer, that Margaret Anderson, who had published Ernest's earliest mature stories in *The Little Review*, was penniless and trapped in Occupied Paris, thanks to her having stayed behind to nurse a onetime lover stricken with terminal cancer. Although himself in bed at his New York hotel with grippe, Papa wrote a check to Margaret for $400 (a handsome sum at the time) and sent it to Solita, together with a note that concluded: "Much love Solita and take care of yourself and don't ever worry because as long as any of us have money we all have money."

Given the criteria that Hemingway applied, it can hardly surprise that the mortality rate among his friendships ran high, and if you inquired about someone who had fallen by the way, Ernest would simply tell you that he or she "didn't measure up." It seems to me, in analyzing this mystique, that the real clue to his lasting relations could be found in the fact that the people who stuck were straight and unphony and formed in their own image. One such durable intimate was Marlene Dietrich, who once told me:

We did not see each other often, but we often wrote and his letters were funny and sad and compassionate and sometimes so overwhelming I could have died. He said remarkable things that seemed to adjust automatically to problems of all sizes.

For example, there was the time I called him on the telephone when I was in New York, and he was on his lovely old farm outside Havana. Ernest was alone in the house; he had finished writing for the day, and being a man who loved good conversation and treated it as an art, he wanted to talk. At one point he asked me what work plans I had, if any. I told him that I had just had a very lucrative offer from a Miami night club, but I was undecided about whether to take it.

"Why the indecision, daughter?" he asked.

"Well," I answered, "I feel I should work. I should not waste my time, it's wrong. I think one appearance in London and one a year in Vegas is quite enough. However, I'm probably just pampering myself, so I've been trying to convince myself to take the offer."

There was silence for a moment, and I could visualize Ernest's beautiful face poised to thought. "Daughter," he said, "don't do what you sincerely don't want to do. Never confuse movement with action." In five words he gave me a whole philosophy.

I had always thought of Ernest as indestructible, but in 1960 his health began to deteriorate. He had suffered innumerable injuries in his reckless desire to live life to the fullest, and they began to exact their toll. He became periodically moody and irrational, and was hospitalized at the Mayo Clinic in Rochester, Minnesota.

It was there that I saw him last. I was shocked by his appearance. His once-burly figure had shrunk to 173 pounds, and his hair and beard were white. Yet he talked cheerfully of the good times we had had together. When it came time to go, he walked me to the elevator. "Good Old Hotch," he said. "Put you through a lot, haven't I, boy?" "Through the best times I ever had," I said.

I was hurrying through a Madrid hotel lobby to catch a plane for Rome when a friend told me that Ernest had taken his life at his ranch in Idaho. I did not go to the funeral. I could not say good-by to Ernest in a public group. But that night, thinking about him, I recalled something that editor Ernest Walsh had written of Hemingway back in the twenties, when he had published some of Ernest's first stories in *This Quarter*, an obscure little Paris magazine. "His rewards will be rich," Walsh said. "But thank God he will never be satisfied. He is of the elect."

A.E. HOTCHNER

11

1 8 8 9

THE
EARLY
YEARS

———

1 9 2 1

GRANDPARENTS, PARENTS, SIBLINGS

Ernest Miller Hemingway first saw life at 8 A.M. on the 21st of July 1899. The elder son of an eldest son, he represented the third generation of his family to reside in Oak Park, Illinois, an enclave of puritanical respectability forming part of the western suburbs of Chicago. The name Ernest came from his maternal grandfather, Miller from a great-grandfather. The eponymous Ernest had run away from farm life in the wake of his family's migration to Iowa from England. Following distinguished service in the Civil War, Ernest Hall went on to make a fortune in the wholesale cutlery business. His wife died when their only daughter, Grace, was twenty-three and their son, Leicester, still in his teens. A passionately musical young woman, Grace studied singing in New York and even attempted an operatic career as a contralto, making her debut at Madison Square Garden in 1895. However, poor health, traceable to a childhood bout of scarlet fever, took her back to Illinois, where, in October 1896, she married Clarence Ed-

3

1

1. The turreted and wide-verandaed Hall house at 439 Oak Park Avenue, where Grace and Ed Hemingway lived with her father until he died on May 10, 1905. Ernest, as well as three of his sisters, would be born there.

2

monds (Ed) Hemingway, the studious young doctor across the street. After the wedding, the couple resided with Grace's widowed father, in his large, verandaed, turreted house at 439 North Oak Park Avenue.

Although the beneficiaries of a prosperous real-estate business in Chicago, Ed's father, Anson Hemingway, another Civil War veteran, and his English-born wife, Adelaide, had chosen to rear their children in Oak Park, at a safe, teetotaling distance from the fleshpots of the big city. By the time of his marriage, Ed Hemingway, from whom Ernest inherited his deep, dark, pensive eyes, had already begun to practice general medicine while specializing in obstetrics. A sober, God-fearing man, Dr. Hemingway once took Ernest and his elder sister on a visit to the Illinois State Prison, warning them that children who did not obey their parents ended up

14

2. The Hemingways: Anson, the first of his line to settle in Oak Park, and his English-born wife Adelaide, seated in the presence of five of their six children. Ernest's father is tall, bearded Dr. Ed Hemingway standing at the center. After serving in the Union Army during the Civil War, Anson Hemingway became a successful realtor in Chicago.

3. The Halls: Ernest Hall, the widowed maternal grandfather for whom the novelist would be named, with his two children: Grace, who married Dr. Ed Hemingway, and Leicester. The senior Hall made a small fortune in cutlery, a trade he had learned in his native Sheffield, England. With age, Hall became increasingly English in both manner

4. Ernest Miller Hemingway, some months after his birth on July 21, 1899, the second child and first son of Dr. Ed and Grace Hemingway. "The robins," his mother wrote, "sang their sweetest songs to welcome the little stranger into this beautiful world." However, he would soon disdain the kind of frilly attire seen here to display a strongly masculine voice, along with his dimples and big, alert brown eyes. As Grace wrote at a later point in the scrapbook she kept for Ernest, "[he] delights in shooting imaginary wolves, bears, lions, buffalo, etc. Also likes to pretend he is a 'soldser.' . . . He storms and kicks and dances with rage when thwarted and will stand any amount of rough usage when playing. . . . He is perfectly fearless. When asked what he is afraid of, he shouts out 'fraid of nothing' with great gusto'."

and accent. Grace would always refer to her father and brother as the two finest men she ever knew.

5. Grace Hall dressed as if ready for one of the many singing concerts she gave, including a debut at New York's Madison Square Garden. Gifted with a fine contralto voice and strong musical instincts, Ernest's mother aspired to a career in opera, but her poor eyesight would not tolerate powerful stage lighting. Still, she earned a handsome income as a music teacher and choir director in Oak Park, becoming the principal breadwinner during the early years of her marriage, before Dr. Hemingway built a large practice.

6. Dr. Ed and Grace Hemingway in 1906, with their four eldest children. Six-year-old Ernest and seven-year-old Marcelline stand to the left and right of their parents, who hold Ursula and Sunny, the last-born, on their knees.

7. Grace Hemingway with her second-born, Ernest, at Walloon Lake, Northern Michigan, in early September 1899, just weeks after the child's birth in Oak Park.

there. On less threatening occasions, young Ernest learned from his father, who had learned from *his* father, the gentlemanly craft of fly fishing, as well as bait casting, hunting, and love of unspoiled nature. Perhaps it was generous feeling for and understanding of life in the wild that prompted a confident three-year-old Ernest Hemingway to proclaim himself "fraid a nothing." One challenge he never took on was the household drudgery—cooking and marketing—that his long-suffering father endured, the consequence of a marriage agreement that left Grace Hemingway free to cultivate her artistic interests, mainly teaching music, directing a church choir, and staging family chamber concerts, with a reluctant Ernest recruited for the cello.

8

As this would suggest, Grace Hemingway embodied the new woman of her time. Robust, even formidable in her figure, she was

stuccoed structure—complete with a balconied music room, a doctor's office, rooms for all the children, and space for two live-in servants—reflected the emerging Prairie Style then being developed by a neighbor and pioneer architect, Frank Lloyd Wright.

9

10

an independent-minded suffragette and a fervent disciple of that practical social Christian, Jane Addams. Liberated by her housekeeper, a nanny for her five children, and a husband to oversee the kitchen, Grace could indulge her passion not only for music but also for religion. With his strong-willed mother determined that her brood grow up pious and creatively engaged, Ernest found little chance to escape duty at church, choral singing, or the cello.

After her father died Grace sold the old house in order to build a splendid new one at 600 North Kenilworth Avenue. Although she designed it herself, the broadly eaved,

Thanks to Grace's punctilious habit of keeping thorough scrapbooks on her children, much is known about Ernest in his early and adolescent years. The second-born of Grace and Ed, he had to endure three more of his mother's pregnancies before the brother he longed for finally arrived. This was Leicester, the sixth and last child, too young to be of much interest to the sixteen-year-old Ernest. Their sisters were, in chronological order, Marcelline, Madeline, Ursula, and Carol. Of these, Ursula became her brother's favorite; tragically, along with Dr. Hemingway, Leicester, and Ernest himself, Ursula was destined to commit suicide.

8. The big house at 600 North Kenilworth Avenue, Oak Park, which Grace Hemingway designed and built with the proceeds from her father's estate. Vaguely reflecting the "Prairie Style" of domestic architecture then being perfected by Oak Parker Frank Lloyd Wright, the new house contained not only rooms for six children and two live-in servants but also an office for Dr. Ed and a music "conservatory" for Grace.

9. The parlor of the Hall house, where the young Hemingway family lived with Grace's widowed father until 1906. Leicester Hall sits at his sister's grand piano, while a portrait of their mother hangs at the right.

10. Ernest with Marcelline, his elder sister whom Grace held back a year in school so that she and her brother could be "twinned" from grade to grade.

11

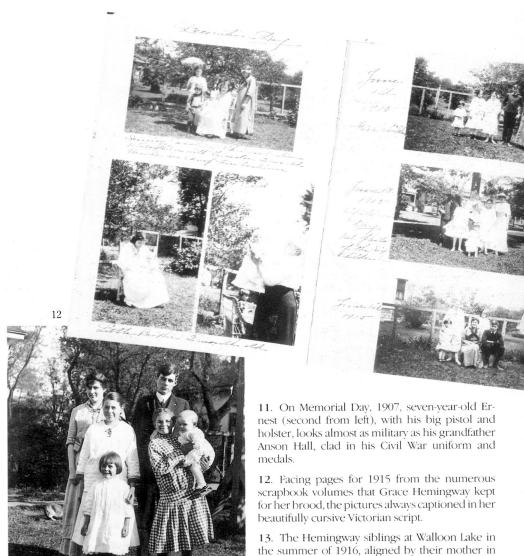

12

11. On Memorial Day, 1907, seven-year-old Ernest (second from left), with his big pistol and holster, looks almost as military as his grandfather Anson Hall, clad in his Civil War uniform and medals.

12. Facing pages for 1915 from the numerous scrapbook volumes that Grace Hemingway kept for her brood, the pictures always captioned in her beautifully cursive Victorian script.

13. The Hemingway siblings at Walloon Lake in the summer of 1916, aligned by their mother in staggered stairstep order, beginning with one-year-old Leicester and proceeding upward with Carol, Sunny, Ursula (Ernest's favorite sister), sixteen-year-old Ernest, and Marcelline.

13

DR. ED HEMINGWAY

As a boy, Ernest enjoyed a special relationship with his father, the two of them becoming intimate co-adventurers dedicated to exploring the outdoor life that still abounded on every side. In the short story "Fathers and Sons," Hemingway vividly recalled the impact his father had on him:

Hunting this country for quail as his father had taught him, Nicholas Adams started thinking about his father. When he first thought about him it was always the eyes. The big frame, the quick movements, the wide shoulders, the hooked, hawk nose, the beard that covered the weak chin, you never thought about it—it was always the eyes. They were protected in his head by the formation of the brows; set deep as though a special protection had been devised for some very valuable instrument. They saw much farther and much quicker than the human eye sees and they were the great gift his father had. His father saw as a big-horn ram or as an eagle sees, literally.

His father came back to him in the fall of the year, or in the early spring when there had been jacksnipe on the prairie, or when he saw shocks of corn, or when he saw a lake, or if he ever saw a horse and buggy, or when he saw, or heard, wild geese, or in a duck blind; remembering the time an eagle dropped through the whirling snow to strike a canvas-covered decoy, rising, his wings beating, the talons caught in the canvas. His father was with him, suddenly, in deserted orchards and in new-plowed fields, in thickets, on small hills, or when going through dead grass, whenever splitting wood or hauling water, by grist mills, cider mills and dams and always with open fires.

The quail country made him remember him as he was when Nick was a boy and he was very grateful to him for two things: fishing and shooting. His father was as sound on those two things as he was unsound on sex, for instance, and Nick was glad that it had

been that way; for someone has to give you your first gun or the opportunity to get it and use it, and you have to live where there is game or fish if you are to learn about them, and now, at thirty-eight, he loved to fish and to shoot exactly as much as when he first had gone with his father. It was a passion that had never slackened and he was very grateful to his father for bringing him to know it.[1]

In the late 1920s Dr. Hemingway suffered a series of devastating humiliations, losing his health to diabetes and his money in the Florida real-estate bubble. A physician unable to heal himself, afraid of becoming an invalid, and trapped with costly interest payments on the Oak Park house and no income flowing from the investments it had been mortgaged to pay for, Dr. Hemingway took his father's .32 revolver and shot himself behind the right ear on December 6, 1928. By this desperate act, he hoped that a life-insurance settlement would solve the problem of supporting his wife, their sixteen-year-old daughter, Carol, and the thirteen-year-old Leicester. At first, it was Dr. Hemingway's brother, a wealthy realtor and bank director, who received the

blame, for having refused to extend requested financial aid. Progressively, however, Ernest tended to hold his mother responsible, citing her "selfish" independence and the extravagant household it entailed, but also her domination of a husband who, driven to self-destruction, seemed to have been guilty of terminal cowardice. The suicide of his father was a trauma that would haunt Ernest all his life. In *For Whom the Bell Tolls*, there is this revelatory passage:

I'll never forget how sick it made me the first time I knew he was a cobarde. *Go on, say it in English.* Coward. *It's easier when you have it said and there is never any point in referring to a son of a bitch by some foreign term. He wasn't any son of a bitch, though. He was just a coward and that was the worst luck any man could have. Because if he wasn't a coward he would have stood up to that woman and not let her bully him. I wonder what I would have been like if he had married a different woman? That's something you'll never know, he thought, and grinned. Maybe the bully in her helped to supply what was missing in the other . . . He understood his father and he forgave him everything and he pitied him but he was ashamed of him.*[2]

1. The horse and buggy in which Dr. Hemingway made house calls before he acquired a "Tin Lizzi."

2. Like father like son, Ernest by the age of five had already developed a love of life in the wild that would only deepen with the years.

3. Clarence (Ed) Hemingway during a tramp through the Great Smoky Mountains in 1891, before his marriage to Grace Hall, the vital, tomboyish girl across the street. Ernest wrote that, with his riveting, deep-set eyes, Ed could see "as big-horn rams or as an eagle, literally." This made him a fabulous wing shot, and as father and son together in a large family dominated by women, Ed and Ernest developed a warm relationship in their shared passion for fishing and hunting.

4. A rare photograph of Dr. Hemingway alone with his elder son, taken when the future novelist was about seventeen. Ernest would later write that his puritanical "father was as sound on [fishing and hunting] as he was unsound on sex."

5. Young Dr. Ed Hemingway not long after his graduation from Rush Medical College in Chicago. Now he had become the man Ernest remembered, in "Fathers and Sons," for "the big frame, the quick movements, the wide shoulders, the hooked, hawk nose, the beard that covered the weak chin, you never thought about it—it was always the eyes—deep set as though a special protection had been devised for some very valuable instrument."

1

FRANK LLOYD WRIGHT

No one had a more profound effect on the Oak Park in which Ernest Hemingway grew up than Frank Lloyd Wright (1867–1959), America's greatest architect. It was here that Wright created his first masterpieces—the famous Prairie Houses—after he moved to the suburb in 1889 and opened his studio in 1895, following a seven-year apprenticeship with Denkmar Adler and Louis H. Sullivan, two titans of the Chicago School. But whereas these form-givers concentrated on commercial architecture—office buildings, the first skyscrapers, department stores, warehouses—Wright found domestic architecture to be the most rewarding outlet for his particular genius. In Oak Park alone, he designed and

2

built some twenty-five houses, to one degree or another marked by his love of the Japanese tradition, with its "floating," broadly overhung roofs, its free-flowing interior spaces, its abstract shapes and feeling for materials, especially wood. Equally characteristic of Wright's work was an innate sense of the organic, expressed in a dynamic assemblage of pure line, surface, and volume radiating along cross axes from the central core of a massive hearth while simultaneously converging upon it. Always present were a clear, harmonious relationship of powerful masses and open areas, deep spaces under low-

1. Frank Lloyd Wright, Oak Park's other famous citizen, during the turn-of-the-century years when he lived in the Chicago suburb, maintained his design studio there, and created the first masterpieces among his signature Prairie Houses.

2. The Robie House (1909), the supreme masterwork of all the Prairie Houses that Wright designed in his Oak Park studio. With its simple forms and clean lines, its strongly projecting horizontal planes, the Robie House found a reflection even in the large new home that Grace Hemingway designed for her family on North Kenilworth Avenue in Oak Park.

3. The living room from Wright's Francis W. Little House (Metropolitan Museum of Art, New York), a 1913 work of a sort that found an echo in Grace Hemingway's music room, with its 15-foot ceiling and slatted-wood balcony.

4, 5. Wright's former studio and home in Oak Park.

3

5

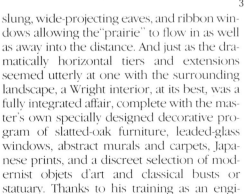

slung, wide-projecting eaves, and ribbon windows allowing the "prairie" to flow in as well as away into the distance. And just as the dramatically horizontal tiers and extensions seemed utterly at one with the surrounding landscape, a Wright interior, at its best, was a fully integrated affair, complete with the master's own specially designed decorative program of slatted-oak furniture, leaded-glass windows, abstract murals and carpets, Japanese prints, and a discreet selection of modernist objets d'art and classical busts or statuary. Thanks to his training as an engineer, Wright proved as innovative in struc-

ture as in aesthetics, pioneering the domestic use of such industrial processes as poured reinforced concrete and steel cantilevers.

Wright's radically modern forms and ideas could be clearly felt in the great three-story, stucco house that Grace Hemingway designed and had built in 1906 for her family on Oak Park's North Kenilworth Avenue. However, after 1909, when Wright ran off with a married woman, he became a "nonperson" in the eyes of his strait-laced neighbors, a fate that would befall Ernest Hemingway once he emerged as a celebrated author of what his own parents considered obscene books.

SCHOOL AND
EARLY SPORTS

Oak Park High was a community showpiece. Built in 1903 at a cost of $300,000, it boasted a class of 150 in the year that Ernest Hemingway graduated as the Class Prophet. Although a star in English, Ernest also excelled at algebra, science, and Latin. One of his English teachers considered him a bit dull, but touching in the way his eyes welled up at the saddest stories. It was in high school that Ernest gave himself the nickname Hemingstein, which stuck for the rest of his life. He edited the school paper and wrote its gossip column, while also contributing to the literary magazine *Tabula*. The newspaper became his vehicle for cultivating the style of his idol, Ring Lardner, the Chicago sports writer famous for his sardonic humor and idiomatic,

or racy, language and imagery. Perhaps still more influential on young Hemingway's writing were Rudyard Kipling and his poems as well as stories of masculine grace under fire.

Ernest tried his best in sports, but his gangly size and consequent lack of coordination defeated him. He went in for the swimming, cross-country, and football teams, with the most disheartening results. The football coach constantly berated him for his slowness at pulling guard. The sole satisfaction that Ernest experienced in sports may have come from a token event, plunging—diving from poolside and floating along as far as possible without coming up for air.

Literary critics later maintained that Ernest benefited in his writing from an unhappy childhood, but he refuted the allegation vehemently:

I never had an unhappy day I can remember! I was no good at football, but does that make an unhappy boyhood? Zuppke put me at center but I never knew what a digit was—I skipped third grade so never found out about digits—so I couldn't figure out the plays. I used to look at my teammates' faces and guess who looked like they expected the ball. I was called Drag-ass when they put me at guard. I wanted to play backfield but they knew better. There was one guy on the team beat me up in the locker room every day for two years, but then I grew up to him and I beat the shit out of him and that was the end of that.

Ernest pestered his father for boxing lessons until the Doctor finally gave him, as a fourteenth-birthday present, a series of lessons at a Chicago gym. At the first one, Hemingway was asked if he'd like to go a few minutes with Young A'Hearn, who was then a high-ranking middleweight in training for a big fight. After punching him playfully in the ribs and promising to take it easy, A'Hearn actually gave Hemingway the full treatment and sent him to the canvas with a broken nose. Later Ernest told a friend:

"I knew he was going to give me the works the minute I saw his eyes."

"Were you scared?" the friend asked.

"Sure," Hemingway answered, "he could hit like hell."

"Well, then, why did you go in there with him?"

"I wasn't that scared."

Hemingway didn't know it, but the first-day treatment he had received was standard procedure, and very few students, despite having

paid in advance, came back for the rest of their lessons. But not Hemingway, who surprised the management when he walked in the following day, ready to finish his course, with a heavy bandage over his busted nose.

Besides sports, Ernest debated in the Burke Club, shot for the Boys' Rifle Club, and played a cello in the high-school orchestra.

Inspired by former war correspondent Richard Harding Davis' *Stories for Boys*—particularly one story about a young reporter—Ernest decided not to go to college but, rather, to become a newspaper reporter. His father and grandfather, both Oberlin graduates, exerted great pressure on him to follow the family's academic tradition, which had already sent Ernest's elder sister, Marcelline, to the Ohio college. But Ernest resisted their entreaties, preferring to concentrate on a possible reporting job he had heard about at the *Kansas City Star*. In the meantime, he bided his time during an indolent post-graduate summer alone in Michigan at Walloon Lake.

4

5

1. Oak Park High School, built in 1903 and the pride of the suburban community. After completing its strong, traditionally academic curriculum, Ernest and his sister Marcelline graduated together in the class of 1917.

2. Oak Park High's football team, with Ernest seated in the second row from the right. By his own admission, he was a "Drag-ass" guard.

3. Oak Park High's class of 1917. Ernest and his sister Marcelline are both in the front row, he second from the right and she third from the left.

4, 5. The Valentine issue of *The Tabula* for February 1916. As the table of contents and Grace Hemingway's caption indicate, it carried Ernest's story entitled "The Judgment of Manitou."

6. Ernest had a bit more success on the Oak Park High swimming team, but even in water sports he excelled mainly at "plunging."

7. Ernest Hemingway's report card halfway through his junior year at Oak Park High, showing him to have been not only a very good student but also "impov[ed]" both in attitude and work," at least as far as Latin was concerned.

6

7

1

WALLOON LAKE

It was in the wilderness world of northern Michigan, at the edge of cold, spring-fed Walloon Lake, that the Hemingways had established their warm-weather getaway, the place where Ernest spent every one of his first seventeen summers. Nearby stood a small sawmill town and a settlement of Ojibway Indians. Until the Hemingways bought an automobile, they traveled north by steamer across Lake Michigan and then by train to their holiday home. There, in the year of Ernest's birth, Ed and Grace had bought an acre and built the first of two cottages, which survive today, still used by Hemingway descendants. In honor of her favorite author, Sir Walter Scott, Grace named the cottage Windemere. As the family grew, so did the property, which soon included a three-room cabin for the kids to sleep in, although Ernest preferred to camp out in a tent. After her father died, Grace used part of her inheri-

3

tance to buy a forty-acre farm across the lake, where a teenage Ernest would work hard to harvest corn, potatoes, and orchards full of plums and Jonathan apples. Ernest's boyhood experiences at Walloon Lake became the rich, raw material for many of his most haunting short stories, among them "The Three-Day Blow," "Up in Michigan," "Ten Indians," "Fathers and Sons," and "The End of Something."

Although a model family in appearances, the Hemingways were actually beset by growing tensions. The parents quarreled about money, which Grace spent in lavish amounts, and they also disagreed about how to raise the children, which Grace preferred to entrust to others. In 1911 the senior Hemingways occupied separate bedrooms in their summer cottage, where Ed could afford to spend only a few weeks each summer. Years later, Ernest captured this estrangement with telling effect in two short stories: "The Doctor and the Doctor's Wife" and "Indian Camp." Such marital strife became all the more poignant for being set within a natural paradise, the limpid beauty of which Hemingway evoked in another story, "Fathers and Sons":

[The Indian camp] was reached by a trail which ran from the cottage through the woods to the farm and then by a road which wound through the slashings to the camp.... First there was the pine-needle loam through the hemlock woods behind the cottage where the fallen logs crumbled into wood dust and long splintered pieces of wood hung like javelins in the tree that had been struck by lightning. You crossed the creek on a log and if you stepped off there was the black muck of the swamp. You climbed a fence out of the woods and the trail was hard in the sun across the field with cropped grass and sheep sorrel and mullen growing and to the left the quaky bog of the creek bottom where the killdeer plover fed. The spring house was in that creek. Below the barn there was fresh warm manure and the other older manure that was caked dry on top. Then there was another fence and the hard, hot trail from the barn to the house and the hot sandy road that ran down to the woods, crossing the creek, on a bridge this time, where the cat-tails grew that you soaked in kerosene to make jack-lights with for spearing fish at night....

But there was still much forest then, virgin forest where the trees grew high before there were any branches and you walked on the brown, clean, springy-needled ground with no undergrowth and it was cool on the hottest days.... [1]

Lake Superior

Two Hearted River / Little Two Hearted River

Fox River · Seney

Lake Michigan

Mackinaw City

Lake Huron

Little Traverse Bay · Harbor Springs
Charlevoix · Petoskey
Horton Bay · Walloon Lake
Lake Charlevoix · Boyne City
Grand Traverse Bay

· Mancelona

MICHIGAN

2

24

5

6

4

1. Walloon Lake, the forested wilderness in northern Michigan where Ed and Grace Hemingway bought an acre of land in 1899 and built the cottage that would become the family's vacation home. Ernest spent every one of his first seventeen summers there, and would continue to visit until he left for Paris in late 1921. It was in this natural paradise that his revered father imparted to him a lifelong passion for fishing and hunting, swimming and tramping through rough country. For Ernest, the unspoiled beauty of the region and the simple, informal lifestyle of the people who inhabited it offered a welcome respite from the Victorian propriety of Oak Park. Here, too, Ernest found the rich material for his first stories.

2. Northern Michigan, where the Hemingways spent their summers in the cool, wooded region centering on Walloon Lake, but ranging afield as far as Harbor Springs, Petoskey, Boyne City, Charlevoix, and Horton Bay, in whose little Methodist church Ernest would make his first marriage vows in September 1920.

3. Ernest deep in the virgin hemlock forest near Walloon Lake in the summer of 1916, walking "on the brown, clean, springy-needled ground. . . ."

4, 5. Windemere, the cottage that Ed and Grace Hemingway built on the shore of cold, spring-fed Walloon Lake and that Grace named in memory of her ancestral England. As their family grew and grew, the couple added a kitchen wing and then a bedroom annex. Still, Windemere remained rustic and isolated, as Marcelline, Ernest's elder sister, would later write: "It consisted of a living room with window seats on each side of the huge brick fireplace, a small dining room, kitchen, and two bedrooms. There was a roofed-over porch with a railing, and a hooked, hinged double gate across the front steps, which led down to the lake. The outside was white clapboard and the interior white pine. No plumbing, of course. A well was dug to the right of the cottage in the front yard. Visiting and communication were by water."

6. Since Dr. Hemingway did much of the cooking and canning for his large family, it seems fitting that he should sound the lunch hour from the porch of Windemere Cottage.

7. Barn-raising on the farm of Henry Bacon, from whom the Hemingways had bought their acre of shore-front land on Walloon Lake. It was during this event, which his parents attended, that one-year-old Ernest walked alone for the first time.

7

8, 9. At Walloon Lake, Ernest found his earliest opportunity to cultivate an innate love of writing, expressed in frequent letters and cards to family and friends back home. But he also kept a regular diary, there noting ideas for stories, and wrote as well as set his first mature fiction in Northern Michigan.

10. At five Ernest Hemingway was already a master angler along the streams and lakes of Northern Michigan. In this photograph he could be Huckleberry Finn, with his oversized straw hat, his fringed buckskin shirt and trousers, his bamboo fishing pole and wicker basket. For his son's third birthday, Dr. Hemingway took Ernest fishing for the first time, a sport that the novelist would pursue with mounting ardor virtually all over the world, from Wyoming and Utah to Florida, from the Caribbean to Spain, Africa, and the Indian Ocean.

11. In the summer of 1917 the Hemingways made their annual trek to Walloon Lake by car for the first time. Here, Grace, Ernest, and two-year-old Leicester posed for Dr. Hemingway during a roadside rest top. Late in his seventeenth year, Ernest was already six feet tall and weighed 150 pounds.

12. Cold as the spring water may have been in Walloon Lake, all the Hemingways loved to swim in it. After dark, the children were even allowed to skinny-dip. Here, in 1919, they are in daylight bright enough that Grace protected her weak eyes with dark glasses. Marcelline sits high at the center, while Ernest is submerged up to his neck on the far right.

10

11

8,9.

12

KANSAS CITY

In October 1917, when Ernest Hemingway left Oak Park and boarded the train for Kansas City, he entered upon what would become a life of insatiable wanderlust. It started with the offer of a job, on a trial basis at $15 a week, as a reporter for the *Kansas City Star*. Luckily, this was one of the nation's very best newspapers, inspired by the crusading spirit of its founder, William Rockhill Nelson, in reaction to a modern, burgeoning, industrial complex that, for all its beautiful shade trees and cultural efforts, had yet to shed the rowdiness of its early days as a rough and ready frontier town. Ernest called Kansas City a place where "crime was rife and justice crude." For him, it all made an exhilarating contrast to the arid gentility of Oak Park. Moreover, Ernest experienced his new urban environment from the bottom up, assigned as he was to a beat that included the police and railway stations plus the main hospital, all of which brought him into contact with the crime and violence, the accidents, heroism, death, and suicide that would evolve into the all-important themes of his mature fiction.

The energetic and fast-learning Hemingway also benefited quite particularly from the example of the *Star*'s Lionel Moise, a famous reporter who, as Ernest later wrote, "could carry four stories in his head and go to the telephone and take a fifth and then write all five at full speed to catch an edition." Like many another newsman and writer, Ernest was also to be influenced by the *Star*'s celebrated manual of style, especially its advocacy of concise, vigorous English and, in the treatment of subject matter, veracity, immediacy, and compression with clarity. After long, sedulous practice, Hemingway would eventually transform these elementary principles into his lean, innovative prose. Among the numerous unsigned pieces that the *Star* subsequently attributed to Hemingway, many reveal a constant in all his journalism, and this was the search for larger meaning—situation or character—through action rather than facts routinely reported.

At the *Star* Hemingway took up with another young reporter, Ted Brumback, who had just returned from several months of driving an American Field Service ambulance in war-torn France. When rejected by the military, owing to faulty vision, Ernest satisfied his eagerness to see action by joining Brumback and volunteering for overseas duty with the Red Cross. Thus, on April 30, 1918, Hemingway left the *Kansas City Star*, after seven months, and by early May he was in New York, ready to be commissioned and assigned to Europe.

Meanwhile, the atmosphere that the eighteen-year-old Hemingway absorbed in Kansas City would re-emerge in a pair of isolated short stories—"A Pursuit of Race" and "God Bless You Merry, Gentlemen"—as well as in the anthology *In Our Time*.

1. The city room at the *Kansas City Star*, where eighteen-year-old Ernest Hemingway had his first writing job. The opportunity came to him through his uncle Tyler Hemingway, a local resident and a close friend of the *Star*'s chief editorial writer. Ernest worked there as a cub reporter from October 1917 to the end of April 1918, when he departed for service overseas with the American Red Cross.

2. Union Station in Kansas City, where Ernest, as a *Star* reporter, picked up whatever stories he could, mainly political corruption, petty crime, and traveling celebrities. He also covered the police station and the city hospital, reporting the latest deaths and acts of violence.

3. In addition to such temples of high civilization as the William Nelson Rockhill Art Gallery, Kansas City in the second decade of the century could boast a rowdy night life that, along one notorious street, offered some twenty-five blocks of dives lined up three and four to a block on either side.

4. By the time Ernest Hemingway arrived in Kansas City, the town was already famous for its exploding abundance of bands specializing in a rather wild form of jazz.

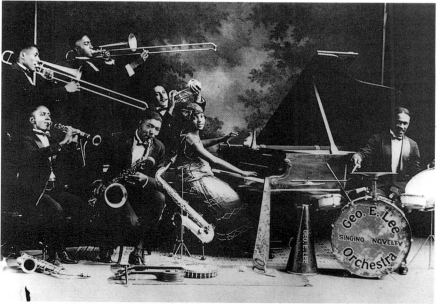

THE GREAT WAR

World War I—the tragically unnecessary Great War that poisoned the 20th century virtually at its source—exploded in August 1914, after a Serbian nationalist assassinated Archduke Franz Ferdinand, the heir to the imperial throne of Austria-Hungary, while he and his morganatic wife were on an official visit to the Montenegrin city of Sarajevo. When Austria-Hungary responded by declaring war on Serbia, the unstable two-headed empire set off a chain reaction throughout Europe's complex of interlocking alliances. Ironically, it was this network of mutual-protection agreements that, except for the Franco-Prussian War of 1870, had kept the Continent relatively peaceful since the Battle of Waterloo (1815) brought an end to the Napoleonic wars. This time, unfortunately, the multiple entente had the opposite effect, for by requiring that Russia enter the fray on Serbia's side, it automatically committed Germany to re-arm in support of Austria-Hungary and France to attack Germany for the sake of her ally, Russia. When this sent German troops across Belgium for an invasion of France, Great Britain declared war on the German Reich. With the Ottoman Empire joining the Central Powers (Germany-Austria-Hungary) and Japan as well as Italy signing up with the Allies (France-Britain-Russia), the whole of Europe had, by 1916, become engulfed in a four-year-long, deadly, but stalemated struggle. The Great War would be marked by the unprecedented inhumanity of rat-infested, dysentery-inducing trenches, gas attacks, aerial bombardments, and the wholesale slaughter of troops—"the flower of Victorian England"—swept by hailstorms of bullets from batteries of rapid-firing machine guns.

Until 1917 the United States had remained officially neutral, selling munitions to whichever side could afford to pay for them. But after German U-boats began torpedoing ships in the Atlantic—even the defenseless passenger liner *Lusitania*—President Wilson had little difficulty mobilizing American public opinion to support him in his call for war against Germany, which Congress declared on April 6, 1917. By entering the conflict, the United States, with her almost unlimited supply of arms, raw materials, credit, and manpower, assured an Allied victory, which, Wilson asserted, would "make the world safe for democracy."

Nearly two months after the United States had become an active belligerent, Heming-

way reached Paris, by way of Bordeaux, on his way to begin service with the Red Cross in Italy. To his delight, the French capital was under seige from the Germans' notorious super-*Kanon*, known as Big Bertha. But hardly had Ernest seen a shell burst on the façade of the Madeleine Church when he and Ted Brumback, another *Kansas City Star* alumnus, were on a train to Milan. Here, in Lombardy, the American Red Cross had been struggling to help the Italians cope with the dreadful aftermath of Caporetto (now part of Yugoslavia), the battle, against Austro-Hungarian troops, that had dealt Italian forces their worst defeat in modern history.

1, 2, 3, 4, 5. The number of brilliant, hortatory, patriotic posters created by every side suggests the universality of the Great War that exploded with the "guns of August" in 1914.

6. French forces held the line against the Germans in the first Battle of the Marne (September 6–9, 1914), thanks to a vast fleet of Paris taxis dispatched to the front. Such was the primitive level at which this first of the modern mechanized wars was fought.

7. The Madeleine Church in Paris after its façade had been struck by a shell from the Germans' Big Bertha. To his delight—and fright—Ernest was there when it happened. A fellow Red Cross volunteer described him "as excited as if he'd been sent on special assignment to cover the biggest story of the year."

8. The "oh, what a lovely war" mood of 1914 soon evaporated when the horrors of trench warfare became known on the home front.

9. "Big Bertha," the great German *Kanon* that was still shelling Paris when Ernest Hemingway arrived there in early June 1918 on his way to Italy for service as a Red Cross volunteer.

THE ITALIAN FRONT

The United States did not declare war, in reaction to German aggression against the Atlantic sea lanes, until April 1917, but well before this occurred a rapidly growing number of Americans had become actively involved with the Allied cause. Some young men shipped out with the Canadian armed forces, which, as part of the British Empire, had been called up soon after the outbreak of hostilities. Others, in 1916, organized the famous Lafayette Escadrille, which, as a wing of the French air service, not only saw much front-line action but also suffered heavy casualties. Meanwhile, men and women alike were volunteering in vast numbers for service in the Red Cross, which soon received vigorous support from the American government. A month after the German Army commenced its devastating advance across Belgium, the American Red Cross dispatched the first mercy ship to Europe. By the time the United States officially entered the war, the ranks of the Red Cross had swelled to almost 300,000, which enabled the relief organization to set up base hospitals and ambulance corps all along the Western front and deep into northern Italy. In one week during May 1917, a fund-raising campaign launched by the presidentially appointed War Council for the American National Red Cross succeeded in generating contributions totaling $115 million. As part of the effort, Ernest Hemingway, a freshly com-

missioned second lieutenant in the American Red Cross, marched down Fifth Avenue in a parade of 75,000 volunteers reviewed by President Wilson himself. Afterwards, in an ebullient mood, Ernest wrote a friend in Kansas City that "by virtue of his manly form and perfect complexion," he had been chosen as right guide to the first platoon, which in turn gave him the best possible position for reviewing the Chief Executive.

Hardly had Ernest disembarked in Milan when he found himself gathering up and bearing away the remains of human beings

blown to bits by an explosion in an armaments factory. Two days later, he began regular duty with an ambulance unit established just east of Lake Garda at Schio, soon renamed the Schio Country Club by "Hemingstein" and his associates. There, during a three-week stay, Ernest drove tall, top-heavy Fiat ambulances to evacuate the wounded behind the lines, ran into John Dos Passos (the future novelist who too was from Chicago), contributed a witty Ring Lardner parody to *Ciao*, the camp newspaper, and, for the first time, drank his fill of red wine. Then, as a way

of getting still closer to the real action, he volunteered to operate an emergency canteen in the trenches along the Piave River north of Venice.

Although the Piave assignment required him to do little more than dispense chocolates and cigarettes, Ernest was now so exposed to danger that near midnight on July 8, 1918, at Fossalta di Piave, he was seriously wounded. According to a Red Cross report, a shell "landed about three feet from him, killing a soldier who stood between him and the point of explosion, and wounding others."

1. Childe Hassam, *Red Cross Drive*, May 1918 (Eleanor and C. Thomas May Trust for Christopher, Sterling, Meredith, and Laura May). There may be a tiny, poinpoint portrait of Ernest Hemingway in this throng of humanity marching down New York's Fifth Avenue in May 1918, for one of his first duties as a freshly commissioned second lieutenant in the American Red Cross was to serve as right guide in the parade's first platoon. The colorful riot of fluttering flags, together with the presence of President Wilson, and the "manly form and perfect complexion" of Lieutenant Hemingway helped launch a week-long drive that raised $155 million for the American Red Cross' War Council.

2. Red Cross nurses marching past the reviewing stand in Madison Square where President Wilson stood as 75,000 volunteers—Hemingway among them—joined in a parade organized to raise funds for the Allied cause in Europe.

3. The Lafayette Escadrille, one of the many volunteer efforts by young Americans eager to aid the Allies long before the United States declared war on Germany. Named for the great French aristocrat who had provided crucial aid to the American colonies in their revolution against Great Britain, this all-American wing of the French air service fought bravely at the front and suffered heavy casualties.

4. Red Cross ambulances assembled in the piazza before the façade of Milan's Gothic cathedral, the great Duomo.

5, 6. The Schio Country Club, as the American Red Cross volunteers called their ambulance unit at Schio just east of Lake Garda.

One of these had both legs blown off, and Ernest himself was riddled with shrapnel throughout much of his right leg. Yet, although only semi-conscious, this young man—not yet nineteen—managed to pick up one of the wounded and back-pack him to the first-aid dug-out. For this astonishing performance the Italians awarded Hemingway not only the Croce di Guèrra but also the far more exclusive Medaglia d'Argento al Valore. Meanwhile, the hero himself had to be evacuated to a base hospital in Milan, where the wounds and the recovery from them became one of the major turning points in both his life and his work. Years later Hemingway spoke about it thus:

I used to keep a bowl by the side of my bed, full of the metal fragments they took from my leg, and people used to come and take them as good luck souvenirs. Two hundred twenty-seven pieces. Right leg. True count. Got hit with a Minenwerfer that had been lobbed in by an Austrian trench mortar. They would fill these Minenwerfers with the goddamnedest collection of crap you ever saw—nuts, bolts, screws, nails, spikes, metal scrap—and when they blew, you caught whatever you were in the way of. Three Italians with me had their legs blown off. I was lucky. The kneecap was down on my shin and the leg had caught all that metal but the kneecap was still attached. The big fight was to keep them from sawing off the leg. They awarded me the Croce al Mèrito di Guèrra, with three citations, and the Medaglia d'Argènto al Valore Militare. I threw them into the bowl with the other scrap metal.

7. Italian and French military watching together along the Piave River north of Venice. It was here, in a trench like this one, that on July 18, 1918, Ernest was seriously wounded when an Austrian shell struck about three feet away. A noncombatant, he had been dispensing chocolate and cigarettes from a little one-man canteen in what was a high-risk area inside the war zone.

8. One of the American Red Cross' tall, top-heavy Fiat ambulances on the kind of narrow mountain road that Ernest drove during his three-week assignment at Schio.

9, 10. As a Red Cross ambulance driver, Ernest worked behind Italian-Austrian battle lines that ran right through the roughest kind of Alpine terrain.

34

10

12

11. A convalescent Ernest proudly posed for a Milanese photographer in his new tailor-made uniform on which he had replaced Red Cross insignia with his Italian medals and stripes.

12. Chink Dorman-Smith, the genial, greyhound-lean Irish aristocrat and career officer in the British Army whom Ernest met in Milan and with whom he remained close for many years. For Ernest, indeed, Chink represented a kind of masculine ideal—military, brave, disciplined yet also witty, worldly, intellectual, and cultivated. Not only would the busy Chink, in between his martial duties, join Hemingway in numerous adventures throughout the early twenties—backpacking over the St. Bernard Pass and following the bullfights in Spain—but he would also serve as godfather to Ernest's first son, coupled with Gertude Stein and Alice Toklas as joint godmothers.

11

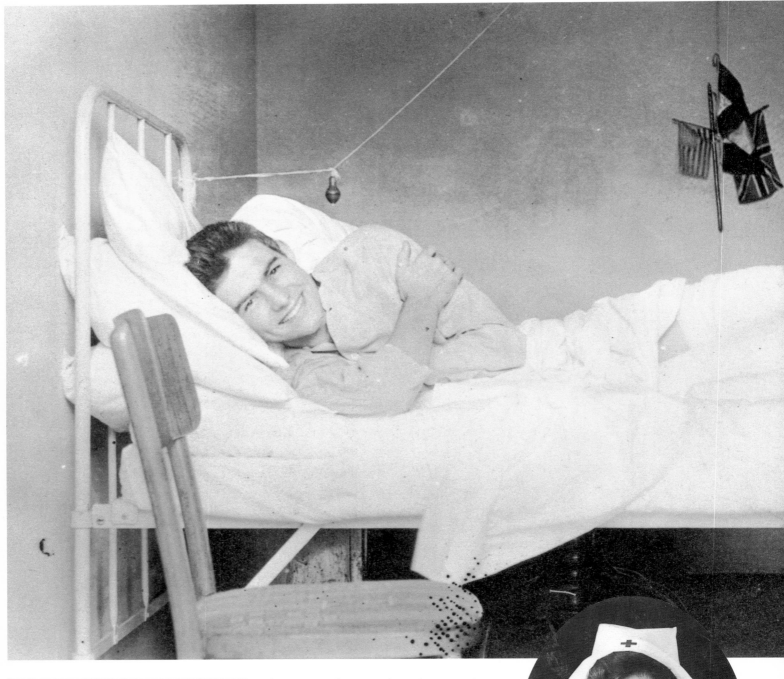

AGNES VON KUROWSKY

Evacuated to Milan, the severely wounded Hemingway found himself convalescing in what had been a luxurious mansion near the great Duomo. As Henry Villard, a fellow patient, wrote: "It had all the earmarks of a country club. Under the striped awnings, which could be rolled up or down according to the temper of the sun, patients were able to lounge at ease and have their meals brought to them.

There were large wicker chairs, a chaise longue, green potted plants, and on the balustrade, decorative flower boxes." It was here that Ernest became passionately enamored of a tall, beautiful, vivacious nurse named Agnes von Kurowsky (1892–1984). A volunteer from the Germantown section of Philadelphia, Agnes was six years older than Ernest, but won over by his ardor and devotion—not to mention the good humor, animal charm, and masculine good looks that everybody commented on—she arranged to work nights in order to spend them in his room.

2

1. Ernest Hemingway seems never to have looked more handsome than during his convalescence in a Red Cross hospital in Milan, perhaps because he had fallen in love for the first time, with one of his American nurses, Agnes von Kurowsky.

2. Nurse Agnes von Kurowsky, the pretty twenty-six-year-old Red Cross volunteer with whom nineteen-year-old Ernest Hemingway fell in love during his convalescence in Milan. Agnes had been born in Philadelphia, the daughter of a German émigré, but grew up, in relatively privileged circumstances, in Alaska, Vancouver, and Washington, D.C., becoming something of a free spirit along the way. Fluent in German and French, she had made a career change from librarianship to nursing, training for the latter in New York's Bellevue Hospital. With her sparkling blue-gray eyes,

Indeed, patient and nurse found themselves to be kindred souls. But while Ernest would forever insist that they also discovered mutual fulfillment in his hospital bed, during the quiet hours of her night duty, Agnes protested, in later life, that their relationship never developed beyond "the kissing stage." Still, it inhabited and grew in his imagination until the Milanese affair blossomed as *A Farewell to Arms*, the 1929 novel of war and love that sealed Hemingway's reputation as one of the greatest American writers of his generation.

3. Ernest and Agnes, flanked by two other Red Cross nurses, at Milan's San Siro racetrack. Their affair began shortly after the seriously wounded Ernest arrived on July 17, 1918, at the American Red Cross hospital in Milan and climaxed just as Agnes departed on October 15 for an emergency

Later in life, Agnes insisted that their romance never got beyond "the kissing stage." Not, however, according to Ernest, who, while on a visit to Milan in the 1950s, spoke at length about his time at the hospital, describing his affair with Agnes von Kurowsky and leaving no doubt that she had been his first great love, a love fully consummated during the many nights that she managed to stay in his bed, undisturbed by calls from the handful of other patients then being treated.

As Ernest gradually recovered enough to move about on crutches or cane, the lovers

curly reddish-blond hair, and flirtatious personality, Agnes made a quick—and enduring—impression on the emotionally vulnerable and sexually awakening Ernest. And she warmed to his dimpled, ear-to-ear grin, Latin coloring, animal magnetism, and unruly wit checked by gentle gravity.

assignment in Florence. It concluded abruptly in mid-March of 1919, when Agnes shocked Ernest, now back home in Oak Park, with a letter announcing her engagement to an Italian army officer, which itself soon foundered on the objections of the suitor's ducal family.

4

shared more than his bed. Together they visited the high-vaulted Gothic Duomo, the Scala opera, the Café Nuovo, the soaring iron-and-glass Galleria, and even the races at San Siro, reached by the romantic means of an open carriage.

After Agnes was transferred, in the late months of the year, to Florence and then Treviso, she and Ernest carried on an avid correspondence. Both wrote as frequently as twice a day, with her addressing him as "The Light of My Existence, My Dearest and Best, Most Ernest of Ernests, More Precious Than God, My Hero." Moreover, she never tired of telling him how much she missed him. "Gosh," Agnes declared in one missive, "if

you were only here, I'd dash in and make you up about now, and you'd smile at me and hold out your brawny arms—what's the use of wishing?"

Following a surprise pre-Christmas visit to Agnes at Treviso, Hemingway returned to America in January 1919, with the understanding that he would quickly get a job and send for her so that they could get married. But before he was able to settle down, Ernest received a letter from Agnes telling him that she had been mistaken, for she was now in love with another, a titled Italian colonel whom she intended to marry.

After jilting Ernest, Agnes herself suffered the same fate at the hands of her Italian suitor.

Hardly consoled, Ernest felt bitter and distraught over her rejection of him and subsequently gave vent to his feelings in "A Very Short Story." In the two pages of this little piece, the author caught the essence of his relationship with Agnes. Incredibly, the story contains the basic elements for what would become his second important novel, *A Farewell to Arms* (1929), whose heroine found her unmistakable prototype in Agnes von Kurowsky. The Great War, with the combined physical and romantic wounds it inflicted upon him, would indeed prove to be the first of the major turning points in both the life and the work of Ernest Hemingway.

38

GATHERING IN HONOR OF
LIEUT. ERNEST HENINGWAY
FEB. 16, 1919

Photo by
N.O. GRANATA
930 BLUE ISLAND AVE.

6

5

4. Ernest (second from the left) supporting himself on crutches while taking the sun, with his fellow convalescents, on an upper terrace of the palatial mansion in which the American Red Cross had established its small Milanese hospital.

5. Energetic and avidly curious as always, Ernest explored Milan despite wounds that almost cost him a leg.

6. No one made more fuss over Oak Park's brave veteran of the Italian campaigns than the Italian-American community in Chicago. Here one group had arrived to sing Ernest's praises in the huge, balconied studio where Grace Hemingway staged recitals, organized family chamber concerts, and gave voice and piano lessons. Backed by his parents and sisters, a uniformed Ernest sits beaming at the center of his exuberant well-wishers.

1 9 2 2

THE
PARIS
YEARS

—

1 9 2 8

PARIS IN THE TWENTIES

Americans had been traveling to Europe virtually since the first colonists arrived at Jamestown and Plymouth Rock. The reasons for returning whence they or their ancestors had come were manifold, ranging from the revolutionary politics of Benjamin Franklin and Thomas Jefferson through the title-seeking of Gilded Age millionaires to the release sought by creative individuals trapped in what they viewed as a spiritual/aesthetic wasteland intolerant of every value save those of puritan stuffiness and vulgar materialism. It is the artists and thinkers, of course, whose reverse migration across the Atlantic became the most storied, as well it should, given that American painters, musicians, dancers, and writers who succeeded in the Old World—or in the New World because of their experience and favorable reception abroad—included the likes of John Singleton Copley, Gilbert Stuart, and Mary Cassatt, Nathaniel Hawthorne, Edith Wharton, Henry James, Bret Harte, and Robert Frost, Louis Moreau Gottschalk, Edward MacDowell, Geraldine Farrar, and Isadora Duncan, T.S. Eliot, Ezra Pound, and Gertrude Stein. But spectacular as this roll call may be, it represents no more than a trickle of expatriating talents compared to the flood tide of intellectually, artistically, or socially aroused Americans who in the 1920s chose Europe as the place where they could best satisfy their craving for self-fulfillment.

What opened the gates to the allures of the Old World, and made it seem a new frontier, was the Great War itself, which had drawn hundreds of thousands of young people overseas—not only army recruits but also Red Cross volunteers like Ernest Hemingway, John Dos Passos, and Agnes Von Kurowsky—and there exposed them to a culturally and historically richer, less narrow-minded or philistine civilization than the one they had known in the Babbitt realm of provincial America. Moreover, the disparity between the possibilities encountered abroad and those rediscovered at home proved depressingly obvious just after the war, when the "return to order" that gripped the entire world took a particularly harsh and reactionary turn in the United States. While the notorious "Palmer Raids" against an invented "Red Scare" trampled on all manner of civil liberties, the ratification in 1919 of the Eighteenth Amendment to the United States Constitution—a cause pressed by the temperance movement

during the absence of servicemen fighting in Europe—prohibited the manufacture, sale, and transportation of alcoholic beverages. Since not even the stern Volstead Act could suppress Americans' thirst for strong drink, the Eighteenth Amendment served mainly to make bootlegging criminals rich and hypocrisy a debilitating national disease. Evidence of the latter proved indisputable for the small subculture of advanced literati when, in February 1921, Margaret Anderson and Jane Heap, publishers of *The Little Review*, were charged with obscenity, tried in a New York court, found guilty, and fined after they began serializing James Joyce's *Ulysses*. Distressed by the unhealthy American situation after World War I, Harold Stearns, a thirty-one-

year-old Harvard graduate, published a bitter indictment of it in a symposium book entitled *Civilization in the United States* (1922). Here, a group of sober, nonradical professors, critics, and writers—men like H.L. Mencken, Lewis Mumford, Van Wyck Brooks, Conrad Aiken—concluded that scarcely any aspect of American life—art, politics, theater, humor, journalism, advertising, medicine, scholarship—had escaped the general decline towards nadir. Confronted with cheerless, universal cliché, mediocrity, standardization, and spiritual shallowness or outright dishonesty—with "emotional and aesthetic starvation"—the gifted American, Stearns announced, had no choice but to flee his own country, if he was to entertain any hope of

1, 2. Designed over the centuries as the setting for Europe's oldest and most powerful monarchy, Paris by the 1920s—long after the departure of kings and emperors—possessed a tree-lined, wide-boulevard elegance that its heritage of magnificent architecture rendered all the more gracious. Yet despite its grandeur, "Paris, in each shape and gesture and avenue and cranny of her being," e.e. cummings wrote, "was continually expressing the humanness of humanity." This could be felt as much as the Opéra, in the Right Bank quarter dominated by the kind of wealthy bourgeois embodied in Proust's Swann, as in the Boulevard Saint-Germain on the Left Bank, which runs through Proust's *quartier noble*, fictionally reigned over by the Duchesse de Guermantes in *Remembrance of Things Past.*

3. With their artful, color-coordinated displays of fruits, vegetables, pâtés, and delicious, wand-like breads, the open markets of Paris contributed to the charm and beauty of the French capital quite as much as the landscaped gardens, the broad avenues lined with chestnuts trees, or the Impressionist masterpieces in the Luxembourg Palace.

4, 5. The Boulevard du Montparnasse, whose spreading, crowded cafés—the Dôme, the Rotonde, the Select, la Coupole—with their expatriate mob of writers, painters, composers, journalists, publishers, and well-read, opinionated loafers, became a veritable university for countless young Americans in 1920s Paris. Malcolm Cowley, a noted historian of the period and scene, called Paris' cafés "the heart and nervous system of the American literary colony." Many of its members—some very talented—found café life so satisfying that their mastery of it developed into the only work of art they created in the French capital. Gertrude Stein called them the "lost generation." But, as the journalist Bruce Bliven wrote, "it may well be the case that of ten Latin Quarter aesthetes, one genuine artist may be produced, it may also be true that this one artist has a real need for the sort of life the Left Bank offers. In that case, the nine who provided the milieu may well be excused for the sake of the tenth." Hemingway was a ten, and to become one he diligently wrote in out-of-the-way cafés—such as the Closerie des Lilas—and frequented the popular terraces only for relaxation.

6. The dome of the Pantheon, the late-18th-century church subsequently secularized and dedicated to the great men and women of France, crowned the Montagne Sainte-Geneviève quarter in which the young Hemingways lived in 1922–23.

7. Harold Stearns, who published *Civilization in America* in 1922, a symposium book that generally deplored the United States as a place of "emotional and aesthetic starvation." After fleeing to Paris, Stearns became a legendary presence at the

Select, a cerebral alcoholic who wrote neither poems nor novels but, rather, a racing column, which the Paris *Tribune* published under the name Peter Pickem. In *The Sun Also Rises* Hemingway would re-create Stearns as Harvey Stone, "balancing his disreputable life like a comic juggler."

having his musical compositions performed and attended, his poems, stories, and novels published, reviewed, and read, his canvases and sculptures exhibited and bought. In 1925, Scott Fitzgerald would put it thus: "America is so decadent that its brilliant children are damned almost before they are born." Of course, some of them became brilliantly productive because of their damnation, as Fitzgerald himself demonstrated better than anyone. So too did Eugene O'Neill, who stayed home and worked with the Provincetown Players to offer one powerful drama after another—*Beyond the Horizon*, *The Emperor Jones*, *Anna Christie*, and *Lazarus Laughed*, to cite only a few of the author's plays from the twenties. But Harold Stearns, unwilling to work against the American grain, declared his own independence on July 4, 1921, and, like Hemingway five months later, sailed for Paris, the *ville lumière* that would attract expatriating Americans like moths around a flaming candle.

Hemingway never tired of skiing in the Austrian Vorarlberg, of following the bullfights in Spain, or of revisiting the northern Italy of his Red Cross days, but when it came to settling down for good living and artistic development, he chose Paris, as did most of his fellow expatriates in the 1920s. Paris was an irresistible magnet for many reasons, beginning with its unparalleled openness and freedom of spirit, reflected in the airy, glittering beauty of the city itself, a place of wide, tree-lined boulevards, magnificent historical architecture, the graceful meander of the Seine dividing the capital into Left Bank and Right Bank. Even the outdoor markets, with their ingenious displays of fruits, vegetables, pâtés, and brown-crusted breads, vied for aesthetic distinction with the dazzling horticulture in the numerous public parks or indeed with the colors in a painting by Monet. Fundamental to this sweet and nurturing environment was the entire history of modernism, which Paris had given birth to and cradled, from the paintings of Delacroix and David, the music of Berlioz and Chopin, the literature of Hugo, Balzac, Flaubert, Proust, and Gide, to the triumphs of late 19th-century Impressionism, of Cézanne, Seurat, van Gogh, and Gauguin, of Debussy, Fauré, and Ravel, of Matisse's Fauvism and Picasso's Cubism, of Diaghilev, Nijinsky, Stravinsky, and the Ballets Russes. As this would suggest, Paris encouraged the genius of foreigners and Frenchmen alike, relishing every new "scandal," or artistic breakthrough, as if it were life-giving oxygen. Added to all this were extraordinary economic advantages for anyone with dollar-denominated resources, since to re-

cover from the ravages of war, France had inflated her economy, making francs fire-sale cheap relative to the greenback, at the same time that she had also imposed rent controls as a device for maintaining a cap on prices. Thus, with only modest means at their disposal, Hemingway and his bride could enjoy a life-style and the liberty to work and grow unlike anything, at any price, known to their counterparts in the United States. This meant

8

dining in good restaurants, drinking decent wine with every meal, betting on horse and bike races, vacationing in the Alps or on the Riviera, and, more important, spending long hours writing or practicing the piano. Further, much of the thinking and creating could be done in a pleasant café—open-air in good weather or snugly enclosed during winter—for little more than the cost of an occasional kirsch, served by efficient, well-wishing waiters. For such purposes, a determined writer like Hemingway might choose the less frequented Closerie des Lilas, but for relaxing or matching wits with peers there were the great, crowded, sprawling cafés of Montparnasse—the Dôme, the Rotonde, the Select, la Coupole. Here, the conversation, the people-watching, and the *fine à l'eau gaseuse* proved so fulfilling that an unfortunate number of Ernest's fellow expatriates invested the whole of their creative capital in such activity, leaving the stories and sonatas to be composed by more disciplined types, among them Hemingway, of course, but also e.e. cummings, Djuna Barnes, and Kay Boyle, Virgil Thomp-

son, Aaron Copland, and George Antheil. Reinforcing them in the high seriousness of their productive resolve was the current artistic ferment of historic ebullition, fed by France's own Cocteau, Radiguet, Aragon, Breton, Valéry, Satie, and Léger, her *maudit* émigré painters Soutine, Pascin, Modigliani, and Chagall, the liberating couturière Coco Chanel, and the composers of *Les Six*: Poulenc, Milhaud, Honegger, Auric, et al. Cultural

9

brilliance of this order drew into its orbit a gathering vanguard of English-speakers, beginning with Gertrude Stein who, with her companion Alice B. Toklas, had long presided over a salon in the rue de Fleurus renowned for its fabulous collection of Cézannes, Matisses, and Picassos and for its advocacy of a new literature as stripped-down and contemporary as Cubist painting. No one benefited more from Stein's tutelage than did Hemingway, but with his exceptional quickness of insight and absorption he also prof-

ited, like no one else, from the advice and encouragement of Ezra Pound, James Joyce, and the avant-garde bookseller Sylvia Beach, all of whom had arrived in Paris only just ahead of the Hemingways and for similar reasons. With his energy and industriousness, and his authentic literary gift and personal magnetism, Hemingway would soon become the star—sometimes as editor as well as writer—of all the "little magazines" that flourished in twenties Paris. Moreover, *transatlantic review*, *The Little Review*, and *This Quarter*, along with the essentially noncommercial publishing houses known as Contact Editions and Three Mountains Press, existed in Paris to serve just such writers as Joyce and Hemingway, whose works were too radical in form or diction to be acceptable in any English-speaking country prior to the later 1920s or even the 1930s.

10

8. The Dôme, the oldest and most favored of the Montparnasse cafés. One writer spoke of it not as a place but rather as an atmosphere, which one could certainly feel and absorb but never describe.

9. Standing witness to the artistic progressiveness of Paris was Rodin's *Balzac*, a magnificent work that survived endless controversy to be installed, finally, just opposite the Café Rotonde on the Boulevard Raspail.

10, 11. Saint-Germain-des-Prés, with its ancient Romanesque church, its numerous bookstores and publishers, throngs of Sorbonne students, delightful cafés—Flore, Deux Magots, Brasserie Lipp—constituted another Left Bank crossroads for the American expatriate in the 1920s (see also fig. 2). Here, as well as in nearby Montparnasse, the French capital, became, as Maria Jolas wrote, the scene of "an extraordinary rendezvous that everybody seemed to have come to almost without realizing it."

12. Bookstalls along the Left Bank quays opposite the flying buttresses of Notre-Dame, where Hemingway bought, at deep discounts, the latest English-language books left in the hotels facing the Seine.

11

The doldrums that overtook postwar America would dissipate once the nation exploded into several years of wild abandon known as the Jazz Age or the Roaring Twenties. Meanwhile, however, Hemingway felt the stultifying dryness of the Oak Park environment as only a restless, romantic veteran of the Italian campaigns could. In the three years between his return to Illinois in late January 1919 and his redeparture for Europe in early December 1921, Ernest ran through the entire gamut of emotions, from euphoric aspiration to suicidal despair, several times and always as a symptom of his confusion about how to become an important and original writer. At first, he reveled in the lavish hero worship accorded him, especially when he donned his uniform, medals, flying Italian officer's cape, and polished cordovan boots. But after wowing his family, the ladies' clubs, the audience at Oak Park High, and Chicago's Italian-American organizations, he collapsed into bitterness, triggered by the arrival in late March of a letter from Agnes von Kurowsky breaking off their engagement and announcing her new love for a young heir to a Neapolitan dukedom. Thereafter Ernest thrashed about in Northern Michigan, quarreled seriously with his mother, and spent several months as a guest of friends in Toronto, where he also began an ongoing journalistic relationship with the *Toronto Star*. Finally, he took a regular, salaried job in Chicago writing for the short-lived *Cooperative Commonwealth*, at the same time that he continued to cobble together his first mature stories, mostly about the deep, lyrical, sometimes violent, and always complicated feelings he harbored for life in the Michigan wilderness. While living with high-spirited literary friends in Chicago, Ernest also met and fell in love with Hadley Richardson, an exquisite young pianist visiting from St. Louis to recover from the experience of nursing her widowed mother through a long, terminal illness. Although eight years his senior, the shy but radiant Hadley captivated the rebounding Ernest even more rapidly and quite as ardently as had Agnes. Hadley rejoiced over her manly suitor's renaissance capacity for "boxing, fishing, writing . . . leaving folks in fits of admiration . . . getting war medals, playing bridge, swirling about in the black cape . . . swimming, paddling, tennis, charm, good looks, knowledge of clothes, love of women, domesticity." After months of daily, endearing correspondence and much traveling between Chicago and St. Louis, the twenty-two-year-old Ernest Hemingway and the thirty-year-old Hadley Richardson were married, among family and friends, in the little country

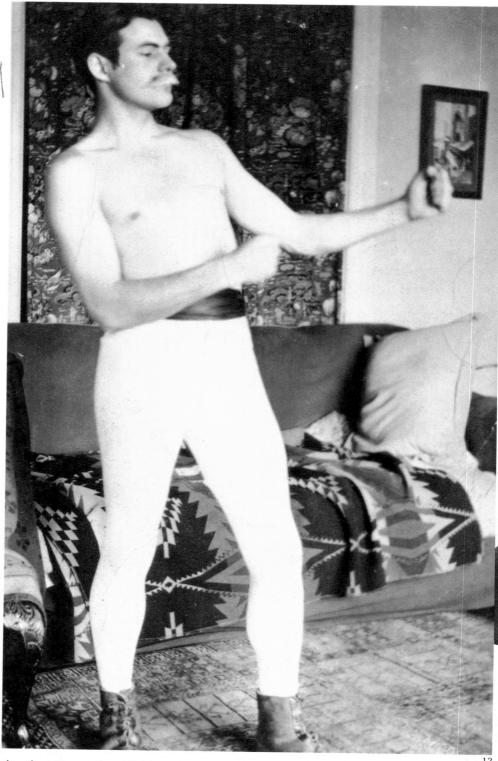

church at Horton Bay, Michigan, on September 3, 1921. Three months later the newlyweds would set sail for France, urged on by Sherwood Anderson, then a resident of Chicago following a long stay in Paris, and armed with the famous novelist's letters of introduction to Gertrude Stein, Ezra Pound, James Joyce, and Sylvia Beach. With $3,000 a year from Hadley's trust fund and Ernest's $1,500 salary as the *Toronto Star*'s European correspondent to support them, the couple declared, as Hadley wrote, "the world's a jail and we're going to break it together."

13

13. A passionate boxer all his life, Hemingway here put on a false moustache, as well as long underwear, bared his chest, and raised his fists in comic imitation of the great John L. Sullivan. Such were Ernest's high spirits on the eve of his departure, with Hadley Richardson, for the life of a budding writer in Paris.

14. Between his return from wartime Italy in 1919 and his re-departure for Europe in late 1921, Ernest spent long months tramping through the wilderness of northern Michigan, often nostalgically attired in his Italian service beret and high combat boots.

15. Ernest and Hadley Richardson in St. Louis during the courtship that led to their marriage in September 1921.

16. Ernest and pals in northern Michigan during the postwar summer of 1920. From left to right: Carl Edgar, Katy Smith, Marcelline Hemingway (Ernest's eldest sister), Bill Horne, Ernest, and Charles Hopkins. Horne was a friend from Red Cross days and Hopkins from the *Kansas City Star* period (1917–18). The witty, sardonic, green-eyed Katy was a longtime summer friend, also from Kansas City. In the 1930s, while visiting Hemingway in Key West, she would meet John Dos Passos and soon marry him. In Florida as well as here, Katy cast a critical eye on Ernest's love of guns.

14

15

16

1

HEMINGWAY IN PARIS

When he wasn't writing, Ernest enjoyed the uninhibited ease of life in Paris, where, with Hadley, his bride of three months, he arrived on December 22, 1921. He would remain, with interruptions, until early 1928. During this period—what the French call the "crazy years"—Hemingway often began the day, according to Carlos Baker, in a café:

He took the shortcut through the Luxembourg Gardens past the bust of Flaubert which seemed both a symbol and a goal. Breakfast coffee and a brioche came to a franc or less at any of the places along the rue Soufflot, and he could write all morning at a back corner table without expectation of prolonged disturbance. Afterwards he could rest strained eyes on the bronze-green of the fountains in the Place de l'Observatoire, where the water flowed thinly over the sculptured manes and shoulders of the horses. With Dos Passos in the winter afternoons he drank hot kirsch, flavored like cherry-pits. He mixed work and play at the six-day bike races. He argued the merits of race-horses with Harold Stearns and Evan Shipman, or went to the prize-fights with Sisley Huddleston and Bill Bird. When the fights were poor, Bird used to remember the brave colored fighters of the past. He had a line modified from Villon which went, "Où sont les nègres d'antan?" When the fights were good, like the Mascart-Ledoux battle at the Cirque de Paris, one yelled himself hoarse and stopped in at Lipp's for a midnight beer on the way home. [1]

Ernest and Hadley first lived at the top of a ramshackle building at 74 rue Cardinal-Lemoine, a narrow, twisting street of scant charm in the Left Bank quarter known as the Montagne Sainte-Geneviève. Here, the couple found themselves perched above a raucous, all-night dance hall or *bal musette* and around the corner from the Café des Amateurs, a sour-smelling hangout for local drunks that Ernest called "the cesspool of the rue Mouffetard." Despite its shortcomings—small, oddly angled rooms, no heat save that provided by a coal-grate fireplace, a recessed-closet bathroom equipped with nothing but pitcher, bowl, and slop jar—the Hemingways remained there until they departed in mid-August 1923 for Toronto, where Ernest would work for the *Toronto Star* and await the birth of his son "Bumby." Upon the family's return to Paris in late January 1924—following the four-and-a-half-month "year in limbo" (i.e., Canada)—they moved into a somewhat better environment than they had known before in Paris. This was at 112 rue Notre-Dame-des-Champs, directly over a noisy sawmill, but in the same Left Bank street with Ezra Pound and a mere step from Gertrude Stein in the rue de Fleurus, the Luxembourg Gardens, and the cafés on the Boulevard du Montparnasse. Owing to the racket from the sawmill, Hadley practiced piano in a basement across the street, while Ernest began writing at his favorite café, the Closerie des Lilas, then beyond the orbit of expatriate Paris.

It was a difficult time financially, and there often was not enough to eat on the table.

2

1. Hadley Richardson Hemingway, the most beautiful and patrician of Ernest's four wives, at the time of her marriage, to a young man eight years her junior. The Hemingways easily rivaled the Fitzgeralds as the handsomest couple among the American expatriates in early 1920s Paris.

3

2. Ernest standing four-square outside the saw-mill that occupied the lower quarters of the building at 13 rue Notre-Dame-des-Champs, where the Hemingways—now a family of three—moved after their return to Paris from Canada in 1924. Nearby lived two of Ernest's most trusted mentors, Ezra Pound, on the very same street, and Gertrude Stein, at 27 rue de Fleurus.

3. Ernest and Hadley were a happy couple in their earlier Paris days, when, thanks to low rent, a powerful dollar, and their indifference to clothes, they could eat well in cafés, bet money on bike and horse races, attend boxing matches, ski in Switzerland and Austria, travel in northern Italy, and spend long summers following the bullfights around Spain. As long as Ernest's writing went well, even the occasional patch of stark poverty did not seriously undermine the cheerful tenor of their lives.

4. The Rue Cardinal-Lemoine, on the Montagne Sainte-Geneviève, one of Paris' oldest, narrowest, and most rancid as well as raucous streets. It was here, at number 74, that the Hemingways, shortly after their arrival in late 1921, rented a tiny flat on the top floor of an ancient tenement. Despite the absence of heat during the winter of record cold and evil-smelling *pissoirs* at every landing, Ernest and Hadley were young, adaptable, and imaginative enough to find even these conditions amusing.

5. The Rue Mouffetard, an extension of the Rue Descartes where Ernest rented a room in which to write, believing (incorrectly) that the *maudit* poet Verlaine had died there. Even more venerable than the Rue Cardinal-Lemoine, where the Hemingways first lived, the steep, turning "Mouff" was, and remains, one of Paris' most picturesque streets.

Hemingway saw his stories rejected one after another, and as the rejection notes dropped through a slit in the sawmill door, he was riled by the letters of rejection which referred to his submissions as "anecdotes" or "sketches" rather than stories. "They did not want them," he said, "and we lived on poireaux and drank cahors and water."

Still, Hemingway persevered because, as he later observed:

I was trying to write then, and I found the greatest difficulty, aside from knowing truly what you really felt, rather than what you were supposed to feel, was to put down what really happened in action; what the actual things were which produced the emotion that you experienced. The real thing, the sequence of motion and fact which made the emotion and which would be as valid in a year or in ten years or, with luck and if you stated it purely enough, always, was beyond me and I was working very hard to try to get it.[2]

In her reminiscenses Hadley evoked those days when they lived over the sawmill in the rue Notre-Dame-des-Champs:

On the opposite side of the street were back entrances to shops on Boulevard Montparnasse. There was a back door into a cellar underneath a bakery and that's where I had my piano. It was so cold in the winter I played the piano wearing several sweaters while Ernest wrote or read manuscripts in a nearby café and kept warm with coffee.[3]

Hemingway's contemporaries viewed him in quite different ways. Burton Rascoe, one of the best-known American journalists of the twenties, wrote:

By all accounts Hemingway is supposed to be very precious and esoteric, and against America and disgruntled and neurotic and a failure. He is not any of these things. He lives in Paris, he told me, for at least three reasons: he finds it cheaper to live there; he can get a change of scene and environment such as would be impossible in America at small expense; and he likes a bit of wine with his meals. He is a robust, hulking sort of chap, with a clear skin and a healthy, ruddy color, who is probably the slouchiest dresser in the Montparnasse quarter. There is nothing decadent, precious, arty, superior, or anti-American about him.[4]

Dorothy Parker's admiration for Hemingway proved boundless. "He works like hell and through it," she observed:

6

7

8

Nothing comes easily to him; he struggles, sets down a word, scratches it out, and begins all over. He regards his art as hard and dirty work, with no hope of better conditions. He has the most profound bravery that it has ever been my privilege to see. He has had pain, ill-health, and the kind of poverty that you don't believe—the kind of which actual hunger is the attendant; he has had about eight times the normal allotment of responsibilities. And he has never compromised. He has never

turned off on an easier path than the one he staked himself. It takes courage.[5]

"He liked to win at everything," the artist Henry Strater said. "At boxing he was very dangerous in the first minute or two. He had a very wicked overhand right, but all you had to do was block it a couple of times and counterpunch from the inside. That would slow him up."

Young Hemingway, it seems, made a strong impression on almost everybody, leaving no one neutral. "When Gertrude Stein talked to me," the artist William Walton once said, "she started in about Teddy Roosevelt being Ernest's real hero. 'After all,' she said, 'Teddy's kind of action is what set the pattern of Ernest's childhood.' And then she threw off the line I later realized she used over and over again. 'Ah, but you see, the trouble about Hem is that he has a wide yellow streak down the middle of his back.' She was having her revenge for some trouble between them that I don't understand."

6, 7. In his early Paris years Hemingway lived so near the Luxembourg Gardens that he passed through them on his way to the café where he often spent the day writing stories, in the traditional blue notebooks still used in French schools. Ernest relished the formal gardens, with their statues of cultural heroes like Flaubert and Delacroix;

moreover, he also spent time in the Baroque palace, built by Queen Marie de' Medici but filled, in the 1920s, with the French national collection of modern art. Hemingway believed that great modern painting, by the radical economy with which it eliminated everything but the essential, helped him get at the heart of what he was trying to achieve—"pure feeling"—even if he didn't "have all those colors" and had to make do "with my pencil in black and white."

8. Place Saint-Michel. In this oddly shaped square, brightened by its openness to the Seine opposite Notre-Dame, Ernest found a café where he could spend the day writing and sipping *café au lait*, when the weather made his regular "study" in the rue Descartes too dark and cold. He preferred the work-conducive anonymity of such a venue—"clean, warm, and friendly"—to the great Montparnasse cafés frequented by the expatriate avant-garde.

9. The memorial bust of Gustave Flaubert often contemplated by young Ernest Hemingway as he passed through the Luxembourg Gardens.

10, 11. Ernest loved attending the horse races at Auteuil and Enghien, the boxing matches at the Cirque d'Hiver, and the six-day bike races both there and in the Vélodrome d'Hiver. He was even lucky enough to get seats for the great Mascart-Ledoux fight staged at the Cirque de Paris in February 1924.

FOREIGN CORRESPONDENT

As the American presence in postwar France grew at an ever-increasing rate, Colonel McCormick of the *Chicago Tribune* could not resist the challenge of launching a Paris edition of his paper to compete with arch-rival James Gordon Bennett, who had the corner on the English-language market with the *Paris Herald*. David Darrah ran the Paris edition of the *Trib* and hired James Thurber and Janet Flanner as correspondents. Meanwhile, Hemingway, to help finance his new expatriate life, arranged with the *Toronto Star*, for which he had been writing since early 1929, to become the newspaper's European reporter, at an annual salary of $1,500, exactly half the income expected from Hadley's trust fund. However, the *Star* insisted on having its money's worth, and barely three months after his arrival in Paris, Hemingway was complaining to Sherwood Anderson that "this goddam newspaper stuff is gradually ruining me." Indeed, it kept him, sporadically, on the rails throughout much of 1922 and 1923, traveling to Genoa for the International Economic Conference, to Milan for an interview with Benito Mussolini, to Constantinople to cover the tragic aftermath of the Greco-Turkish War, and to Lausanne for the concluding peace conference.

Easily, the most dramatic of his assignments came when Hemingway boarded the Orient Express for the Middle East, where war had broken out between the Turks and their would-be Greek overlords. The troubles originated in the 1919 Versailles Peace Conference, where the victorious Allies had awarded Greece the Bulgarian coast on the Aegean and the remnants of European Turkey, including Thrace and the Dodecanese but excluding the zone of the Straits. Izmir, or

1

Smyrna, was to come under Greek administration pending a plebiscite. Thus encouraged by the Allies, the Greeks invaded Asia Minor in 1921, only to be defeated in 1922, as much by the murderous incompetence of their politically appointed military commanders as by the superior will of the Turkish forces led by Kemal Atuturk, the "father of modern Turkey." By the time Hemingway arrived in Constantinople, the Greek Army had been given seventy-two hours to evacuate eastern Thrace. On October 17 Ernest reached Adrianople to observe the retreating forces, in whose wake scrambled a million Christian refugees. For miles he walked along the old stony road across the Maritza Valley towards Macedonia, following a "silent, ghastly procession" of displaced humanity, swaying camels, and groaning ox carts heaped with bedding, furniture, and tethered pigs. Adding to the chaos were periodic trains of ammunition mules and battered Fords speeding forward with cargos of weary Greek officers. All the way to the horizon Hemingway could see nothing but the "slow, rain-soaked, shambling, trudging Thracian peasantry, plodding along in the rain." Not only did Ernest report the scene brilliantly; he would also hold and nurture it in his imagination until the experience would re-emerge in his writing as the Italian retreat from Caporetto in *A Farewell to Arms*. Even sooner, it surfaced as one of the sketches—one of the most memorable—that he assembled for his second book, *in our time*, published in Paris in 1923:

Minarets stuck up in the rain of Adrianople across the mud flats. The carts were jammed for thirty miles along the Karagatch road. Water buffalo and cattle were hauling carts through the mud. No end and no beginning. Just carts loaded with everything they owned. The old men and women, soaked through, walked along keeping the cattle moving. The Maritza was running yellow almost up to the bridge. Carts were jammed solid on the bridge with camels bobbing along through them. Greek cavalry herded along the procession. Women and kids were in the carts crouched with mattresses, mirrors, sewing machines, bundles. There was a woman having a kid with a young girl holding a blanket over her and crying. Scared sick looking at it. It rained all through the evacuation.[1]

During this period, Hemingway was also dispatched to cover the Greco-Turkish Peace Conference in Lausanne, where the twenty-three-year-old reporter very quickly took the measure of one Italian delegate, Mussolini, just three weeks after his "march on Rome." At a press conference, Ernest wrote, "Musso-

2

3

lini sat at his desk reading a book. His face was contorted into the famous frown. He was registering Dictator." Then, on a prankish impulse, Hemingway slipped behind His Excellency to discover what book could so entrance him that he would remain totally unaware of the invited press. "It was a French-English dictionary—held upside down."

In Paris, meanwhile, Hadley prepared to join her husband for a ski holiday in Chamby. Convinced that Ernest would want to work on

1. James Thurber, who brought wry humor to Paris' foreign press corps when he joined in 1924–25 as a reporter for the *Chicago Tribune*.

2. Janet Flanner had become a Parisian expatriate in order to write novels. Although she did publish one piece of long fiction, it was in journalism, originally as a reporter for the *Paris Herald*, that Flanner would make her legendary career. As the pseudonymous Genêt, Flanner became *The New Yorker*'s Paris correspondent in late 1925, and continued to write her "Paris Letter" for the next half-century. After accompanying Ernest to prizefights, where he joined French fans in their argotic yelling at the combatants, Flanner called Hemingway "a natural quick linguist who learned a language first through his ears because of his constant necessity for understanding people and for communicating."

3. In October 1922, Hemingway, as foreign correspondent for the *Toronto Star*, covered the horrific aftermath of the Greco-Turkish War, which forced the Greek Army and a million Christian refugees to evacuate, within seventy-two hours, the entire eastern portion of Thrace.

4. The rather Byronic oil portrait that Henry (Mike) Strater painted of Ernest during their 1923 visit to Rapallo, where Ezra Pound had recently settled.

5. Ernest with the famous biographer Lincoln Steffens, a delegate to the Greco-Turkish Peace Conference in Lausanne, whose interest in Hemingway's writing saved one of his early stories,

his accumulated, but recently neglected, literary output, she packed every typescript and carbon copy she could lay hands on, with calamitous consequences that Hemingway told me about years later:

The suitcase was in a compartment on the train, which was in the Gare de Lyon. While Hadley went to get a bottle of Vittel water, the valise was stolen, and none of the stories or the first draft of a novel that were in it were ever recovered. Poor Hadley was so broken up about it, I actually felt worse for her than for having been robbed of everything I ever wrote. Only story that was salvaged was "My Old Man," which had been sent to a magazine by Lincoln Steffens and had not as yet been returned. After that we called it Das Kapital—my total literary capital. I never really blamed Hadley. She had not hired on as a manuscript custodian and what she had hired on for—wife-ing—she was damn good at.

while all but one other piece disappeared in Hadley's suitcase stolen from a train compartment in Paris' Gare de Lyon. Steffens had sent "My Old Man" to *Cosmopolitan* for possible publication.

1

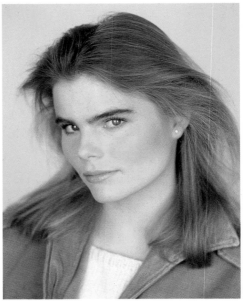

2

3

HADLEY RICHARDSON

Born into a conservative, affluent St. Louis family on November 9, 1891, Elizabeth Hadley Richardson enjoyed a privileged, if sheltered, girlhood, complete with exclusive school, the Mary Institute (a private girl's school founded by T.S. Eliot's grandfather), and society dancing classes. Like Hemingway's mother, Mrs. Richardson played the piano, had strong religious beliefs, earned the reputation of a free and independent thinker, and exerted the dominant influence in her household. The daughter had little in common with her mother, and the two never got along very well. Like the Hemingways, the Richardson family spent their summers away from home, in New England, mostly at Rye Beach in New Hampshire. James Richardson had entered the family pharmaceutical business, but despite his charm and humor, he couldn't abide the rigors of the commercial world. When Hadley was twelve her father committed suicide, as Hemingway's would in 1928.

The red-headed, vividly blue-eyed Hadley evinced an early capacity for talkativeness and affection. In the process of maturing, however, she developed insecurities about herself and became shy, even withdrawn. Like her mother, she played the piano quite well, well enough to be offered, while in high school, the chance to train for a concert career, but she rejected the opportunity and returned to the Mary Institute. In 1910 Hadley graduated at nineteen and went on to Bryn Mawr, only to quit after her first year. Back in

St. Louis, she resumed her piano studies, but rather desultorily. After her mother's death, in the summer of 1920, Hadley gradually became much more social, and in September she accepted an invitation to visit an old school chum in Chicago. Her first night there she met Ernest at a party, and, according to the latter, he decided almost immediately that she was the girl he wanted to marry. Hadley stayed three weeks, spending most of that time with young Hemingway.

A year later, on the 3rd of September, 1921, Hadley and Ernest were married at Horton Bay, in a Methodist church just a few miles from Windemere Cottage on Walloon Lake. Ernest was twenty-two and Hadley thirty. They honeymooned there for two weeks while Grace Hemingway was living in her new cottage across the lake. In the autumn Hadley and Ernest moved into a third-floor flat on North Clark Street, a poor section of Chicago. For months they had dreamt about and saved money for a trip to Italy, but after Ernest quit his job writing for the monthly *Cooperative Commonwealth*, the prospects looked bleak, except for Hadley's $3,000 a year from a trust fund and her $8,000 bequest from an uncle who conveniently died in October 1921. At the persuasion of Sherwood Anderson, then a Chicago resident, the couple decided on life in Paris, where creative people could live cheaply, in stimulating as well as picturesque communion with one another, at the center of the modern world's most sophisticated, cosmopolitan avant-garde. Ernest planned to continue writing for the *Toronto Star*, now as the newspaper's Paris correspondent, and Anderson provided warm letters of introduction to Gertrude

Stein, Sylvia Beach, Ezra Pound, James Joyce, and Lewis Galantière. The new expatriates sailed on December 8th aboard the *Leopoldina* and arrived in the French capital a few days before Christmas.

Ernest and Hadley found their first Parisian apartment on the fourth floor of an old Left Bank building at 74 rue Cardinal-Lemoine, across the street from one of Joyce's early borrowed residences. Next door stood an infamous *bal musette*, a dance hall frequented by sailors and working men. "You can live on less and less," was Hemingway's motto at the time.

Having no place to write, Hemingway rented an unheated room at 39 rue Descartes, where Verlaine was reputed to have died. An attic room, it looked out across the gray panorama of chimneypots, sheet-metal roofing, church towers, and twisted drain pipes, extending all the way from the Sorbonne to the

vast esplanade of Les Invalides. In the winter Ernest sought refuge from cold in a neighborhood café, where, scribbling in blue French lycée notebooks, he composed those first stories of a remembered Michigan. Hemingway wrote home: "It looks like a good winter. Cafés much fuller in the daytime now with people that have no heat in hotel rooms." That first winter was so cold all the fountains froze. Hemingway later typed his stories on a Corona portable that Hadley gave him for his twenty-second birthday.

When Hadley became pregnant in 1923, the couple decided to have the baby in Canada. Just before they left Paris, Ezra Pound met with Hadley to offer her some advice and a present. The gift was his threadbare brown-velvet smoking jacket, which she wore around the house and kept for years; the advice was that she must never try to change her husband, something with which she agreed heartily. Then Pound went on to say that he might just as well say goodbye to her now, for having a baby would change her completely. He thought that motherhood ruined women. But Hadley felt just the reverse. Having a baby, she said, would only give her one more person to love.

Among his friends Ernest did not spare himself in 1926. Having a drink with Bill Bird at the Caves Mura, he blurted out the news that his marriage was breaking up. When Bill asked why, Ernest answered flatly: "Because I'm a son of a bitch."

John Dos Passos once wrote that Ernest Hemingway left his wives "more able to cope with life than he found them." This was certainly true in Hadley's case. The once timid, unhappy girl, looked upon by her mother as

an "invalid who shouldn't even spend a night alone," had blossomed into an independent, self-confident young woman who knew not only how to deal with life but also how to enjoy it. Her interests increased, her vision and understanding deepened, but most of all Ernest had endowed his beautiful first wife with a belief in herself.

Five years after they had moved to Paris, Hadley left Ernest, who was having an affair with her best friend, Pauline Pfeiffer. Hadley issued an ultimatum: Pauline and Ernest weren't to see each other for a hundred days, following which she would consent to a divorce provided they were still in love. Three months into the trial separation, Hadley graciously wrote Ernest not to delay divorce proceedings any longer. In January 1927 the Paris decree became final. Hadley moved with her three-year-old son John, nicknamed Bumby, and F. Puss, the cat, to 35 rue de Fleurus, near the home of Gertrude Stein and Alice Toklas. When Ernest carried her things there, Hadley recalled, he was "weeping down the street and I know he was very sorry for himself."

After an extended visit to the USA, Hadley returned to Paris, where she met *Chicago Daily News* bureau chief Paul Scott Mowrer, who had received the first Pulitzer Prize ever awarded for foreign correspondence. They were married on July 3, 1933, in London. Following a period in Chicago, they returned, towards the end of World War II, to Paris, where Paul reported for the *New York Post*.

"The memory of each person who has lived in Paris differs from that of any other," wrote Hemingway.

1. The lovely but shy and withdrawn Hadley Richardson, seated second from right in the front row of her graduating class (1910) at Mary Institute in St. Louis.

2, 3, 4. The beauty of Hadley Richardson, the thirty-year-old woman whom Ernest Hemingway married in 1921, would be inherited by her son, the handsome Jack, and passed along to his two famous daughers: Margaux and Mariel Hemingway.

5. Hadley Richardson, second from the right in the front row, posed with the class of 1910 at St. Louis' Mary Institute, a private school for gentlewomen founded by T.S. Eliot's grandfather.

6. At their Northern Michigan wedding, September 3, 1921, the handsome new Hemingway couple radiate all the glamour of movie stars. On the bride's right: Ernest's sisters Ursula and Carol; to the groom's left: Grace Hemingway, her youngest child Leicester, and Dr. Ed Hemingway.

JOSEPHINE BAKER

In 1925, *La Revue Nègre* epitomized the growing influence of jazz and blacks on Paris during *les années folles*. It starred Josephine Baker, the "ebony Venus" from St. Louis who became a Jazz Age icon after startling Paris with a costume that consisted of nothing more than a pink flamingo feather between her fabulous brown legs. Into the French language went *up-to-date*, *un jazz band*, *un cocktail*, and *le jazz hot*. An exhibition of the new dance, the *Char-Less'ton*, attracted unprecedented crowds to Claridge's on the Champs-Élysées. The "Shimmy" and the "Black Bottom" became other popular dances. Meanwhile, expatriates flocked to black cabarets like Le Bal Nègre.

Hemingway frequented a Paris nightclub called Le Jockey, which, he said, had the best orchestra, the best drinks, a wonderful clientele, and the world's most beautiful women. On one of our visits to Paris, Ernest informed me:

Was in there one night with Don Ogden Stewart and Waldo Peirce when the place was set on fire by the most sensational woman anybody ever saw. Or ever will. Tall, coffee skin, ebony eyes, legs of paradise, a smile to end all smiles. Very hot night but she was wearing a coat of black fur, her breasts handling the fur like it was silk. She turned her eyes on me—she was dancing with the big British gunner subaltern who had brought her—but I responded to the eyes like a hypnotic and cut in on them. The subaltern tried to shoulder me out but the girl slid off him and onto me. I introduced myself and asked her name. "Josephine Baker," she said. We danced nonstop for the rest of the night. She never took off her fur coat. Wasn't until the joint closed she told me she had nothing on underneath.

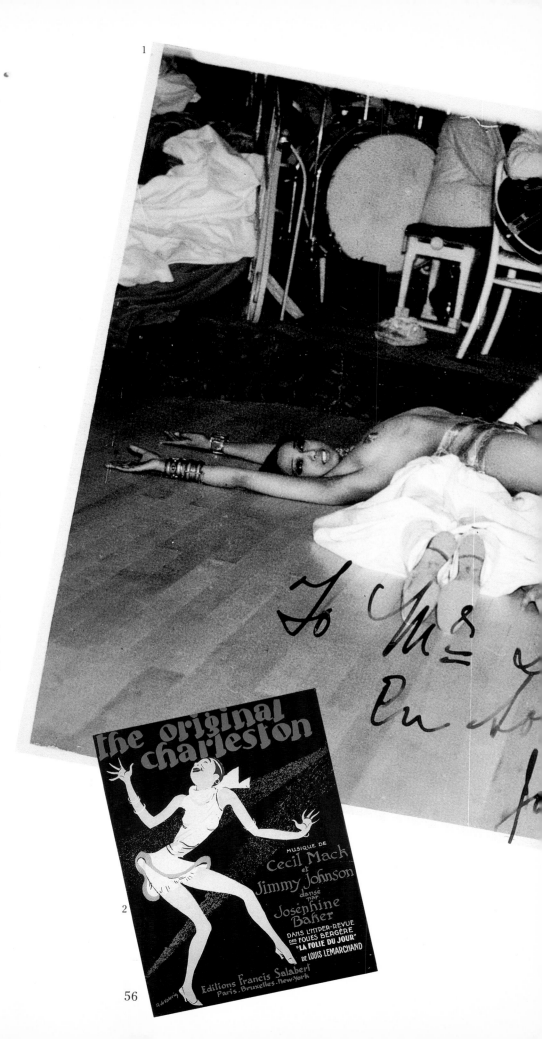

1. Josephine Baker in performance at the height of her fame as an exotic dancer who had become the rage of Paris after her sensational debut there in 1925 in *La Revue Nègre*. Janet Flanner, an eye witness to that historic opening night, would later write of the event as if it had happened only hours before: "She made her entry entirely nude except for a pink flamingo feather between her limbs; she was being carried upside down and doing the split on the shoulder of a black giant. Midstage he paused, and with his long fingers holding her basket-wise around the waist, swung her in a slow cartwheel to the stage floor, where she stood, like his magnificent discarded burden, in an instant of complete silence. She was an unforgettable female ebony statue. A scream of salutation spread through the theater. Whatever happened next was unimportant. The two specific elements had been established and were unforgettable—her magnificent dark body, a new model that to the French proved for the first time that black was beautiful, and the acute response of the white masculine public in the capital of hedonism of all Europe—Paris."

2. A poster for one of the many starring vehicles that the Folies-Bergère mounted for Josephine Baker during the late 1920s and 1930s.

3. Josephine Baker as portrayed by Jean Dunand, the leading *peintre-décorateur* of France's Art Deco period. Here, the attitude struck by the bronze-colored star seems to be the one she used for her first celebrated entrance upon the Parisian stage, when Janet Flanner called her "an unforgettable female ebony statue." After dancing with Baker at a nightclub, Hemingway described her as "tall, coffee skin, ebony eyes, legs of paradise, a smile to end all smiles."

1

1. La Closerie des Lilas, one of Hemingway's favorite cafés in Paris. He liked it in part because few, if any, of the expatriate crowd wandered that far along the Boulevard du Montparnasse from their preferred haunts near the Boulevard Raspail: le Dôme, la Rotonde, le Select, etc.

2. When Hemingway fell behind in his payments on Miró's magnificent painting called *The Farm*, purchased as a birthday gift for Hadley, the Closerie waiters raised the money among themselves and lent it to the "sad-ass," impecunious writer.

2

CLOSERIE DES LILAS

Ernest once took me on a tour of the neighborhood where he and Hadley had once lived, beginning on the rue Notre-Dame-des-Champs, the locus of their little apartment over a sawmill. We worked our way past familiar restaurants, bars, and stores to the Jardin du Luxembourg and its great Baroque palace, then France's museum of modern art, where, Ernest said, he fell in love with certain paintings that taught him how to write.

Hemingway was especially fond of the Closerie des Lilas, a restaurant situated on the Boulevard du Montparnasse, around the corner from his simple digs.

They were good to me at the Lilas when I needed it. Like that time with the Miró. Miró and I were good friends; we were working hard but neither of us was selling anything. My stories would all come back with rejection slips and Miró's unsold canvases were piled up all over his studio. There was one that I had fallen in love with—a painting of his farm down south. It haunted me, and even though I was broke I wanted to own it, but since we were such good friends I insisted that we do it through a dealer. So we gave the picture to a dealer, who, knowing he had a sure sale, put a price of two hundred dollars on it. Damn steep, but I arranged to pay it off in six installments. The dealer made me sign a chattel mortgage, so that if I defaulted on any payment, I would lose the painting and all money paid in. Well, I skimped and managed okay until the last payment. I hadn't sold any stories or articles, and I didn't have a franc to my name. I asked the dealer for an extension, but, of course, he preferred to keep my dough and the painting. That's where the Closerie came in. The day the dough was due, I came in there sad-ass for a drink. The barman asked me what was wrong, and I told him about the painting. He quietly passed the word around the waiters, and they raised the money for me out of their own pockets.

SHERWOOD ANDERSON

When Ernest and Hadley decided on Paris rather than Italy, they were following the advice of Sherwood Anderson (1876–1941), then a prolific, middle-aged writer as much esteemed for his novel *Winesburg, Ohio* (1919) as for the romantic history of how he had entered literature. Wretched in

his marriage, disgusted by his successful paint factory, and smothered by the small Ohio town in which he lived and worked, Anderson simply walked out of his office one day in 1912—and then kept on walking. After recovering from the nervous breakdown this sudden, radical behavior announced, Anderson swore that the remainder of his days would be devoted to writing. With his love of stylistic simplicity packed with complex yearnings, his passion for sports and women, his eternally rebellious, adolescent spirit and contempt for the falseness of suburban respectability, Anderson had an impact reminiscent of Mark Twain in *Huckleberry Finn*. Hemingway loved him for all those reasons, and Anderson returned the feeling once the two met in Chicago in late 1921, shortly before Sherwood and Tennessee, his second wife, left for a sojourn in Paris. Straight away, the two writers seemed to evince a literary father-son identity, with the result that when Anderson returned from Paris, spoke glowingly of his encounters with Gertrude Stein, Ezra Pound, James Joyce, and Sylvia Beach,

and urged Ernest to go forth and partake of an exciting world where literature's future was being shaped, the Hemingways needed to hear no more. Furnished with their mentor's letters of introduction, in which the author characterized Ernest as "a young fellow of extraordinary talent" who was "instinctively in touch with everything worth-while going on," they booked passage on the French liner *Leopoldina* scheduled to depart New York for France during the second week of December.

The unhappy consequence of the Anderson-Hemingway relationship was the comparison that early critics invariably drew between the works of the two Chicago writers. Determined to assert independence, Hemingway expressed his very real dislike of Anderson's 1925 novel *Dark Laughter* by parodying it in a book-length satire called *The Torrents of Spring*, which Scribner's published in 1926. A blatant act of treachery against a generous benefactor, *The Torrents of Spring* hurt Anderson, of course, and Hemingway would live to regret it, as he admitted in later years:

I did it because I was righteous, which is the worst thing you can be, and I thought he was going to pot the way he was writing and that I could kid him out of it by showing him how awful it was. He had written a book called Dark Laughter, *so I wrote* The Torrents of Spring *to poke fun at him. It was cruel to do, and it didn't do any good, and he just wrote worse and worse. What the hell business of mine was it if he wanted to write badly? None.*

He had written good and then he lost it. But then I was righteous and more loyal to writing than to my friend. I would have shot anybody then, not kill them maybe, just shoot them a little, if I thought it would straighten them up and make them write right. Now I know that there is nothing you can do about any writer ever. The seeds of their destruction are in them from the start. I'm sorry I threw at Anderson. It was cruel and I was a son of a bitch to do it. The only thing I can say is that I was as cruel to myself then. But that is no excuse. He was a friend of mine, but that was no excuse for doing it to him.

1. Sherwood Anderson, the first important writer of fiction whom Ernest Hemingway met, in 1921 while both were living in Chicago. The young Hemingway greatly admired Anderson's masterful novel *Winesburg, Ohio* (1919), a plain-spoken evocation of the frustrated longings suffered by sensitive souls in small-town Middle America. Thus, when Anderson returned from Paris and announced that there was where the future of English literature was being fashioned, Ernest and Hadley could scarcely wait to depart, fortified with generous letters of introduction from Anderson to Gertrude Stein, Ezra Pound, James Joyce, and Sylvia Beach.

2. *The Torrents of Spring* (1926), Hemingway's brief, witty, but vindictive satire of Anderson's *Dark Laughter*, a book that Ernest thought fell below his old mentor's standard. By its very savagery, *The Torrents of Spring* was also meant to declare the author's literary independence of Anderson, with whom critics persisted in comparing the younger writer.

THE TORRENTS OF SPRING

A ROMANTIC NOVEL IN HONOR OF THE PASSING OF A GREAT RACE

ERNEST HEMINGWAY
AUTHOR OF "IN OUR TIME"

GERTRUDE STEIN
AND ALICE TOKLAS

Born in Allegheny, Pennsylvania, reared in Europe and Oakland, California, and finally educated at Radcliffe and Johns Hopkins, Gertrude Stein (1874–1946) moved to Paris in 1903 at the age of twenty-nine. There, with her brother Leo, she established a home at 27 rue de Fleurus, which soon became a magnetic salon devoted to writing and the modern arts in general. Hemingway and Sherwood Anderson, among many others, came to her for guidance. At one of her gatherings, Stein remarked that the only geniuses she had ever known were God, Picasso, and herself. The personal claim to greatness had much to do with her immediate grasp of the momentous innovations being carried out by Matisse and Picasso during the first decade of the 20th century. Even more, however, it was the importance that Stein attached to what she considered her comparable experiments in English prose. These consisted, in essence, of drastically simplified syntax and diction, all designed to liberate writing from the dead weight of traditional literary language. Simultaneously, Stein hoped to convey emotion more directly or subtly through the repetition of key words, rhythms, or sounds, as in the famous line: "A rose is a rose is a rose." Unfortunately, she had no patience for editing or revising her work, which left much of it too obscure or too drawn-out to be publishable. However, Stein was certain of her general principles and brilliant in her exposition of them, especially when she had a rapt and impressionable pupil like Hemingway, who, with his iron discipline and drive to succeed, could use her ideas to even better effect than she could.

Alice Toklas had arrived in Paris from San Francisco in 1907, when she met Gertrude Stein. In 1910, Alice moved into the rue de Fleurus apartment, and four years later Leo moved out. The two women came to be known as the Steins, and Gertrude made their life together the subject of her only commercially successful book, the ironically titled *Autobiography of Alice B. Toklas* (1933). In *A Moveable Feast*, Hemingway wrote that his friendship with Stein soured after he overheard a lesbian exchange between her and Alice, with Gertrude pleading with "Pussy" not to force her to do something, presumably sexual.

Yet, not too long after he met Stein and had been given the run of her place, Hemingway could write to Sherwood Anderson: "Gertrude Stein and me are just like brothers." For him truly to become a writer, Gertrude told Ernest, he would have to give up journalism. "If you keep on doing newspaper work you will never see things, you will only see words and that will not do. . . ." When he showed Gertrude the first draft of *The Sun Also Rises*, it was, in her opinion, little more than travelogue and dialogue. "Start over again, and concentrate," was the advice she offered. Hemingway rewrote the novel, following Stein's critique.

As his reputation grew, Ernest no longer played the devoted pupil eagerly seeking the

3

literary counsel of Gertrude Stein. The pupil was becoming better known than the teacher, an intolerable situation for Gertrude. But Hemingway continued to attend her salons, fully aware that a breach was imminent.

1. Gertrude Stein sitting—or rather squatting—for Jo Davidson's life-size portrait sculpture. The posture is the very one that Stein habitually adopted during her long dialogues with disciples like Hemingway.

2. When Picasso painted the protrait of Gertrude Stein in 1905–06, the work became one of the great "breakthrough" moments in the history of modern art, liberating the artist from the soft sentimentality of his Blue and Rose periods and into something much tougher. Stein wrote that after eighty sittings, Picasso abandoned the picture with the face scraped away. Returning to Paris from a summer in Spain, where he came under the spell of archaic Iberian sculpture, Picasso resumed work on the portrait and painted the face from memory, but in a style totally different from the rest. Thanks to the face's primitive, mask-like simplifications, the overall image seems all the more to evoke the power so many, including Hemingway, felt in the presence of Gertrude Stein. Stein, in fact, believed that her own radical experiments in English prose composition made her the literary counterpart of Picasso, the innovative Cubist.

3. Gertrude Stein and Alice Toklas in the salon of their pavilion located in the courtyard of 27 rue de Fleurus, surrounded by the glory of their assembled Cézannes, Matisses, and Picassos. "My wife and I," Hemingway wrote in *A Moveable Feast*, " . . . loved the big studio with the great paintings. It was like one of the best rooms in the finest museum except there was a big fireplace and it was warm and comfortable and they gave you good things to eat and tea and natural distilled liqueurs made from purple plums, yellow plums, or wild raspberries. These fragrant, colorless alcohols . . . all tasted like the fruits they came from, converted into fire on your tongue that warmed you and loosened it."

THE STEIN COLLECTION

1

2

The art-collecting Steins were four in number: siblings Michael, Leo and Gertrude and Michael's wife Sarah or Sally. Although they considered themselves Californians, the Steins had deep roots in Europe as well as in Pittsburgh and Baltimore. Indeed, Michael, Leo, and Gertrude were all born in western Pennsylvania, and before the large family settled in Oakland in 1880, they had spent four years in Vienna and a year in Paris. When the senior Stein died in 1891, three years after his wife, Leo and Gertrude, the two youngest children, were only twenty and eighteen, which made them the wards of twenty-five-year old Michael. By this time the family had shifted their investments from clothing to stocks, real estate, and San Francisco cable cars, which, once divided among the heirs, left each of them comfortable but none truly affluent. While Michael managed the clan's finances and slowly learned to appreciate modern art, his wife and sister followed the precocious Leo and became passionate modernists, all of which developed after Leo and Gertrude graduated from, respectively, Harvard and Radcliffe and began making long sojourns in Europe.

Oddly enough, the Steins' "modernization" began in Florence, where Leo immersed himself in the near-mathematical perfection of the grand figural compositions painted by the *quattrocento* master Piero della Francesca. Then, in London in 1902, Leo took a brave step and bought not a Japanese print or an objet d'art—the sort of thing he and his family had always collected—but rather an oil by the English Impressionist Wilson Steer. Having made a commitment to modern painting, Leo decided to settle in Paris, where he leased the courtyard studio at 27 rue de Fleurus that would become the art-filled salon well known to Hemingway and so many others within the 20th-century vanguard. In the spring of 1904 Bernard Berenson arrived in the French capital and announced that Leo should know Cézanne, an artist whose paintings could be seen at Vollard's in the Rue Lafitte. For a connoisseur already steeped in the classicism of Piero della Francesca, Cézanne, as Leo said, was easy, and so he bought one. The following summer, Leo had a veritable "Cézanne debauch" in Florence, where he spent long hours studying the Cézannes in the pri-

3

vate collection of another American, Charles Loeser. Now Gertrude joined him, and after brother and sister moved into the Rue de Fleurus, they pooled funds to buy a second Cézanne and a Delacroix. This was in the spring of 1905, and by the time the Autumn Salon opened a few months later, the Steins had leaped so far ahead in their grasp of the new in painting that they purchased the very canvas for which the term *Fauve* ("Wild Beast") was invented—Matisse's *Woman with the Hat*. Leo called it "a thing brilliant and powerful, the nastiest smear I had ever seen." Furthermore, he soon acquired from Clovis Sagot, another adventurous dealer, his first Picasso, *The Acrobat's Family with a Monkey* now in Göteborg.

At first Gertrude disliked Picasso's work, but as her writing evolved towards abstraction, she increasingly identified with the audacious moves the Spaniard was making into Cubism. Meanwhile, the Michael Steins, who had taken up residence in the Rue Madame, became to Matisse what Leo and then, mainly, Gertrude were to Picasso—all-important propagandists as well as serious collectors. Ironically, just as 20th-century modernism approached its "heroic" phase, Leo started to hang back, falling victim to his brilliant capacity for so many compelling interests that none could hold him very long. Thus, despite his clairvoyance about the earlier innovations made by Picasso, throughout his Blue and Rose periods, Leo scorned

1. Paul Cézanne. *Bathers.* c. 1895. Oil on canvas, 10⅝ × 18⅛″. Baltimore Museum of Art (Cone Collection).

2. Henri Matisse. *Open Window, Collioure.* 1905. Oil on canvas, 21¾ × 18⅛″. Collection Mrs. John Hay Whitney, New York.

3. Henri Matisse. *Olive Trees.* 1905. Oil on canvas, 18⅛ × 21⅝″. Metropolitan Museum of Art, New York (Robert Lehman Collection).

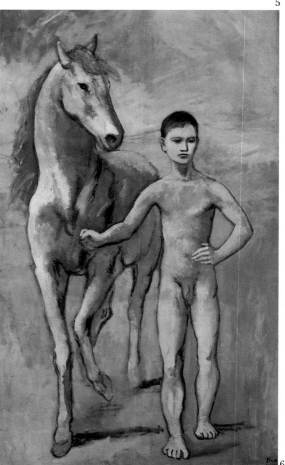

4

5

6

64

Cubism as mere "funny business." Still, by 1913, when Leo abandoned Paris for life in Tuscany, leaving Gertrude alone with Alice Toklas, who had joined the Rue de Fleurus household in 1910, the walls of the courtyard studio were hung three deep with Cézannes, Matisses, and Picassos, not to mention individual works by artists like Manet, Renoir, Manguin, Bonnard, and Vallotton. Even after brother and sister divided the collection, with Leo taking most of the Cézannes and Gertrude keeping the Picassos, there remained a plenitude of pictorial marvels for Hemingway and the "lost generation" to admire when they arrived in the 1920s. However reduced by comparison with what they had been in 1913, the Stein holdings in the Rue de Fleurus remained one of the premiere collections of modern art anywhere, a stunning hoard of the boldest aesthetic statements ever made, assembled at a time when few regarded the experiments of Matisse and Picasso as anything more than crude jokes or mud in the public's eye.

Vollard, a dealer notoriously particular about whom he would sell paintings to, liked dealing with the Steins because they alone, among all his clients, bought pictures "not because they were rich, but despite the fact that they weren't."

4. Pablo Picasso. *Young Girl with a Basket of Flowers*. 1905. Oil on canvas, 61 × 26″. Private collection, New York.

5. Pablo Picasso. *The Acrobat's Family with a Monkey*. 1905. Gouache, watercolor, pastel, and India ink on cardboard, 41 × 29½″. Göteborgs Konstmuseum, Göteborg, Sweden.

6. Pablo Picasso. *Boy Leading a Horse*. 1906. Oil on canvas, 86¾ × 51½″. Museum of Modern Art, New York (gift of William S. Paley).

7. Pablo Picasso. *The Reservoir, Horta de Ebro*. 1909. Oil on canvas, 23¾ × 19¾″. Collection Mr. and Mrs. David Rockefeller, New York.

8. Pablo Picasso. *The Architect's Table*. 1912. Oil on canvas mounted on panel (oval), 28⅝ × 23½″. Museum of Modern Art, New York (gift of William S. Paley).

7

8

1

SYLVIA BEACH, SHAKESPEARE AND COMPANY

With characteristic fearlessness, Sylvia Beach (1887–1962) once declared: "My loves were Adrienne Monnier and James Joyce and Shakespeare and Company." Daughter and granddaughter of Presbyterian ministers, Nancy Woodbridge (who in adolescence renamed herself Sylvia) went to France in 1916 with her sister Cyprian, intending to read French literature after a two-year tour of Europe. During the Great War she worked for the Red Cross in France, traveling between Paris and Belgrade, where she distributed pajamas to Serbian troops. In 1919 Sylvia opened a bookshop on the rue Dupuytren in Paris, then moved it to 8 (later 12) rue de l'Odéon, where she sold and lent the latest avant-garde English-language literature and established a salon rivaling those of Pound and Stein.

Hemingway wrote that "Sylvia had a lively, shapely sculptured face, brown eyes that were as alive as a small animal's and as gay as a young girl's, and wavy brown hair that was brushed back from her fine forehead." A woman of rare courage, she found the resources to edit and publish James Joyce's *Ulysses* (1922). Moreover, she bobbed her hair, smoked continually, walked about Paris unaccompanied, and bartered with sign makers, window washers, and booksellers, all of which established her as one of the first liberated women of the century.

"Although she was hostess, publisher, booklender, and bookseller," a Beach biographer has noted, "her greatest achievement was as a pump-primer, who provided access to current and experimental literature; made American works available to the French for reading, translation, and criticism; brought artist and public together; and united artists from a dozen countries. She encouraged young writers to write critical essays, influenced their reading, found them printers and translators, rooms and protectors, received their mail, lent them money, collected money due them and solicited funds for their support."[1]

The opening of Shakespeare and Company impressed the French, since it was the first combination English-language bookshop and lending library in Paris. Sylvia's velvet smoking jacket charmed the local citizenry, as did the black-and-white woolen Serbian rugs on the hardwood floor of her shop. No prices on books, no great profits, and permission for customers to sit down and read a book before deciding to buy. Stein met Pound, Anderson, and Joyce there. Hemingway called Sylvia "Madame Shakespeare," and relished the privilege of borrowing her books free of charge.

2

3
4

1. Sylvia Beach, the parson's daughter from Princeton, N.J., who after the Great War opened her English-language bookstore/lending library on the Left Bank and thereby emerged as one of the pivotal figures among the vanguard expatriates of twenties Paris. She was an enthusiastic advocate of many experimental authors, most famously James Joyce. Grateful for her steadfast support of him in the difficult days of his early Paris life, Hemingway devoted a chapter to Beach in *A Moveable Feast*. "She had pretty legs," he wrote, "and she was kind, cheerful and interested, and loved to make jokes and gossip. No one that I ever knew was nicer to me."

2. Sylvia Beach, Hemingway, and two friends outside Shakespeare and Company at 12 rue de l'Odéon in March 1928. Characteristically, Beach has adopted a worshipful attitude, this time towards a baleful-looking hero wounded by nothing more, or less, than a skylight that had fallen on his head.

3, 4. Shakespeare and Company as it exists today, not far from the original shop on the Rue de l'Odéon.

5. Ernest Hemingway never looked more like the serious young poet—which he actually was—than in this photograph made at Shakespeare and Company soon after he first called there in early 1922.

6. James Joyce's *Ulysses*, in the edition that Sylvia Beach courageously undertook to publish in 1922 and promote through her Left Bank bookstore, Shakespeare and Company.

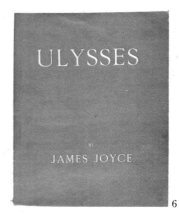

ULYSSES

BY

JAMES JOYCE

6

5

1

EZRA POUND

When Hemingway spoke of Ezra Pound as "the most generous writer I have ever known and the most disinterested," he was expressing gratitude towards the person who, more than anyone else, had enabled him to get his early work published. Indeed, by the time Ernest presented his letter of recommendation from Sherwood Anderson, Pound had already made an important career of discovering and tirelessly promoting remarkable talents, both literary and artistic. Meanwhile, Pound was, in his own right, an immensely gifted and productive poet, devoting a half-century to his *Cantos*, which evolved as one of the masterpieces of 20th-century literature.

Critic and editor as well as poet, Ezra Pound (1885–1972) was born in Hailey, Idaho, and educated at the University of Pennsylvania and Hamilton College, with romance languages as his specialized, enduring interest. As early as 1908, the intense, restless Pound abandoned college teaching and left for Europe, where he published his first book on poetry in Venice before moving on to London. Such was his brilliance and unerring sense of the new that he soon became a leading figure in the British capital's literary life. Closely allied with William Butler Yeats and Ford Madox Ford, Pound also launched the movement known as Imagism, which he soon celebrated in an anthology that included, together with his own verse, poems by William Carlos Williams, Hilda Doolittle, and Richard Aldington. However, it was through his association with "little magazines" that Pound could best satisfy his love of advancing the cause of needy, worthwhile writers. During his London period he served as literary editor of the *Egoist*, a British publication, as foreign correspondent for Harriet Monroe's Chicago-based *Poetry*, and as London editor of *The Little Review*. In 1913, at the advice of Yeats, Pound wrote to James Joyce in Trieste and invited him to submit some of his work. Declaring it "great stuff," he had the *Egoist* serialize *A Portrait of the Artist as a Young Man*. But after persuading Margaret Anderson and Jane Heap to make *The Little Review* an American vehicle for excerpts from *Ulysses*, a New York court found the editors culpable of obscenity, which prompted them to follow the trend and move their operations to Paris.

By 1920, Pound himself had taken up residence in the French capital, believing it to be the "one live spot in Europe" likely to yield "a poetic serum to save English literature from postmature and American literature from premature suicide and decomposition." Eager for an injection of it, T.S. Eliot arrived in Paris in 1921, barely recovered from a nervous breakdown, and, as Eliot himself phrased it, "placed before [Pound] the manuscript of a sprawling, chaotic poem called *The Wasteland*, which left his hands, reduced to about half its size, in the form in which it appears in print." Grateful to Pound for his inspired editing, Eliot later wrote: "I should like to think that the manuscript, with the suppressed passages, had disappeared irrevocably; yet on the other hand, I should wish the blue pencilling on it to be irrefutable proof of Pound's critical genius."

A few months later, in early 1922, young Ernest Hemingway appeared, with Hadley, at Pound's small Paris studio at 70bis rue Notre-Dame-des-Champs. Ernest listened quietly while Pound talked and drank what seemed to Hadley at least seventeen cups of tea. Soon Pound was visiting the couple regularly at their small apartment. Proud of the interest the great man took in her husband's work, Hadley wrote to Grace Hemingway: "Ezra Pound sent a number of Ernest's poems to Thayer, of the *Dial*, and has taken a little prose thing of his for *The Little Review*, an American magazine." Although in the end the *Dial* pieces would all be rejected, Hadley felt that "it is surely most flattering" that they had been recommended by Pound. While a massive, athletic Ernest taught the string-bean, carrot-topped, goateed Ezra to box, the latter helped his new protégé to perfect the severe economy of style for which he would become famous. Ezra, moreover, spared no effort to see Ernest's writing published, not only in the journals he advised but also in book form, through Bill Bird's Three Mountains Press, a Paris-based English-language publisher of vanguard texts that gave Hemingway his first contract. Thanks to Pound, Ernest also became associate editor to Ford Madox Ford for a new, extremely ambitious little magazine called *transatlantic review*, it too headquartered in Paris.

Pound involved Hemingway in his continuing, and ultimately unwelcome, campaign of assistance to Eliot. As Hadley recalled it: *Ezra Pound suggested a venture to relieve T.S. Eliot of his onerous job at Barclay's Bank so that he might devote full time to poetry. Miss Natalie Barney was to offer the initial donation, the remaining funds to be subscribed through a society known as Bel Esprit. According to Ernest, who was recruited away from Gertrude Stein's rival salon, you either had bel esprit or you did not. Pound solicited Hemingway's help in collecting subscriptions. The imprint on the society's stationery was a logo of the Temple à l'Amitié in Nancy Barney's garden, symbol of the spirit behind the enterprise. Hemingway accepted his fundraising obligation with little enthusiasm, but he admired Pound and was willing to assist in the altruistic scheme despite a supercilious attitude about Greek temples in Left Bank gardens and saving poets from banks. When the society collapsed (Eliot escaped his bank job by other means, with the help of an English patron), Hemingway took the money he had put aside for Bel Esprit to the racetrack at Enghien, where he wagered all on a drugged horse in a steeplechase, and lost.[1]*

By 1924 Pound had tired of Paris, with its demanding, gossipy throng of literary expatriates, and returned to Italy, where he would become tragically caught up in Fascist politics. This climaxed in the treasonous anti-American, anti-Semitic broadcasts that Pound made during the Second World War, an activity that forever compromised the reputation of one of the 20th century's greatest poets and most selfless advocates of fellow artists' work.

1. Ezra Pound at Shakespeare and Company, where, in February 1922, Hemingway accidentally met the great poet even before he could present his letter of introduction from Sherwood Anderson. By this time Pound had secured his place in history, not only for the originality and erudition of his own verse, but also for his tireless championing of younger poets, foremost among them T.S. Eliot. In exchange for Pound's help with his writing, Ernest taught Pound, at his request, to box. Pound was probably the most important of Hemingway's early literary mentors, thanks to his detailed critique of specific manuscripts, as well as to his vigorous efforts to get Hemingway into print. Pound, Ernest declared, had taught him more about "how to write and how not to write than any son of a bitch alive." Even after Pound turned maniacally pro-Fascist in wartime Italy, Hemingway remained a loyal friend, preferring to remember "what a great, sound and fine poet he was" and forget the "utter rot, nonsense and balls" of his later political, economic, and racist pronouncements.

2, 3. Natalie Barney and the Temple à l'Amitié in the garden of her exquisite house in the Square Furstemberg, where she maintained an important salon devoted to the arts. The temple appeared on the brochure for Bel Esprit, the foundation that Pound and Barney had conceived in the hope of raising sufficient funds to enable T. S. Eliot to chuck his London bank job and become a full-time poet. Out of loyalty to Pound, Hemingway—according to his account in *A Moveable Feast*—did all he could to generate capital for Bel Esprit, but only, he explained, from those who already had Bel Esprit in their own right.

4. T.S. Eliot, who gave Ezra Pound the manuscript of "a sprawling chaotic poem called 'The Waste Land'" and received it back edited into the masterpiece the world has known since its publication in 1922.

JAMES JOYCE

Ingenuous as always, James Joyce wrote: "Is it not extraordinary, the way I enter a city barefoot and end up in a luxurious flat?" Arriving in Paris for a fortnight's visit, Joyce remained twenty years, and it was during those years that Hemingway became Joyce's protégé cum drinking companion.

James Joyce (1882–1941) was born in Rathgar, a Dublin suburb, one of sixteen children. In the course of his education in Jesuit schools, he read incessantly, won prizes for essays, and studied Latin, French, and Italian. After taking a bachelor's degree from Dublin's University College in 1902, Joyce left for Paris. "I will not serve that in which I no longer believe, whether it calls itself my home, my fatherland, or my church," he later wrote in *A Portrait of the Artist as a Young Man*. Almost penniless and starving, Joyce spent most of his time writing plotless sketches and frequenting Parisian cafés. Called back to Dublin in 1903, he stayed by his dying mother's bedside for four months. After her death he lingered in Dublin through 1904, renting cheap rooms and earning a scant amount from teaching. That same year, Joyce met the witty and charming Nora Barnacle and, after marrying her, headed for Switzerland, where a promise of employment proved to be false. Eventually, Joyce landed a job in Trieste teaching English. His son Giorgio was born there in 1905 and a daughter, Lucia, in 1907. It was in this year that Joyce saw the publication of *Chamber*

3

1, 4. James Joyce, the nearly blind Irish writer, whom Hemingway met at Sylvia Beach's Shakespeare and Company in March 1922 and whom he once claimed to have respected even more than his active mentors Ezra Pound and Gertrude Stein. While Hemingway contributed to the cause of Joyce's *Ulysses*, by discovering a way to smuggle copies into puritanical America, he also learned much from Joyce's example about the fine literary art of paring away all but the essential and of allowing this to suggest rather than state meaning.

2. Sylvia Beach and James Joyce at the entrance to Shakespeare and Company in the Rue de l'Odéon around 1922.

3. Even though penniless, Joyce had it in his extraordinary genius to attract patrons rich enough to support him and his family—the famous Nora, his wife and the model for Mollie Bloom, and their two children, Giorgio and Lucia, both born in Trieste—in relatively high style. This included dining almost every night in a good restaurant, preferably the expensive Michaud's, where they could be overheard chatting together in Italian. Indeed, this was how they were when Ernest and Hadley first glimpsed Joyce, before Sylvia Beach introduced Hemingway to him at Shakespeare and Company.

Music, a slender volume of poems composed during his last months in Ireland.

In 1914 Joyce returned home briefly to publish his *Dubliners* himself after two editors broke contracts, put off by the author's use of the names of actual persons, places, and institutions. In London, meanwhile, Ezra Pound asked Joyce's permission to anthologize a poem from *Chamber Music*, whereupon Joyce sent, in addition, the manuscript for *A Portrait of the Artist as a Young Man*, which Pound serialized in the *Egoist*. Joyce began writing *Ulysses* in 1914, but not until Pound persuaded him to move to Paris did he make real progress with the great experimental novel, finishing it in 1921. Although parts of the enormous manuscript appeared in English and American magazines, no book publisher would touch the whole. This brought Sylvia Beach to the rescue, and on Joyce's fortieth birthday she presented him with the first of a thousand numbered copies. Subsequently *Ulysses* would be reprinted, banned, burned, confiscated by customs authorities, smuggled across borders, and finally published in the United States in 1934.

In addition to his impoverished existence, Joyce also suffered from poor health, having had ten major eye operations without benefit of anaesthetics. He was, in fact, nearly blind. Joyce seemed never without a cigarette or thin cigar, and he restricted his drinking to white wine, but never touched it during the day. Joyce adored dancing—flinging himself

about in gyrations of his own invention—and he loved to sing even though the quality of his voice left something to be desired. Tall, slender, ramrod straight, he was described as quiet, self-contained, and courteous, almost courtly. According to *Twentieth-Century Authors*, "he dressed with conservative elegance, beringed hands being his only exoticism aside from his inevitable walking-stick. Sometimes he wore a black patch over his left eye beneath the almost spherical lens of his glasses. Greeks, he believed, brought him good luck; nuns, bad luck. He feared thunder, dogs, and riotous waters."

"I knew James Joyce from 1921 til his death," Hemingway once informed me:

In Paris he was always surrounded by professional friends and sycophants. We'd have discussions which would get very heated and sooner or later Joyce would get in some really rough insults; he was a nice man but nasty, especially if anyone started to talk about writing, nasty as hell, and when he really had everything in an uproar, he would suddenly depart and expect me to handle the characters in his wake who were demanding satisfaction. Joyce was very proud and very rude—especially to jerks. He really enjoyed drinking, and those nights when I'd bring him home after a protracted drinking bout, his wife, Nora, would open the door and say, "Well, here comes James Joyce the author, drunk again with Ernest Hemingway."

4

1. Wyndham Lewis, a leading British modernist not only in literature but also in painting. As rivals for Pound's critical attention and in their common distaste for Sherwood Anderson's *Dark Laughter*, with the American parodying it in *The Torrents of Spring* (1926) and the Briton in *Paleface* (1927), Lewis and Hemingway entered upon a love/hate relationship that ended only with the posthumous publication of *A Moveable Feast*. Here Ernest likened his old adversary to "a frog, not a bullfrog, but just any frog," for which "Paris was too big a puddle."

2. Wyndham Lewis, *Portrait of Edith Sitwell*, 1923–25 (oil on canvas, 33⅛ × 42⅞"; Tate Gallery, London). Hemingway's negative opinion notwithstanding, Lewis was a modernist painter of significance, more for his Vorticist abstractions of 1914–15 than for his twenties portraiture, where he modified Vorticism's Cubo-Futurist radicality into a stylishly effective, mechanistic streamlining of an otherwise rather conventional image.

Wyndham Lewis, Ford Madox Ford, Archibald MacLeish, John Dos Passos, and Robert Mc-Almon figured large among the contemporaries who shared Hemingway's Paris existence. Wyndham Lewis (1882–1957), the polymath British artist, novelist, essayist, and editor, had worked with Ezra Pound in prewar London editing *Blast*, a brief-lived journal (1914–15) passionately devoted to Vorticist—really Cubo-Futurist—aesthetics. Although his Vorticist paintings made him one of the foremost modernists in England, Lewis achieved a major literary reputation with the publication of his novel *Tarr* in 1918. He enjoyed the fervent support of Ezra Pound, while T.S. Eliot proclaimed him to be "one of the permanent masters of style in the English language." In his critical writings, Lewis alternately praised Hemingway as "the greatest writer in America" and damned him for his indifference to politics and ideas, for his characters with the soul of a "dumb ox," and for his indebtedness to Gertrude Stein: "This brilliant Jewish lady has made a clown of him by teaching Ernest Hemingway her baby-talk.... [She has] strangely hypnotized him with her repeating habits and her faux-naif prattle...[though] he has never taken it over into a gibbering and baboonish stage as has Miss Stein." Hemingway, who could easily match Lewis in ego and hypersensitivity, if not in outright paranoia, gave as good as he got, declaring in *A Moveable Feast* that he "had never seen a nastier-looking man" than Wyndham Lewis, who, in the twenties at least, actually cut quite a good figure. Meanwhile, Lewis was almost alone among critics in finding favor with *The Torrents of Spring*, Hemingway's cruel parody of Sherwood Anderson's *Dark Laughter*.

Ford Madox Ford (1873–1939), also British, was a noted novelist, critic, and poet who had enjoyed connections with the Pre-Raphaelites, Henry James, Stephen Crane, Ezra Pound, D.H. Lawrence, and, especially, Joseph Conrad. As editor of the Paris-based *transatlantic review*, he courageously supported many new writers, among them Hemingway, whom he too called "the best writer in America at this moment (though for the moment he happens to be in Paris).... " Ford even hired Ernest to help edit *transatlantic review*, later placing him in charge during his own absence on a fund-raising tour of the United States. But not only did Ernest betray this trust by publishing opinions and pieces

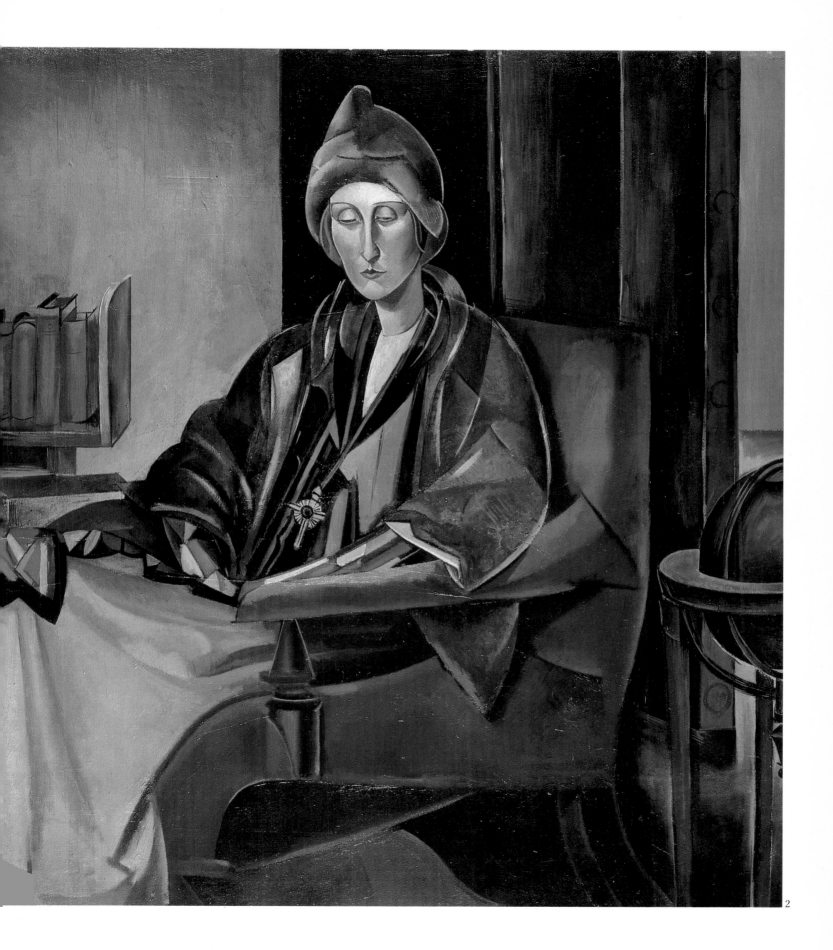

that Ford subsequently felt obliged to repudiate, he would also satirize Ford in both *The Torrents of Spring* and *The Sun Also Rises*. Worst of all, Hemingway decided to serialize Gertrude Stein's *The Making of Americans*, an interminable mass of rhythmically repetitious prose that finally helped sink the *transatlantic review*.

The Illinois-born Archibald MacLeish (1892–1982) would eventually emerge as something of an American poet laureate—distinguished for his long, patriotic poems, several important verse dramas, and essays advocating liberal democracy. In his mature years MacLeish served as Librarian of Congress and held the Boylston Professorship at Harvard, but from 1923 to 1928 he formed part of the expatriate avant-garde in Paris. His poem about Ernest captured the subject as he was in those heady postwar days:

> *The lad in the Rue de Notre Dame des Champs*
> *At the carpenter's loft on the left-hand side going down—*
> *The lad with the supple look like a sleepy panther—*
> *And what became of him? Fame became of him.*
> *Veteran out of the wars before he was twenty:*
> *Famous at twenty-five: thirty a master—*
> *Whittled a style for his time from a walnut stick*
> *In a carpenter's loft in a street of that April city.*[1]

Harvard-educated John Dos Passos (1896–1970) was an American novelist whose literary reputation at one time almost rivaled Hemingway's, following the complete publication of his *U.S.A.* trilogy (1930–37), with its daring kaleidoscopic technique at interweaving narration, stream of consciousness, and excerpts from contemporary periodicals. After he and Hemingway, a fellow Chicagoan, met briefly at Schio in 1918, Dos Passos surged ahead with the successful publication of the war novel *Three Soldiers* (1921). By 1924 the two writers had become Paris buddies, and "Dos" one of Hadley's favorites among the literary pals Ernest brought home. Much later he married Hemingway's childhood friend Katy Smith and remained on good terms with Ernest even into the thirties. Dos Passos recalled:

Hem and I would occasionally meet at the Closerie des Lilas at the corner of Saint-Michel and Montparnasse to drink some such innocuous fluid as vermouth cassis while we talked about the difficulties of putting things down on paper. We both were reading the Old Testament. We read to each other choice passages. The song of Deborah and Chronicles and Kings were our favorites. . . . My story was that basing his wiry short sentences on cablese and the King James Bible, Hem would become the first great American stylist.[2]

Although now a mere footnote to the story told here, Robert McAlmon (1896–1956) wielded considerable power among the expatriate literati of twenties Paris, thanks to

3. Robert McAlmon, whose Contact Editions brought out Hemingway's first book, the 58-page *Three Stories and Ten Poems* that appeared in a 300-copy edition in August 1923.

4. Ford Madox Ford, the British novelist, critic, poet, and, in the mid-twenties, editor of the Paris-based *transatlantic review* that published some of Hemingway's earliest stories. A bold stylistic innovator in his own right, one from whom Pound admitted he had "learned more . . . than from anyone else," Ford consistently praised Hemingway as the master of " . . . perhaps the most delicate prose that is today being written." Nevertheless, Hemingway called his generous, if rumpled, portly, and somewhat pompous, mentor "the golden walrus," satirized him in *The Torrents of Spring* and *The Sun Also Rises*, and finally devoted a savage chapter to the long-departed man in *A Moveable Feast*: "It was Ford Madox Ford [who suddenly appeared at the Café des Lilas] . . . and he was breathing heavily, through a heavy, stained mustache and holding himself as upright as an ambulatory, well clothed, up-ended hogshead."

5. Archibald MacLeish in 1926, a time in expatriate France when Hemingway's involvement with the relatively affluent, Harvard Law-educated poet appeared symptomatic of the transition that Ernest was making in his life and career. Within one year he would move from the "little magazine," tight-budget days of his marriage with the gentle Hadley to the famous novelist, fast-living, high-style period of his life with Pauline Pfeiffer, the wealthy Arkansas woman who would become the second Mrs. Ernest Hemingway in 1927.

6. John Dos Passos, the nearsighted writer from Chicago whom Hemingway met briefly at Schio in 1918 and then came to know very well in Paris in 1924. By this time "Dos" had already published *Three Soldiers* (1921), his war novel, but had much to learn, in part through long café discussions with Ernest, before he would produce his masterpiece, the *U.S.A.* trilogy of 1930–37. With his Choate and Harvard background, he too, like MacLeish, provided a bridge between the pinched bohemia of Hemingway's earlier Paris years and the worldly expansiveness that would come with the creation and publication of *The Sun Also Rises* in 1926.

7. Edmund Wilson in the mid-1920s. The decisively favorable notice that this powerful critic gave Hemingway's first, small-edition books—*Three Stories and Ten Poems* (1923) and *in our time* (1924)—did much to establish their author's reputation as a serious writer.

8. The "American" (August 1924) issue of *transatlantic review* edited by Hemingway, who included writing by himself, John Dos Passos, and Gertrude Stein, among others.

money received from his marriage of convenience to the wealthy English novelist Bryher, which enabled him to publish such promising but risky efforts as Hemingway's first book, *Three Stories and Ten Poems* (1923). Often ridiculed, or simply dismissed, in memoirs of the period, McAlmon nonetheless received this appreciation from Morley Callaghan:

Of all the Americans who had been in Paris— those who appear in memoirs and movies— McAlmon is the overlooked man. Not only

did his Contact press first publish Hemingway, but it published Gertrude Stein's The Making of Americans. *He had the friendship of Joyce and Pound as well as William Carlos Williams.*[3]

When *Three Stories and Ten Poems* came out it was in an edition limited to 300 copies, none of which generated much interest outside the English-speaking Paris colony. Still, Edmund Wilson reviewed the collection in the *Dial*, giving Hemingway the first favorable comment made on his work by an important critic.

F. SCOTT FITZGERALD

According to Morley Callaghan, "the friendship between Hemingway and Scott Fitzgerald (1896–1940) was based more on common literary interests than any natural affinity."

They admired one another's work and enjoyed one another's company—the enjoyment more on Fitzgerald's side than on Hemingway's—but there was a strain to the relationship from the beginning. At their first meeting in the Dingo Bar, Fitzgerald praised his fellow author in embarrassingly extravagant terms, then very quickly lapsed into a kind of drunken paralysis after a single glass of champagne. Hemingway did not think much of a man who could not hold his liquor; then, there was something about Fitzgerald's mouth, a pretty-boy look to his face, that disturbed Hemingway. As for Zelda, Hemingway thought she was jealous of Scott's writing and would do anything to keep him from his typewriter.

A flaw in Fitzgerald's character, according to Hemingway, was Scott's awe of and attraction to the rich. In a hurt letter, Fitzgerald denied any such obsession, despite the evidence from his stories and novels, which were very much concerned with the ethos of affluence.[1]

Morley Callaghan and Hemingway had struck up a friendship at the time of their common employment on the *Toronto Star*. In Paris they boxed together at the American Club during the summer of 1929, a friendly competition to which Callaghan brought the advantage of his days as a collegiate pugilist. At one of their bouts, Joan Miró, dressed in his old-fashioned suit, striped shirt, and bowler hat, sat as time-keeper. On another occasion, Scott Fitzgerald provided a similar service, only to allow one round to exceed the two-minute limit. After Callaghan decked his opponent, Hemingway angrily accused Fitzgerald of deliberately and maliciously allowing the round to run over. Isabel Paterson picked up the story for her book column in the New York *Herald Tribune*, but reported, erroneously, that Hemingway had been knocked out, not down. This item shattered the relationship between Callaghan and Hemingway. Thus, according to Callaghan:

... Fitzgerald foolishly allowed another lapse to be scored against him when he drunkenly related to Hemingway a story going the rounds in New York, spread by Robert Mc-Almon, that Ernest was a homosexual and

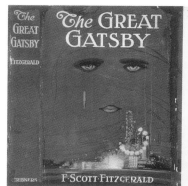

1. Scott Fitzgerald, having already published *This Side of Paradise* (1920), *The Beautiful and the Damned* (1922), and *The Great Gatsby* (1925), was the golden boy of postwar writing when Ernest Hemingway met him in Paris in April 1925. The two most brilliant new talents in American literature made a study in opposites: the one wealthy from instant success, physically handsome but fragile, undisciplined in work, out of control in his drinking, and pathetically dependent upon his wife, the unstable Zelda; the other, economically pressed, unknown except within the world of expatriate "little magazines," ruggedly attractive and physically powerful, regular in his writing habits, proud of his ability to hold liquor, and still wholesomely integrated in his family life. While Ernest seems to have pittied Scott from the start, he quickly understood the genuineness of his rival's gifts, sought his critical opinion, and welcomed his assistance in making successful contact with Scribner's, which accepted both *The Torrents of Spring* and *The Sun Also Rises* for publication in 1926.

2. Zelda Fitzgerald, as slender, golden, and verbally gifted as her husband, aroused Hemingway's enmity from the start. But while Ernest saw Zelda as a jealous castrator, eager to destroy Scott by taunting him into endless alcoholic partying, she retaliated by characterizing Hemingway's bond with Fitzgerald as homoerotic. Having long outlived the tragic couple, Hemingway had the last word in *A Moveable Feast*, where he remembered a perfect Riviera dinner at which Zelda—"her hawk's eyes . . . clear and calm"—leaned forward and whispered her great secret: "Ernest, don't you think Al Jolsen is greater than Jesus?"

3. While the Hemingways lived in a toiletless, cold-water flat over a sawmill, the Fitzgeralds spent Christmas 1925 in a well-furnished apartment near the Étoile. But for all its comforts, Ernest described the place as "gloomy and airless" with "nothing in it that seemed to belong to them except Scott's first books bound in light-blue leather with the titles in gold." Inevitably, it seems, Hemingway would end up lording it over Fitzgerald, who repaid Ernest with near-blind hero-worship.

4. *The Great Gatsby*, the masterpiece that Scribner's published in April 1925, just two weeks before the author met Ernest Hemingway at the Dingo Bar in Paris.

Pauline [who in 1927 had become the novelist's second wife] a lesbian. Hemingway's bull rage over the slander was scattershot and all-inclusive; Fitzgerald was somehow associated with McAlmon, who was "too pitiful to be beaten up" (though Hemingway had every intention of doing so), and Fitzgerald suffered the fate of those messengers who bear ill-tidings to the king. After 1929 the blood-brotherhood of 1925 could never be the same.

Then Fitzgerald began to reveal that no matter what might have happened between them, he still kept some wide-eyed loyalty to his own view of Ernest. Whether he was secretly hurt, feeling pushed aside and not heeded, didn't matter. He began to tell me about all Ernest's exploits and his prowess and his courage. He told the stories as if he were making simple statements of fact. It seemed to give him pleasure to be able to tell stories about a man whose life was so utterly unlike his own. He gave Ernest's life that touch of glamour that he alone could give, and give better than any man. Ernest and the war. His wound. The time when Ernest thought he was dead. As he talked about bravery and courage, I grew impatient. These legends, this kind of talk, spoiled Ernest for me. I had as much affection for him as Scott had. I liked him for being the poet and storyteller he was, and I liked him for his warmth and availability to me, and the sweetness in him . . . . So I sat there, feeling that Scott was belittling himself.[2]

Yet, the fact remains that it was Fitzgerald who, at the outset of their friendship, gave Hemingway a leg up by writing to his editor at Scribner's, the legendary Max Perkins:

This is to tell you about a young writer named Ernest Hemingway, who lives in Paris, writes for the transatlantic review, and has a brilliant future. I'd look him up right away. He's the real thing.

1. Margaret Anderson, founding editor of *The Little Review*, who in 1920 risked jail to begin serializing James Joyce's *Ulysses*. After an American judicial panel ruled the editor guilty of obscenity, Anderson and her associate Jane Heap moved *The Little Review* to Paris and left *Ulysses* to be issued there by Sylvia Beach's Shakespeare and Company. As early as 1922 Hemingway began publishing both poetry and prose in *The Little Review*.

2. The spring 1923 or "Exiles" issue of *The Little Review*, in which coeditors Ezra Pound and Margaret Anderson presented the first six chapters of Hemingway's *in our time*, the second of his published books.

3. At a planning session for the *transatlantic review*, Ford Madox Ford, the new journal's editor, seated at the center of his principal supporters: Ezra Pound (standing) and James Joyce on the left and, on the right, John Quinn, the New York Irish-American attorney who had long been an active "angel" to avant-garde causes.

LITTLE REVIEW EXILES' NUMBER

PARIS' "LITTLE MAGAZINES"

The main outlet for the creative life of Paris' expatriate literati was the "little magazines," so called because of their tiny, select audience, shoestring budgets, and writer's fee of one dollar a page. However, such littleness stood in inverse relation to the immense influence the journals exercised, since a good eighty percent of the important new writers of the postwar era were, like Hemingway, first published in these vehicles. Not concerned with advertisers, stockholders, or subscribers, little-magazine editors could experiment, encourage innovation, and let quality alone determine policies and decisions. As a consequence, the mass-circulation journals of the first half of the century have now been mostly forgotten, but names like *The Little Review*, *transatlantic review*, and *This Quarter*, live on in the annals of 20th-century American literature.

The mother of them all was *The Little Review*, founded in Chicago in 1914 by a beautiful and courageous woman named Margaret Anderson. Soon she would be joined by a close collaborator, Jane Heap, after which the two of them published *The Little Review* from bases in San Francisco and New York. It was here, in February 1921, that a judicial panel found Anderson and Heap guilty of obscenity for having published the Nausicaa section of Joyce's *Ulysses*. The effect of this historic judgment was to send them and their journal off to Paris, where Sylvia Beach would undertake to have her Shakespeare and Company publish the whole of *Ulysses* in February 1922. Meanwhile, Pound, Stein, Joyce, and Hemingway all appeared in the pages of *The Little Review*, which expired only with the world economic collapse in 1929.

The short-lived but all-important *transatlantic review* came into being in 1922 under the editorship of Ford Madox Ford, who had arrived in Paris the year before, following a long and distinguished literary career in London. Drawing on the artistic advice of Ezra Pound and James Joyce and on the financial resources of John Quinn, a wealthy New York attorney with a consuming interest in the modern arts, Ford promised to make his new monthly journal an outlet for young writers. When finally established in a small office on the Île-Saint-Louis, above Bill Bird's Three Mountains Press, he lived up to his commitment by publishing, right along with Pound, Joyce, Cocteau, Tristan Tsara, and René Crevel, the cream of expatriate Paris: Gertrude Stein, John Dos Passos, William Carlos Williams, Djuna Barnes, Robert McAlmon, and Hemingway. Not only did Hemingway get three stories into *transatlantic review*, he soon became its associate editor and, finally, acting editor, once Quinn's death required that Ford go to the United States in search of a new backer. But the old one proved irreplaceable, and *transatlantic review* ceased publication in 1925, after only fifteen issues. Meanwhile, it had given Hemingway invaluable exposure and experience, including the historic opportunity to have *transatlantic review* serialize Gertrude Stein's *The Making of Americans*, an interminable piece of writing so obsessively stylized in its numbing rhythms and repetitions that Wyndham Lewis exploded in *Time and Western Man* (1927): "It is a little difficult to understand how she could be so stupid.... Creaking, groaning, and repeating itself in an insane iteration, it

grows, flowers heavily, ages and dies.... Slab after slab of this heavy, insensitive, common prose-song churns and lumbers by.... It is mournful and monstrous, composed of dead and inanimate material." Hemingway, as the editor of Stein's turgid narrative, may have been the only member of his generation who ever read *The Making of Americans* all the way through to the dropsical end.

As *transatlantic review* expired, *This Quarter* was born in May 1925, the child of the Irish-American writer Ernest Walsh and his wealthy patron, the Scottish heiress Ethel Moorhead. To salute Pound and his contribution to new art and letters, just as the American was preparing to leave Paris for life in Italy, Walsh dedicated the first issue to him. Hemingway, who had worked hard to help

launch *This Quarter*, contributed a short piece entitled "Homage to Ezra":

So far, we have Pound the major poet devoting, say, one fifth of his time to poetry. With the rest of his time he tries to advance the fortunes, both material and artistic, of his friends. He defends them when they are attacked, he gets them into magazines and out of jail. He loans them money. He sells their pictures. He arranges concerts for them. He writes articles about them. He introduces them to wealthy women. He gets publishers to take their books. He sits up all night with them when they claim to be dying and he witnesses and dissuades them from suicide. And in the end a few of them refrain from knifing him in the back at the first opportunity.

Hemingway also recommended that *This Quarter* publish Stein, as well as an excerpt from Joyce's *Work in Progress* (later *Finnegans Wake*); moreover, he gave the journal two of his own stories: "Big Two-Hearted River" and "The Undefeated." In *A Moveable Feast*, Ernest called Walsh "The Man Who Was Marked for Death," which reflected the belief of many in the Montparnasse crowd that the editor had conned his way in Paris through Irish charm and a romantically doomed look. But the look was no put-on, as Hemingway confirmed after having witnessed one of Walsh's tubercular hemorrhages: "It was legitimate, and I knew that he would die all right."

4. 29 quai d'Anjou, the 17th-century house on the Île-Saint-Louis, where, in 1923–24, Hemingway found not only his first two book publishers, Robert McAlmon's Contact Editions and William Bird's Three Mountains Press, but also an important, if largely unpaid, job as associate editor of *transatlantic review*. Eight years later he would write about the "teas" that Ford Madox Ford, *transatlantic review*'s editor-in-chief, gave on the premises every Thursday afternoon: "You should have seen those Thursday teaparties! The French speak of 'la semaine à deux jeudis'...the week with two Thursdays in it. Mine seemed to contain dixty, judging from the noise, lung-power, crashing in, and denunciation. [Guests] sat on forms—school benches—cramped round Bird's great hand press. They all shouted at me: I did not know how to write, or knew too much to be able to write, or did not know how to edit, or keep accounts, or sing 'Franky and Johnny' or order a dinner. The ceiling was vaulted, the plane-leaves drifted down on the quays outside, the grey Seine flowed softly."

5. The debut issue of *This Quarter*, the whole of it dedicated to Ezra Pound on the eve of his departure from Paris for life in Italy. The issue included Hemingway's "Homage to Ezra."

6. Ernest Walsh, the publisher *This Quarter*.

HEMINGWAY AND PAINTING

During his Paris years Hemingway developed a discerning eye for the major trends in the visual arts, which attained a momentary climax in 1925, when the French capital hosted the International Exhibition of Decorative and Industrial Arts, thereby establishing Art Deco as the successor to Art Nouveau and the hallmark style of the twenties and thirties. Meanwhile, Dada had burned itself out, only to produce the fantastic phoenix of a movement known as Surrealism, proclaimed in 1924. The following year the Galerie Pierre gave Surrealist painters their first important group show, an exhibition that brought together works by Paul Klee, Hans (Jean) Arp, Man Ray, Pablo Picasso, and Joan Miró. Presiding over the entire development was André Breton, the poet and unofficial Surrealist "pope" who called Surrealism "psychic automatism in its pure state, by which one proposes to express—verbally, by means of the written word, or in any other manner—the actual functioning of thought . . . .in the absence of any control exercised by reason, exempt from any aesthetic or moral concern." "Surrealism," he continued, "is based on the belief in the superior reality of certain forms of previously neglected associations, in the omnipotence of dream, in the disinterested play of thought."

Picasso whose Blue, Rose, and Cubist pictures Hemingway knew well from the Stein collection, had abandoned the Neoclassicism of his early twenties manner, as well as his commitment to design sets and costumes for Diaghilev's Ballets Russes. Further, he had, in his painting, begun to make ever-more daring and imaginative departures from observable reality. Yet, despite the formal and psychological boldness of his new works—all encouraged by Breton's faith in "the omnipotence of dream, in the disinterested play

of thought"—and his often intimate involvement with the Surrealists, Picasso remained too independent to consider himself a true member of the Breton circle.

Miró's *The Farm*, a proto-Surrealist masterpiece executed in 1921–22, was hanging in a Montparnasse café when Hemingway saw the canvas and wanted to buy it as a birthday present for Hadley. The poet Evan Shipman also wanted to acquire *The Farm* and offered to roll dice for the privilege of buying it. Hemingway won, though he didn't have the money and had to scramble around to borrow 5,000 francs ($250). Ernest wrote: "In the open taxi the wind caught the big canvas as though it were a sail and we made the driver drawl along . . . At home we hung it and everyone looked at it and was very happy." Hemingway felt that Miró had put into *The Farm* his deep and abiding affection for Spain—"all that you feel about Spain when you are there and all that you feel when you are away and cannot go there"—emotions that Ernest himself was trying to express in his attempt at a first novel. He was just back

from the San Fermín festival at Pamplona, where he had introduced a circle of Montparnasse pals to the tragedy and beauty of bullfighting, just as he himself had been introduced to the corrida by Gertrude Stein.

Stein also brought Ernest together with the art and artists of his generation, teaching him to discover the mysterious things in great paintings that produce deep emotions. In her salon he met Picasso, Matisse, and Masson, among others, but the painter for whose work and persona he, as well as Stein, developed the greatest affinity was the Spanish Cubist Juan Gris.

When Ernest went to a museum it was never to look at the pictures in general, but only at particular canvases. Sometimes he would seek out one picture and then leave. He might walk across an entire room of Titians, not looking at any except the one he wanted to view, and then stand in front of that one picture, absorbed in it, peering at the work for as long as his emotions demanded. On one occasion I was with him at the Accademia di Belle Arti in Venice when he stopped in front of Veronese's *Feast in the House of Levi* for twenty minutes. Another time, in Paris, we went to the Jeu de Paume—then crammed with Impressionist paintings—to look at a particular Cézanne. Ernest said it had been his life's ambition to write as good as that picture. "Haven't made it yet," he admitted, "but getting closer all the time."

The knowledge Ernest had of the artists he respected and of their works came from prodigious reading, his natural eye for form and color, his familiarity with the people and the places painted. In the case of masters like Miró, Picasso, Matisse, Braque, Gris, Masson, and Monet, who had been his contemporaries and acquaintances, he gained remarkable insight into their personalities, their drives, and their philosophy of living. Ernest always tried to locate the heart of a painting, what he called "the pure emotion," and the real thing the artist set out to achieve. He identified with the difficulty of the artist's task, believing that as a writer he had the same struggle to achieve the same pure emotion—with the difference, however, that "artists have all those great colors, while I have to do it on the typewriter or with my pencil in black and white."

One day at the Prado Ernest took me to see certain paintings by Bosch, Botticelli, Velázquez, El Greco, and Goya, with particular emphasis on Goya's huge group portrait of Charles IV and his family. "Is it not a masterpiece of loathing?" Ernest asked:

3

4

5

Look how he has painted his spittle into every face. Can you imagine that he had such genius that he could fulfill this commission and please the King, who, because of his fatuousness, could not see how Goya had stamped him for all the world to see. Goya believed in movement, in his own cojones, *and in everything he ever experienced and felt. You don't look at Goya if you want neutrality.*

As we were leaving, Ernest asked if I wanted to see the girl whom he had loved longer than any woman in his life. He led away from the main hall and into a small room where his girl waited inconspicuously: Andrea del Sarto's *Portrait of a Woman.* Er-

nest stood back for a moment while I approached her; then he came up beside me. His mouth was slightly smiling and his eyes proud, he breathed in deeply, and as the sigh escaped he said, "My beauty." Ernest remained transfixed, so lost in his reverie for this girl of the 16th century that a Prado guard had to tap him on the arm and twice insist that the museum was closing.

In later years Hemingway would be the proud possessor not only of hunting trophies but also of a splendid collection of modern paintings, among them the Miró, of course, a Klee, Gris' *The Guitarist* and *The Torero,* several works by Masson, and a Braque, the latter unfortunately stolen in the 1960s.

1. Paolo Veronese. *The Feast in the House of Levi.* 1573. Oil on canvas, 18'3" x 42'. Galleria dell'Accademia, Venice.

2. Andrea del Sarto. *Portrait of a Woman (Lucrezia?).* c. 1514. Oil on panel, 28¾ x 22". Prado, Madrid.

3. Paul Cézanne. *The Maincy Bridge.* 1879. Oil on canvas, 23½ x 28¾". Musée d'Orsay, Paris.

4. Paul Cézanne. *Self-portrait.* 1880–81. Oil on canvas, 26 x 15". Musée d'Orsay, Paris.

5. Joan Miró. *The Farm.* 1921–22. Oil on canvas, 4'½" x 4'7¼". National Gallery of Art, Washington, D.C.

Morley Callaghan remembered that "when Hadley became pregnant, Hemingway went immediately to Gertrude Stein to announce, in the tone of defeat and self-pity he sometimes affected: 'I'm too young to be a father'." After getting used to the idea, he then began to worry about finances. Because they didn't want the baby to be born in Europe, the couple moved in 1923 to Canada, where Ernest took a salaried job with the *Toronto Star*, for which he had been writing, as well as reporting, off and on, since early 1920. The paper was as aggressive and raffish a news sheet as could be found in a North American city. Unfortunately, the editor under whom Ernest worked in 1923 was a tyrant who treated him, according to Callaghan, a fellow victim, "as a paid hireling, put into the harness." The harness was a beat of reporting typical daily events. Despite plans to remain a year, Hemingway lost patience after a few months and resigned.

John Hadley Nicanor Hemingway was born in the early morning of October 10, 1923, his third name (Spanish for Nicholas) taken "not after anyone in particular so much as in memory of our wonderful trip to Spain

2

this summer," Hadley explained to Ernest's parents. Hemingway was not present at the birth, having been sent on assignment to cover the British Prime Minister's visit to New York. He arrived at the hospital in Toronto the next morning, half-crazed with anxiety and exhaustion.

When the inevitable clash between Hemingway and his Canadian editor finally came, Ernest took his family back to Paris in January of 1924, preferring to survive on Hadley's $50 a week rather than endure Toronto on a weekly salary of $125. They moved into a flat at 113 rue Notre-Dame-des-Champs, close to Ezra Pound's studio, and entered the period

1

3

of their greatest poverty, since Ernest had decided to follow Gertrude Stein's advice and give up all newspaper work, even as foreign correspondent, for the sake of making the most of his gift for writing fiction.

Ernest now became the "Papa" he would always remain, while mother and son picked up his frolic with nicknames, calling him Tatie, or Tiny, or Wax Puppy. Hadley continued to be Hash varied with Feather-Kitty or Cat. Morley Callaghan wrote: "They were always making up little verses for each other, nonsense rhymes, like this one: 'Little wax puppy/ Hanging on the wall/Won't somebody take me down/I'm not happy at all'." The infant went through many sobriquets, but "Bumby" stuck. However, it was under his real names that Bumby went to be christened at the St. Luke's Episcopal Chapel in Paris, with Gertrude Stein, Alice Toklas, and Eric Edward Dorman-Smith as godparents. Gertrude added her own nickname for little Hemingway, Goddy.

1, 2. John Hadley Nicanor Hemingway being fussed over, first by his mother, Hadley, and, then, by his two godmothers, Gertrude Stein and Alice Toklas, whom the handsome Jack would remember in later life as "two of the ugliest creatures I could conceive."

3. Hemingway with Bumby, his first born, in Paris in 1925. Sylvia Beach remembered Ernest at Shakespeare and Company with Bumby in tow, "holding his son carefully, though sometimes upside down," as he stood in the middle of the shop poring over the latest journals.

4. Frequently referred to as "the beautiful Bumby," Hemingway's eldest son not only inherited his mother's extraordinary good looks; he also passed them on to his own daughters, the film stars Margaux and Marial Hemingway.

4

SKIING IN THE VORARLBERG

With finances an ever-present constraint, the Hemingways, in the winter of 1924, discovered that a family of three could live for an absurdly low sum—possibly make money by subletting their Paris apartment—in the Austrian Vorarlberg. This was at the Pension Taube in Schruns, a comfortable, simple, family-style place, offering hearty, plentiful food and a bar stocked with thirty-six kinds of beer. Ernest and Hadley skied, but also went on excursions up to the Madlener Haus on a huge snow field above the town. According to John Dos Passos, who joined the Hemingways in 1925, "this was a sort of ski club with

roaring fires and hot food. The people were as nice as they could be. Everyone cried 'Grüss Got' when they met you." Ernest grew a beard to join his moustache, an embellishment that Hadley thought "quite good-looking, quite fierce-looking. The peasants in the mountains called him 'The Black Christ,' and some of them, who came down to the local Bierstube, varied it with 'The Black Kirsch-drinking Christ'." Ernest played poker with the locals and read books he had borrowed from Sylvia Beach, while Hadley knitted. Towards the end of their stay in 1924 came the good news that *In Our Time*, a collection of short stories, had been accepted by Boni and Liveright in New York. It would be Hemingway's third published book and the first to be brought out by a commercial house.

"Hadley was the one who liked skiing, who really liked doing things," Ernest once told me:

I remember one winter Hadley and I went skiing in Germany at a lodge run by a Herr Lint. I was an instructor, and we earned our keep that way, but the previous season eleven of Herr Lint's fifteen guests had been lost in an avalanche—Herr Lint had warned them about the snow, but they had disregarded his advice. Well, losing eleven guests is a very poor advertisement for a ski school, so the season I was there with Hadley there were no guests at all, and to make matters worse there were terrible snowstorms, one right on top of the other. During the storms there were all-night poker games, sans voir to open, and the principal antagonists at the poker table were Herr Lint and the proprietor of a rival ski lodge. Herr Lint lost his lodge, all the ski equipment, and a piece of property he owned in Bavaria. Have an account of that in "The Snows of Kilimanjaro." Call him Herr Lent. Of course, Herr Lint couldn't pay me, but I was able to live on checks I got from the Toronto Star—eleven dollars for straight pieces and between eighteen and twenty-one bucks for a Sunday spread complete with photos. Not much, but the kronen was seventy thousand to the dollar, and for three hundred and fifty thousand kronen you lived pretty good.

1. Hemingway at Schruns, which he called "a good place to write. I know because I did the most difficult job of rewriting I have evern done there in the winter of 1925 and 1926, when I had to take the first draft of *The Sun Also Rises*, which I had written in one sprint of six weeks, and make it into a novel." It was, however, in this paradise, where they "slept together in the big bed under the feather quilt with the window open and the stars very bright," that eventually "new people" came into their lives "and nothing was ever the same again."

2. The Hemingways in 1925 at the Taube ski resort in Shruns in Austria's Vorarlberg. Very soon after their arrival in Europe, Ernest and Hadley became avid skiers, making a two-week trip to the Alpine slopes near Chamby, Switzerland, before they had really settled into Paris. Because they could live very well and more cheaply in Schruns than in Paris, while deriving needed income from their sublet apartment, the young couple would arrive about Thanksgiving and stay until nearly Easter, sustained by a store of books borrowed from Sylvia Beach's generous lending library.

3. The Hotel Taube and its complete staff at Schruns, Austria. Herr Lint, the owner, ran an excellent inn and ski academy, but, owing to the loss of fifteen skiiers who had ignored warnings about avalanches, Ernest, Hadley, and Bumby, their little son, found themselves virtually the only guests during one wintry period.

4. Snow sports in the Vorarlberg in the early 1920s.

1. Gerald and Sara Murphy, with their three children, at Houlgate on the Normandy coast in 1922. So gifted and accomplished were the Murphys in the fine art of living well that they captivated many of the most creative people in France during the 1920s: Stravinsky, Picasso, and Léger, the Fitzgeralds, the MacLeishes, the Philip Barrys, John Dos Passos, and the Hemingways.

2. The Villa America at Cap d'Antibes, where the Murphys entertained, with effortless grace and infinite affection, in an airy, light-filled house scented with fresh-cut oleanders, tulips, roses, mimosa, heliotrope, jasmine, and camelias. Delicious, inventive meals, served with flawless but unobtrusive care, were taken on the parquet terrace surrounded by a garden planted with date palms, Arabian white-leaf maples, pepper trees, olives, ever-bearing lemons, black and white figs. "At night the whole place throbbed with nightingales," according to Calvin Tomkins.

3. The Murphys virtually pioneered the now-maniacal summer cult of the French Riviera, where until the early 1920s no one fashionable thought of going save in winter. By removing a thick overgrowth of seaweed, Gerald Murphy created the Riviera's first beach, at la Garoupe. Here, in 1924, the Murphys entertained a group that included Pablo and Olga Picasso, the painter's mother from Barcelona, and the rather Proustian couple, Count and Countess Étienne de Beaumont.

4

GERALD AND SARA MURPHY

Symptomatic of the leap Hemingway made in the mid-twenties, from the narrow bohemia of his early Parisian life to world fame as a glamorous, bestselling novelist, was the eagerness with which he and Hadley were taken up by Gerald and Sara Murphy, a now-legendary couple who reigned at the social pinnacle of expatriate France. These well-to-do New Yorkers had moved abroad primarily to experience a more gracious and culturally rewarding mode of existence for themselves and their three children. Charming, gifted, and infinitely civilized, they moved into Gounod's former home in Paris and bought an elegant villa on the Riviera, where they pioneered as summer, sun-worshipping residents at a time when fashionable society still considered the Mediterranean coast too hot to visit except in winter. In Paris, Gerald and Sara became leading patrons of Diaghilev's Ballets Russes, then a magnet for the greatest talents of the day, not only composers on the order of Stravinsky, Satie, and Milhaud, but also painters like Picasso, Matisse, and Léger. Conceivably the most fabulous party thrown in Paris during *les années folles* was the large, beautifully orchestrated event the Murphys gave on Sunday evening, June 17, 1923, as a gala celebrating the premiere of *Les Noces* or *The Wedding*. For this landmark ballet Stravinsky had prepared the score, Bronislava Nijinska the choreography, and Natalia Goncharova the sets and costumes. In keeping with the radical departures made by the production itself, the Murphys chose a restaurant barge in the Seine as the site of their soirée and assembled guests who, in the words of Calvin Tomkins, "constituted a kind of summit meeting of the modern movement in Paris." Stravinsky himself arranged the place cards, making certain that seated next to him would be Princess Edmond de Polignac, the Singer Sewing Machine heiress who had made a career of supporting great composers—Ravel, Debussy, Satie—and who had in fact commissioned *The Wedding*. When the dazzling company assembled for the champagne dinner, they exulted over a particular Murphy touch. Unable to purchase fresh flowers on Sunday, the hosts had decorated the banquet table with pyramids of fanciful, brightly colored children's toys. The surprisingly effective arrangements so captivated Picasso that he recombined his toys into a real work of art. From time to time during the hours-long feast, five ballerinas danced to piano accompaniment played by the Swiss

2

3

conductor Ernest Ansermet and Marcelle Meyer, a specialist in the music of *Les Six*. A climactic moment arrived when Jean Cocteau slipped into the barge captain's uniform, seized a lantern, and went about the deck poking his head into portholes and solemnly intoning: *On coule!* ("We're sinking!"). To top it all off, Ansermet and Boris Kochno, Diaghilev's secretary, pulled from the ceiling a great laurel wreath inscribed "Les Noces—Homages" and held it while Stravinsky ran across the room and jumped head-first right through the center.

Only in the late winter of 1925, however, did the Murphys and the Hemingways become close in a sort of triadic merry-go-round that had the Fitzgeralds chasing the Murphys, who, put off by Scott's obvious attempt to use them as models for characters, pursued Ernest as a more disciplined, productive, and promising talent. Very soon, the situation became even more complicated once a young woman within the Murphy circle—Pauline Pfeiffer—fell in love with Ernest and precipitated a crisis that reached its dénouement in the summer of 1926, when, during a visit to the Murphys in the South of France, Ernest and Hadley decided to separate.

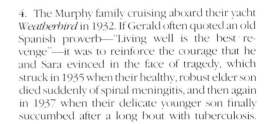

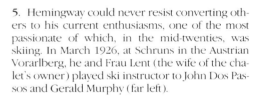

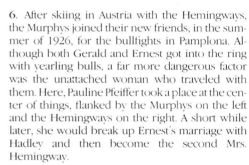

4. The Murphy family cruising aboard their yacht *Weatherbird* in 1932. If Gerald often quoted an old Spanish proverb—"Living well is the best revenge"—it was to reinforce the courage that he and Sara evinced in the face of tragedy, which struck in 1935 when their healthy, robust elder son died suddenly of spinal meningitis, and then again in 1937 when their delicate younger son finally succumbed after a long bout with tuberculosis.

5. Hemingway could never resist converting others to his current enthusiasms, one of the most passionate of which, in the mid-twenties, was skiing. In March 1926, at Schruns in the Austrian Vorarlberg, he and Frau Lent (the wife of the chalet's owner) played ski instructor to John Dos Passos and Gerald Murphy (far left).

6. After skiing in Austria with the Hemingways, the Murphys joined their new friends, in the summer of 1926, for the bullfights in Pamplona. Although both Gerald and Ernest got into the ring with yearling bulls, a far more dangerous factor was the unattached woman who traveled with them. Here, Pauline Pfeiffer took a place at the center of things, flanked by the Murphys on the left and the Hemingways on the right. A short while later, she would break up Ernest's marriage with Hadley and then become the second Mrs. Hemingway.

7. Gerald Murphy, *The Watch*, 1925 (Dallas Museum of Art). Shortly after his arrival in France, Murphy made an instant and totally comprehending connection with the latest in modern art. Untrained but for a few lessons with Natalia Goncharova, he began painting some of the most original and authoritative modern pictures ever produced by an American of his generation. Later explaining that "real objects which I admired had become for me abstractions, or objects in a world of abstraction," the artist succeeded in making a unique synthesis of American close-focus realism, Cubist flat-pattern design, twenties-style Art Deco or "machine" aesthetics to produce heroically scaled, emblematic images of the kind of vernacular objects that Pop artists would glorify in the 1960s.

1

SPAIN AND THE CORRIDA

Even before Hemingway left for his first visit to Spain, in the summer of 1923, friends in Paris—especially Gertrude Stein and Alice Toklas—believed that Ernest would become one of the true *aficionados* of bullfighting. On that initial visit south of the Pyrenees, Hemingway traveled as the guest of his first publisher, Robert McAlmon of Contact Editions, but also in the company of his second publisher, Bill Bird of Three Mountains Press. Right off, Hemingway immersed himself in the world of the corrida, staying in the same *pensións* as the matadors, following them from Madrid to Seville, Ronda, and Granada, and acquiring a rich vocabulary of professional or vernacular terms. Advised by Alice Toklas that his bull-fight education could be enhanced by attending the San Fermín Festival in Pamplona, he went there in July, this time traveling with Hadley, already five months pregnant. For Hemingway the writer and sportsman, the week in the classic white-walled, sun-baked Navarese hill town indeed became an epiphany. For the Hemingways as a couple, it proved to be one of the happiest interludes in their marriage.

Thereafter, for a number of years, Hemingway attended Pamplona's bullfights annually, always surrounded by friends—Chink Dorman-Smith, Donald Ogden Stewart, John Dos Passos, Gerald and Sara Murphy, and, fatefully in 1926, Pauline Pfeiffer. Before them all, as well as crowds of impressed Spaniards, Ernest took delight in joining the free-for-alls at which amateurs were allowed to enter the bullring and challenge yearlings whose

horns had been padded. Gerald Murphy told of one of these sessions in 1926:

When you were with Ernest, and he suggested that you try something, you didn't refuse. He suggested that I test my nerve in the ring with the yearlings. I took along my raincoat and shook it about, and all of a sudden this animal—it was just a yearling and the horns were padded, but it looked about the size of a locomotive to me—came right for me, at top speed. Evidently, I was so terrified that I just stood there holding the coat in front of me. Ernest, who had been watching very carefully to see that I didn't get into trouble, yelled, "Hold it to the side!" And miraculously, at the last moment, I moved the coat to my left and the bull veered toward it and went by me. Ernest was delighted. He said I'd made a veronica. Ernest himself, meanwhile, was waiting for one of the larger bulls, and a lot of people were watching him. *Finally he caught the attention of the bull he wanted, and it came toward him. He had absolutely nothing in his hands. Just as the bull reached him, he threw himself over the horns and landed on the animal's back, and stayed there, facing the tail. The bull staggered on a few steps and then collapsed under Ernest's great weight. After that, to my great relief, we went back to our seats.*[1]

Thanks to such exploits, Ernest began to attract the attention of the international press,

2

FERIAS Y FIESTAS DE SAN FERMIN
Programa de festejos que se celebrarán
del 6 al 18 de Julio

3

and he also began to achieve a cult status in Pamplona, according to another Murphy account:

We drank the very dry sherry and ate roasted almonds, and every time we sat down anywhere we would be surrounded by Spaniards who shot wine into Ernest's mouth from their wineskins. One evening a whole crowd of people suddenly began pointing at Sara and me and shouting, Dansa Charles-ton! Dansa Charles-ton! *Ernest had put them up to it. The Charleston was all the rage in America then, but it hadn't really spread to Europe as yet; Sara and I had just learned it that summer, from a traveling dance team that appeared at the casino in Juan-les-Pins—we invited them for lunch, and they taught the steps to the children and to us. And so right there in the middle of the square in Pamplona, with a little brass band playing some sort of imitation jazz and the crowd just going wild, we got up and demonstrated.*[2]

Meanwhile, for the 1925 pilgrimage that he and Hadley made to Pamplona, Hemingway organized a party of Montparnasse expatriates—Lady Duff Twysden and her cousin Pat Guthrie, Donald Ogden Stewart, Harold Loeb, and Bill Smith. The mix of these personalities was such that it introduced, as Stewart later wrote, that "devil, sex" into what

1. Ernest Hemingway at Manzanares Castle in the late 1920s, during one of his many visits to Spain. Ernest would be forever haunted not only by that country's castles, its yellow, barren plains, its mountain streams ripe for fishing, but also by its proud, spirited people, their language, culture, heady wine, and highly flavored food. Above all, he would be moved by the ritualized gaiety, grandeur, and ultimate tragedy of the bullfight.

2, 3. As these posters from the years 1926 and 1934 reveal, the San Fermín Fiesta at Pamplona very quickly grew from the small ferial celebration it was when Hemingway first attended the annual bullfights to a glamorous international event sought out by the Biarritz glitterati and the world press. Not only did Hemingway's writing—feature articles for the *Toronto Star* in 1923, *The Sun Also Rises* in 1926, and *Death in the Afternoon* in 1932—help make the difference, but so too did his own larger-than-life, publicity-generating persona.

4, 5. The arrival of the bulls in the *plaza de toros* at the end of their run through Pamplona's streets, as photographed in the early 1920s and then as painted by Hemingway's friend and fellow *aficionado*, Waldo Peirce. Courtesy Colby College Museum of Art, Waterville, Maine.

6. Used tickets saved from the San Fermín Fiesta bullfights at Pamplona, which Ernest and Hadley Hemingway first attended in late July and August 1923. Scarcely had Ernest returned to Paris from his initial visit to Spain when, at the advice of Alice Toklas, he backtracked for the fabulous corrida in Pamplona, this time traveling with his pregnant wife.

previously had been a kind of "male revel." It was this interlude at Pamplona that formed the basis of the climactic scenes in *The Sun Also Rises*.

Hemingway eventually achieved such identification with the corrida and such intensity in his writing about it that by the end of the twenties the Hemingway name had become virtually synonymous with the sport.

7. Ernest, Hadley, and friends in 1924 at the end of the San Fermín Fiesta, picnicking on a bank of the Irati River in high Basque country near the ancient site of Roncevaux. Both Hemingways loved the unspoiled area, with its cold mountain streams full of trout, its pine groves and magnificent beech trees.

8. A caricature of "Don Ernesto" painted by Waldo Peirce, a co-conspirator in Pamplona high-jinks who understood Hemingway's passion for the corrida well enough to satirize it with affection. The title page of a watercolor sketchbook, executed in 1927. Courtesy Colby College Library, Waterville, Maine.

9. Ernest relaxing with a sick steer at Pamplona in 1927.

10. A real moment of truth in the Pamplona bullring. Though offensive to many northerners, bullfighting seems to have touched a deeply responsive, Latin chord in the soul of Anglo-Saxon Hemingway, who once wrote that the *faena* gave "him an ecstasy that is, while momentary, as profound as any religious ecstasy."

11, 12. One of the free-for-alls in the Pamplona bullring at which amateurs were permitted to act out moments of truth with yearlings that had been run through the streets. Hemingway—the one in white pants—always participated with gusto, often becoming the news-making star of the event.

7

DON ERNESTO EN PAMPLONA

8

9

12

10

11

1, 2. The Crillon, an elegant hotel on the Place de la Concorde (Right Bank), and the Café Select on the Boulevard Montparnasse (Left Bank), both settings for crucial encounters in *The Sun Also Rises*: "At five o'clock I was in the Hôtel Crillon waiting for Brett. She was not there, so I sat down and wrote some letters. They were not very good letters but I hoped their being on Crillon stationery would help them. Brett did not turn up, so about quarter to six I went down to the bar and had a Jack Rose with George the barman. Brett had not been in the bar either, and so I looked for her upstairs on my way out, and took a taxi to the Café Select. Crossing the Seine I saw a string of barges being towed empty down the current, riding high, the bargemen at the sweeps as they came toward the bridge. The river looked nice. It was always pleasant crossing bridges in Paris."

3. At Pamplona for the San Fermín Feria of 1925, Lady Duff Twysden, with her sphinx-like smile, gray cat's eyes, swan's neck, Mona Lisa pose, tweed skirt, and man's fedora hat, sits at the center of celebrating friends, flanked by Ernest and Hadley Hemingway. Characteristically, the men sport Basque berets. During this vintage summer "of erupting feuds, damaged friendships, tight lips, and thin skins"—all of which sparked the creation of *The Sun Also Rises*—Hadley did not invariably wear her radiant and familiar smile. Oddly enough, it was she, not Duff Twysden, whose effect upon a brilliant young matador—inspiring him to present her with both his cape and his bull's ear—gave Hemingway the idea of an affair between the fictional Brett Ashley, modeled on Duff, and the novel's Pedro Romero.

4. Lady Duff Twysden, whose alluring presence at the center of rivalrous male admirers, both in Montparnasse and in Pamplona, fired Hemingway's imagination to produce his first novel, *The Sun Also Rises*. For all her steady drinking and miscellaneous love life, Duff Twysden at thirty-two offered a fresh- if long-faced, bobbed-hair, elegantly tailored figure, a person of natural chic, insouciant wit, and low, murmurous laughter that the smitten Harold Loeb described as having the "liquid quality of the lilt of a mockingbird singing to the moon." Without significant funds of her own, Duff seems to have survived on remittances sent her cousin, Pat Guthrie, a dissipated Scotsman with whom she was generally inseparable in 1925. After *The Sun Also Rises* appeared, the living prototype of Lady Brett Ashley evidently took her time about reading it. Then, rather than resent her fictional reincarnation in a notorious *roman à clef*, Duff merely complained that she had not in fact slept with "the bloody bullfighter." Even though Ernest's obvious infatuation with Duff Twysden offended Hadley, it was probably never consummated, for, as Brett says in the novel, "deciding not to be a bitch" is "what we have instead of God." Still, the union between writer and subject was close enough that Hemingway captured her words and mannerisms with an uncanny accuracy instantly recognized by Montparnasse's expatriate avant-garde.

THE SUN ALSO RISES

In 1925, for his third visit to the San Fermín Fiesta in Pamplona, later immortalized in *The Sun Also Rises*, Hemingway traveled with a group that included the humorist Donald Ogden Stewart, a wealthy, rather alcoholic friend, Pat Campbell, Lady Duff-Twysden, and Harold Loeb, a Guggenheim heir. The five friends were destined to become the principal characters in the book, with Hemingway, himself, in a strange way, as the model for Jake Barnes, the first-person narrator and protagonist. In *The Crazy Years*, William Wiser wrote:

[Hemingway] exploited the tense relationships and outright hostilities the trip inspired, documenting the fiesta and earlier sequences of Montparnasse life in a fresh and unadorned style that would be the cornerstone of

his reputation. Reactions by the living prototypes of the characters in the novel were mixed. Stewart discovered his own quips and taglines issuing from a fictional counterpart, Bill Gorton, but was probably less amused to be depicted as an amiable alcoholic. As Brett, Lady Duff-Twysden's words and mannerisms were just as carefully recorded, but her complaint was, "I never even slept with the bloody bullfighter." In his minor and fatuous role as Broddocks, Ford Madox Ford must have been dismayed, but he kept his annoyance to himself. Harold Loeb was made miserable by the portrait of himself as Robert Cohn. After he had done so much to further Hemingway's career—admired and respected him as a man and as a writer—to be mirrored as a weak, vain, shallow-minded romantic was a betrayal that soured the remainder of his young life. Hemingway had needed a character to represent everything the new code of

from the working-class Montagne Sainte-Geneviève quarter to the Café Select:

I told the driver to go to the Parc Montsouris, and got in, and slammed the door. Brett was leaning back in the corner, her eyes closed. I got in and sat beside her. The cab started with a jerk.

"Oh, darling, I've been so miserable," Brett said.

The taxi went up the hill, passed the lighted square, then on into the dark, still climbing, then levelled out onto a dark street behind St. Etienne du Mont, went smoothly down the asphalt, passed the trees and the standing bus at the Place de la Contrescarpe, then turned onto the cobbles of the Rue Mouffetard. There were lighted bars and late open shops on each side of the street. We were sitting apart and we jolted close together going down the old street. Brett's hat was off. Her head was back. I saw her face in the lights from the open shops, then it was dark, then I saw her face clearly as we came out on the Avenue des Gobelins. The street was torn up and men were working on the car-tracks by the light of acetylene flares. Brett's face was white and the long line of her neck showed in the bright light of the flares. The street was dark again and I kissed her. . . .

We were sitting now like two strangers. On the right was the Parc Montsouris. The restaurant where they have the pool of live trout and where you can sit and look out over the park was closed and dark. . . .

"Café Select," I told the driver. "Boulevard Montparnasse." We drove straight down, turning around the Lion de Belfort that guards the passing Montrouge trams. Brett looked straight ahead. On the Boulevard Ras-

5. Harold Loeb, a moneyed, Princeton-educated Guggenheim heir whom Ernest first met at Ford Madox Ford's Thursday teas, quickly became a valued tennis and boxing partner, as well as a vigorous literary advocate. In the latter capacity, Loeb successfully interceded for Hemingway while negotiating a contract with Boni and Liveright for the publication of his own first novel, *Doodab*. Yet, even though this enabled Ernest to be published in America for the first time, Harold found himself attacked by his beneficiary, not only during their 1925 Pamplona frolic but also in its imaginative recreation in *The Sun Also Rises*. The causes appear to have been several, among them Loeb's love of romantic fiction, his distaste for the corrida, and his winning manner with Lady Duff Twysden. Thus, when Duff's besotted cousin and keeper suddenly ordered Harold to leave their party and Harold turned to Duff, who said he should remain, Ernest exploded in macho rage. "You lousy bastard," he roared at Loeb, "running to a woman." But after the two antagonists stepped outside, they quickly made up, followed by a contrite note from Ernest. In *The Sun Also Rises*, however, Hemingway transformed his friend into the very kind of weak, vain, sentimentalist that the "lost generation" detested. With this, Loeb became one of the many benefactors whom the great writer would repay with incomprehensible—often anti-Semitic—cruelty.

the lost generation opposed—if not a villain, at least a disagreeable catalyst-figure—and Harold Loeb was his ruthless choice. For all the innovation and effervescence of that vintage year, 1925 marked a season of erupting feuds, damaged friendships, tight lips and thin skins.

The central characters in the novel are Jake Barnes, an American newspaperman whose war wounds have left him capable of desire but physically unable to satisfy it, and Lady Brett Ashley, a promiscuous, elegant English-woman who searches for but cannot find a satisfactory replacement for her attraction to Jake. Early in the narrative, Brett and Jake find melancholy rapport in a taxi as they move

6. The jacket of *The Sun Also Rises*, Hemingway's first novel, a book in which the hero-narrator's observation about the matador Pedro Romero—that he "had the old thing, the holding of his purity of line through the maximum of exposure"—could be taken as an implicit literary ideal. It also became something like a philosophy of life for the "lost generation," which regarded *The Sun Also Rises* as a kind of generational Bible.

7. Caetano Ordóñez, the astonishing young matador who, as Niño de la Palma, so captivated the Hemingways in the summer of 1925 that he presented an overjoyed Hadley with the ear from one of his bulls and then his cape. From this came the climactic episode in *The Sun Also Rises*, the affair between Brett Ashley—in retreat from her tortured love for the sexually incapacitated Jake—and the bullfighter Pedro Romero.

8, 9. Scenes from the 1957 movie version of *The Sun Also Rises*, produced by Darryl F. Zanuck, directed by Henry King, released by Twentieth Century Fox, and starring Tyrone Power, Ava Gardner, Mel Ferrer, and Errol Flynn.

10. *In Our Time*, Hemingway's third book and his first American, or commercially published, volume, appeared in October 1925, just as the author was beginning the final draft of *The Sun Also Rises*. It was an anthology of sketches and stories selected from his first two books, the Paris-published *in our time* and *Three Stories and Ten Poems*, other stories already published in little magazines, and several new pieces. Perhaps more than any other work, *In Our Time* consolidated Hemingway's nascent reputation as a serious artist, prompting one reviewer to laud the prose for its "lyricism, aliveness and energy tremendously held in check" and compare its rhythms to "the triphammer thud" of Stravinsky's *Le Sacre du Printemps*. In this classic collection, Hemingway attained his ideal of fashioning one "true simple declarative sentence" after another, leaving emotion to well up from simple facts simply conveyed.

pail, with the lights of Montparnasse in sight, Brett said, "Would you mind very much if I asked you to do something?"

"Don't be silly."

"Kiss me just once more before we get there."[1]

Then, in contrast to the brave but foiled intimacy of the Parisian episode, Jake describes the riotous start of Pamplona's San Fermín Feria:

When I woke it was the sound of the rocket exploding that announced the release of the bulls from the corrals at the edge of town.... Down below the narrow street was empty. All the balconies were crowded with people. Suddenly a crowd came down the street. They were all running, packed close together. They passed along and up the street toward the bullring and behind them came more men running faster, and then some stragglers who were really running. Behind them was a little bare space, and then the bulls, galloping, tossing their heads up and down. It all went out of sight around the corner. One man fell, rolled to the gutter, and lay quiet. But the bulls went right on and did not notice him. They were all running together.[2]

But whatever the setting, it resonated with the contemporaneity of tenderly absurd, heartbreaking story, told in lean, hard, athletic prose and in dialogue so ear-true that it seemed like cablese.

Hemingway took the title for *The Sun Also Rises* from a passage in Ecclesiastes celebrating the earth, God's creation, which "abideth forever," unlike the shallow, shiftless, yet poignantly true and oddly engaging characters who people it. And so at the beginning of the book Hemingway coupled the Biblical excerpt with a line often uttered by Gertrude Stein: "You are all a lost generation." Years later he explained the dual, interconnected themes during one of our visits to Paris:

Gertrude kept repeating what some garage keeper in the Midi had told her about his apprentice mechanics: une génération perdue. Well, Gertrude... a pronouncement was a pronouncement was a pronouncement. I only used it in the front of Sun Also Rises so I could counter it with what I thought. That passage from Ecclesiastes, that sound lost? "One generation passeth away, and another generation cometh; but the earth abideth forever...." Solid endorsement for Mother Earth, right? "The sun also ariseth, and the sun goeth down, and hasteth to the place where he arose...." Solid endorsement for sun. Also endorses wind. Then the rivers—playing it safe across the board: "All the rivers run into the sea; yet the sea is not full; unto the place from whence the rivers come, thither

they return again." Gertrude was a complainer. So she labeled that generation with her complaint. But it was bullshit. There was no movement, no tight band of pot-smoking nihilists wandering around looking for Mommy to lead them out of the dada wilderness. What there was, was a lot of people around the same age who had been through the war and now were writing or composing or whatever, and other people who had not been through the war and either wished they had been or wished they were writing or

6

7

boasted about not being in the war. Nobody I knew at that time thought of himself as wearing the silks of the Lost Generation, or had even heard the label. We were a pretty solid mob. The characters in Sun Also Rises *were tragic, but the real hero was the earth and you get the sense of its triumph in abiding forever.*

Hemingway began writing *The Sun Also Rises* in late July 1925, just two weeks after the events that inspired it. He composed the initial chapters in Valencia, then continued in Madrid, San Sebastián, and Hendaye, completing the manuscript in Paris on September 21, "toward the last . . . sprinting, like in a bi-cycle race. . . ." Over the next six months, Ernest revised the seven notebooks filled with holograph copy, writing the final draft during three months he spent in snowbound Schruns, Austria.

With *The Sun Also Rises*, Hemingway entered history and even household consciousness as one of the era's most important writers. In an eloquent review, the poet Conrad Aiken praised the book's brilliant dialogue, the "extraordinary effect of honesty and reality," and the "understanding and revelation of character which approaches the profound," all achieved "with a maximum of economy."

When one reflects on the unattractiveness, not to say the sordidness, of the scene, and the (on the whole) gracelessness of the people, one is all the more astonished at the fact that Mr. Hemingway should have made them so moving. These folk exist, that is all; and if their story is sordid, it is also, by virtue of the author's dignity and detachment in the telling, intensely tragic.[4]

Razor-sharp in his instinct for time and place, Hemingway had captured the disequilibrium of postwar life and the romantically disillusioned sensibility it bred. Seeing Brett and Jake as fellow lost souls, the young people of the period so identified with *The Sun Also Rises* that, according to the critic Malcolm Cowley, Smith girls in New York "were modelling themselves after Lady Brett. . . . [While] bright young men from the Middle West were trying to be Hemingway heroes, talking in tough understatements from the sides of their mouths."

8

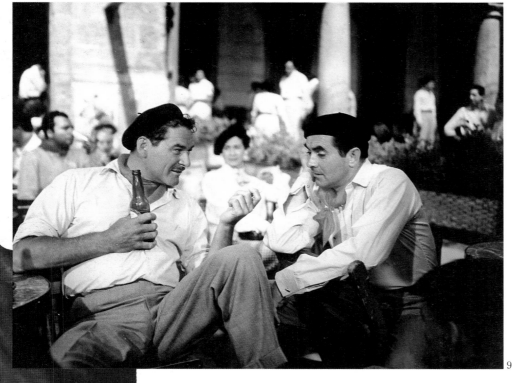

9

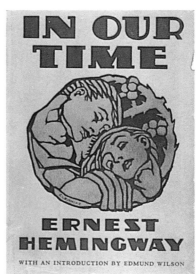

10

95

THE
KEY WEST
YEARS

———

PAULINE PFEIFFER

After the publication of *A Farewell to Arms* (1929), Hemingway's second novel, Scott Fitzgerald speculated that Ernest "needs a new woman for each big book." The new woman at the time *Farewell* appeared was Pauline Pfeiffer, and Fitzgerald's sense of things, while only a theory, boded ill for the marriage she entered with Ernest in May 1927, following an anguished courtship that began as a secret, adulterous affair some fourteen months earlier. However, the pair had known one another since March 1925, when Ernest and Hadley attended a party given by Harold Loeb to celebrate the publication of his first novel, *Doodab*. Among the guests—most of them affluent like the host himself—were Pauline and Virginia (Jinny) Pfeiffer, daughters of a first-generation German-American who reigned like a feudal lord over a 60,000-acre estate near Piggott, Arkansas. Financially, they also enjoyed the generosity of their New York uncle, Gus Pfeiffer, the owner and director of Richard Hudnut Perfumes, Sloan's Liniment, and William Warner Pharmaceuticals. Pauline, in addition, had a job as a fashion reporter for *Vogue*. And such was her chic that Ernest expressed his response to the Pfeiffer girls by saying that he would like to take out the bright-witted Jinny but in her sister's coat, a smashing creation made of chipmunk skins!

Born in 1895, Pauline was older than Ernest—by four years, rather than Hadley's eight—and more pleasant-faced than pretty. But with her slim figure, boyishly bobbed hair, and irrepressible vivacity, she seemed the very embodiment of a youthful, twenties flapper. Robert McAlmon called her "small-boned and lively as a partridge." Although very much at home in expatriate Paris, Pauline came from quite a different environment. Paul Pfeiffer, after making a fortune as a commodities broker in St. Louis, had tired of city life by 1912 and decided to move to California, only to end up in Piggott, when the train broke down there and the surrounding timberland looked ripe for clearing and development. Very soon he would possess almost everything in sight—land, land office, bank, cotton gin, and a vast plantation sown with wheat, cotton, clover, corn, and soybeans. Fully occupied as one of Arkansas' richest landowners, Paul Pfeiffer left the rearing of his two daughters to their mother, a pious but droll, warm-hearted Irish Catholic who maintained a private chapel and kept Pauline and Jinny firmly in the faith. About the time Hadley graduated high school, Pauline

1. Pauline Pfeiffer in 1918, during her high-fashion days as a reporter for *Vogue*.

2. A *défilé de mannequins* at the 1925 Couture Ball, the sort of fashion event that Pauline Pfeiffer covered for Paris *Vogue*.

3. Cover of Paris *Vogue* for November 1926, probably the last issue that Pauline helped prepare before she resigned to marry Ernest Hemingway.

3

2

entered it, also in St. Louis, before moving on to study journalism at the University of Missouri. A job on the night desk at the *Cleveland Star* led to the *Daily Telegraph* in New York and then *Vanity Fair*, whose publisher, Condé Nast, reassigned her to Paris, where she covered the fashion shows for *Vogue*.

At first, it was Hadley who interested Pauline, prompting her to call at the sawmill flat, where she was appalled not only at the condition under which the Hemingways lived but also at the sight of the master himself, loutishly unshaven, undressed, and still sprawled in bed, reading. Gradually, her attitude shifted, as she observed the handsome writer working quietly at the Closerie des Lilas and became enchanted with the deftness of his ready humor. By late 1925 Ernest had begun to enjoy her company and the enthusiastic support she offered, against Hadley and almost everyone else, of his determination to publish *The Torrents of Spring*, a notorious satire of a recent novel by Sherwood Anderson. Once Hemingway warmed to Pauline—to her flattery, of course, but also to her intelligence, style, and studied interest in literature—she became convinced that theirs was a mutually enhancing love "that only about two persons in one or several centuries

get." Moreover, with her wealth, her sense of unique understanding, and her eagerness to accede to him in every way, Pauline felt certain it was she alone who could best help the rapidly maturing novelist to realize the fullness of his genius. The affair began in Schruns, where Pauline joined the Hemingways for skiing, intensified in Paris as Ernest passed through to and from New York in February 1926, and really caught fire during a visit the Hemingways made to the Murphys in the South of France. When Bumby had to be quarantined for whooping cough, Pauline arrived to keep the family company, since she had been immunized by a childhood bout with the disease. "Here it was," Hadley later said, "that the three breakfast trays, three wet bathing suits on the line, three bicycles were to be found." For a while Ernest reveled in his position at the center of two women's lives,

but by the time the *ménage à trois*, together with the Murphys, completed a week at the 1926 Pamplona Festival, the situation had become desperate. Back at Antibes, Hadley and Ernest shocked everyone by announcing their decision to break up. In Paris, Hadley decreed that if the love between Ernest and Pauline could survive a hundred-day cooling-off period, during which the pair must remain apart, she would agree to a divorce. But without *any* woman to inspire or attend him, Ernest could not cope and soon gave way to lachrymose thoughts of suicide. Hadley, meanwhile, proved strong enough to bear her own grief but not his; thus, well before the trial separation had run its course, she wrote Ernest that he was now free to arrange a French divorce on grounds of incompatibility.

On May 10, 1927, in Paris, Ernest Heming-

4. Ernest Hemingway in early 1928, shortly after he pulled a bathroom skylight down on his head while groping for the toilet chain.

5. Pauline with Patrick, her firstborn, and her five-year-old stepson, Bumby, whom she came to love quite as much as she did her own two boys.

6. Pauline and Ernest on the beach at Hendaye in September 1927. Note Pauline's shingled hair, a boyish style that Ernest would soon appropriate for the heroine of his next novel, *A Farewell to Arms* (1929).

7. Hôtel de Luzy, 6 rue Férou, near the Saint-Sulpice Church in Paris. Here, in this Louis XVI mansion, Pauline and Ernest kept an elegant apartment from 1927 until 1931.

8. Pauline attempting to trim her husband's shaggy hair during a stay on Bimini in 1937.

7

way married Pauline Pfeiffer in the Roman Catholic rite, after having persuaded the Church that the anointment he had received in 1918 from an Italian priest passing among the wounded at Fossalta constituted a legitimate baptism. With his new marriage, Hemingway left behind everything he associated with Hadley—Chicago, bourgeois values, domestic bondage, a cold-water loft over a noisy factory, writing in cafés—and embraced the life of a celebrated novelist. Now he would be rich enough to keep up with the Murphys, ski at Gstaad rather than Schruns, hunt lions in Africa instead of following plebeian bike races, and generally make the world his oyster, not just Montparnasse.

A year later Pauline gave birth to Patrick Hemingway on June 27, 1928, followed by the arrival of Gregory Hemingway on November 12, 1931. Despite a long period of genuine happiness together—at their antique-furnished apartment in Paris, in a splendid, well-managed home in Key West, on countless fishing trips in the Caribbean, during hunting season in Wyoming, on safari in Africa—their marriage began to deteriorate as early as 1931. Even Pauline's unwavering resolve to devote herself exclusively to Ernest

—leaving the children to be reared by nannies—could not prevent the divorce that finally came in 1940.

Later, Hemingway would become almost as tender in his feeling for the long-dead Pauline as he did for the still-living Hadley in *A Moveable Feast*, where he bitterly blamed Pauline—as well as Dos Passos and the Murphys!—for the collapse of his first marriage. In an excised passage from the manuscript for the same book, Hemingway wrote: *...I never worked better nor was I happier [than after Hadley remarried]. ...I loved [Pauline] truly and she loved me truly and well. And we had as good a life together for many years as early Paris had been.... That part, the part with Pauline, I have...saved for the start of another book.... It could be a good book because it tells many things that no one knows or can ever know and it has love, remorse, contrition and unbelievable happiness and the story of truly good work and final sorrow.*

As for *A Farewell to Arms*, his new wife figured mainly in the heroine's death, which resulted from a prolonged, wracking labor like that suffered in 1928 by Pauline, who survived thanks only to successful Caesarean section.

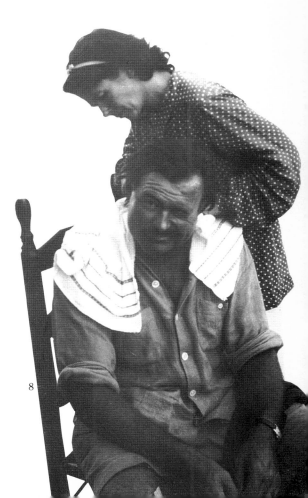

8

101

A FAREWELL TO ARMS

After the stunning critical and popular success of *The Sun Also Rises*, Hemingway felt it imperative that the novel's successor be a work of exceptional quality. With the distractions of divorce, remarriage, and a series of freak accidents, it was not until early 1928 that the long-fermenting memories of 1918 finally began to mature into the vintage prose of *A Farewell to Arms*, judged by many to be the author's crowning achievement. Yet when Hemingway took up the theme he thought it would make a short story. Very quickly, however, his ruminations about the war and the affair with Agnes von Kurowsky assumed a larger, almost aureoled life, beginning with the unforgettable opening paragraph:

In the late summer of that year we lived in a house in a village that looked across the river and the plain to the mountains. In the bed of the river there were pebbles and boulders, dry and white in the sun, and the water was clear and swiftly moving and blue in the channels. Troops went by the house and down the road and the dust they raised powdered the leaves of the trees. The trunks of the trees too were dusty and the leaves fell early that year and we saw the troops marching along the road and the dust rising and leaves, stirred by the breeze, falling and the soldiers marching and afterwards the road bare and white except for the leaves.[1]

The writing progressed steadily through one of the most agitated and traumatic periods in the author's life. In 1948 Hemingway described it thus:

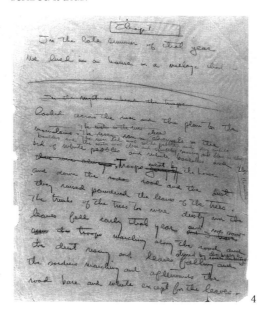

1. The jacket for the first edition of *A Farewell to Arms*, published by Charles Scribner's Sons in New York in 1929.

2,3. Jackets for two later editions of *A Farewell to Arms*, one of the most popular and reprinted of all novels.

4. Ernest's holograph manuscript for the famous opening paragraph of *A Farewell to Arms*, which the author began writing in March 1928, ten years after the war-and-love experiences that inspired it.

5. Lake Maggiore in northern Italy across which the lovers in *A Farewell to Arms* rowed their way to a "separate peace," far from the horrors of war.

6

6. Rock Hudson and Jennifer Jones as Frederic Henry and his English Red Cross Nurse, Catherine Barkley, in the 1957 movie remake of *A Farewell to Arms*, which Ernest also despised.

7. Gary Cooper (Lieutenant Frederic Henry), Helen Hayes (Nurse Catherine Barkley), and Adolphe Menjou (Rinaldi) in Paramount's 1933 movie version of *A Farewell to Arms*, which Ernest hated. He even refused to attend the premiere, held in Piggott, Arkansas, his second wife's hometown.

8. David O. Selznick used *A Farewell to Arms* as the vehicle for his first film in nine years. Here, in 1957, he directs Rock Hudson on location in the Italian Alps, the actual setting of Hemingway's 1929 novel.

7

This book was written in Paris, France, Key West, Florida, Piggott, Arkansas, Kansas City, Missouri, Sheridan, Wyoming, and the first draft of it was finished near Big Horn in Wyoming. It was begun in the winter months of 1928 and the first draft was finished in September of that year. It was rewritten in the fall and winter of 1928 in Key West and the final writing was finished in Paris in the spring of 1929.

During the time I was writing the first draft my second son Patrick was delivered in Kansas City by Caesarean section and while I was rewriting my father killed himself in Oak Park, Illinois. I was not quite thirty years old when I finished the book and the day it was published was the day the stock market crashed.[2]

Hemingway might also have added that he had just collected the five-year-old Bumby at the pier in New York and was on a Florida-bound train when Western Union intercepted him in Trenton to deliver the news of Dr. Hemingway's suicide that morning, December 6, 1928. Entrusting his French-speaking son to the care of a Pullman porter, Ernest, with only $40 in his pocket, left the train at Philadelphia, wired his publishers and friends for money, and, with $100 sent by Scott Fitzgerald, boarded the overnight express for Chicago to join his grief-stricken family. Before Christmas, however, Ernest was back in Key West, desperate to conclude the novel with one of the thirty-two versions he wrote for the ending. When Max Perkins read the essentially final manuscript in late January he pronounced *A Farewell to Arms* magnificent, an opinion seconded by *Scribner's Magazine*, which immediately paid a record $16,000 for serial rights.

Taking his title from a line by the Elizabethan poet George Peele, discovered in the *Oxford Book of English Verse*, Hemingway transformed his experience at Fossalta and his loss of Agnes into a narrative involving Lieutenant Frederic Henry, an American ambulance driver attached to the Italian Army. Wounded in the trenches, Frederic recovers in an American Red Cross hospital in Milan, where he falls in love with Catherine Barkley, a beautiful English nurse. When Frederic returns to the front it is to witness the horror and treachery of the retreat from Caporetto, which Ernest re-conceived, in part, from his coverage of the Greeks' withdrawal across Thrace in 1922. Revolted by the sight of Italian carabinieri shooting their own soldiers, Frederic flees with the pregnant Catherine to Switzerland, rowing their way across Lake Maggiore. There, in a snowbound village

reminiscent of Chamby, where Ernest and Hadley had known great happiness in 1922, the couple enjoy a brief idyll before she delivers a stillborn child and dies, in an achingly stoic—thus all the more romantic—scene of interlinked, love, birth, and death. "And this was the price you paid for sleeping together," the bitter and benumbed Frederic says. "This was the end of the trip. This was what people got for loving each other."

In what may well be the most famous passage ever composed by Hemingway, Lieutenant Henry muses on the futility of war, but, with its denunciation of high-flown rhetoric, the passage could also be seen as a statement

of the author's literary aesthetics:

. . . I was always embarrassed by the words sacred, glorious, and sacrifice and the expression in vain. We had heard them, sometimes standing in the rain almost out of earshot, so that only the shouted words came through, and had read them, on proclamations that were slapped up by billposters over other proclamations, now for a long time, and I had seen nothing sacred, and the things that were glorious had no glory and the sacrifices were like the stockyards at Chicago if nothing was done with the meat except to bury it. There were many words that you could not stand to hear and finally only the names of places had dignity. Certain numbers were the same way and certain dates and these with the names of places were all you could say and have them mean anything. Abstract words such as glory, honor, courage, or hallow were obscene beside the concrete names of villages, the numbers of roads, the names of rivers, the numbers of regiments and the dates.[3]

Thus, the hero would be prepared to make the "separate peace" that he and Catherine claim for themselves, to the everlasting admiration of generation after generation of readers hostile to wars waged by old men for young men to fight and die in.

Helped by almost universal praise from critics, *A Farewell to Arms* became a runaway best-seller, despite the stock-market crash, which occurred in October 1929, one month after the book's publication, not the same day, as Hemingway later stated. However, the most memorable commentary on *A Farewell to Arms* came in an introduction written in 1932, for the Modern Library edition, by Ford Madox Ford, Ernest's old mentor at the *transatlantic review* who overlooked the insult of being satirized as Braddocks in *The Sun Also Rises* to rank Hemingway, with Conrad and W. H. Hudson, as one of "the three impeccable writers in English prose that I have come across in fifty years or so of reading." Noting the American's supreme gift for words, Ford wrote that "one of his pages has the effect of a brook-bottom into which you look down through the flowing water. The words form a tesselation, each in order beside the other."

After Hemingway's death in 1961, Charles Poore, book editor for the *New York Times*, observed:

A Farewell to Arms is generally recognized as the best of all the novels of love and war that have been written by Americans. It is hard to think of a contemporary as the author of a classic. Yet this novel is decidedly a classic by standards of excellence we apply to works of the past. In a way it belongs to the past as well as to the present and the future, since it is about the first World War.

KEY WEST

By 1928 Ernest had an irresistible urge to rediscover America, a longing that came to focus on Key West, Florida, thanks to Dos Passos' evocative memories of a "dreamland" region through which he had once hitchhiked. When the Hemingways arrived there in early April 1928, following a spartan eighteen-day voyage from La Rochelle to Havana on the Royal Mail Steam Packet *Orita*, they found a subtropical island covered with flowering shrubs, coconut palms, pepper, lime, and guava trees. Charming in its seedy dilapidation, Key West also presented a dwindling population of some 10,000 Spanish-speaking and old New England souls, half-

val where bootleg rum and Coca-Cola flowed as if the Volstead Act had never been passed. Here, Ernest would become a celebrated fixture, as he spent many an hour under the ceiling fans at the long, front-to-rear bar, fascinated by the Balzacian motley of patrons ranging from sailors on leave to Cuban millionaires and professional fishermen. All of them readily poured out their stories to the handsome, worldly writer with the dark, penetrating gaze, rough but ready humor, and growing fame. Also, Key West, with its sultry mornings and tradewind-freshened evenings, offered marvelous swimming and fishing, which Ernest took up with the same driving energy he had brought to every one of his recreational enthusiasms, boxing, bullfighting, or wing shooting. Very quickly, he fell into a kind of ideal routine, which con-

paved streets with few cars and numerous bicycles, and a weathered village whose clapboard, iron-balconied houses seemed oddly redolent of Nantucket crossed with New Orleans.

The southernmost island in a chain stretching into the Caribbean from the Florida peninsula, Key West is 1½ miles wide and 4½ miles long, and in 1928 it could be reached only by ferry, either from the American mainland 120 miles away or from Havana, a mere 90 miles eastward. A once prosperous cigar industry had declined, leaving most of its workers to make their way at the naval and military station, which occupied much of the waterfront. For the impoverished locals as well as for the well-heeled owners of cabin cruisers who put into port, distraction could be found at the Navy's two tennis courts, the Cuban coffee shops along Duval Street, a thriving string of brothels, and Sloppy Joe's, a dark, cave-like saloon on Green Street off Du-

sisted of intense work during the early hours, out on the water in the afternoon, and lively social engagement at sundown.

The twelve years during which Hemingway called Key West home would find him at his most productive. The period began with one masterpiece of a novel, *A Farewell To Arms*, published in 1929, and ended with another, *For Whom the Bell Tolls*, which appeared in late 1940. In between he wrote the relatively minor novel *To Have and Have Not*; *Death in the Afternoon*, a treatise on Spain and the corrida; *Green Hills of Africa*, a book-length account of his 1934 safari; the short-story collection entitled *Winner Take Nothing*; *The Fifth Column*, his only play; *The Spanish Earth*, a film propagandizing the Loyalist side of Spain's civil war; and two of his very finest stories: "The Short Happy Life of Francis Macomber" and "The Snows of Kilimanjaro."

Much of this vast work was done at 907 Whitehead Street, where in April 1931 the Hemingways, financed by Pauline's Uncle Gus, bought a magnificent but much-neglected house. Built in 1851 by an antebellum shipping tycoon, the Spanish-colonial mansion had white-stone walls, pine timbers shipped from Georgia, delicate wrought-iron loggias wrapped around both the main and second stories, high ceilings, tall, shuttered windows, fireplaces in several rooms, and a lush, surrounding garden planted with fig, banyan, and lime trees and protected by a high iron fence. Best of all, the property included an old-fashioned carriage house that became a cool and secluded study for the busy writer. Once the extensive restorations had been completed, and Pauline's antique Spanish furniture shipped from Paris, the Hemingway house on Whitehead Street became—and remains today—the showplace of Key West.

1. The waterfront of the Key West village in which Ernest and Pauline Hemingway made their home for a dozen years, beginning in April 1928.

2. The poet Evan Shipman tutoring Hemingway's three sons in the family home at Key West.

3. Heavy, gracefully swaying date palms shaded the Hemingways' swimming pool, in which a large pet turtle made its home.

4. The splendid 1851 Spanish-colonial mansion that the Hemingways bought in 1931 and restored as their family home. Pauline added the 65 × 20-foot swimming pool in 1937, boasting that it was the only saltwater pool between Miami and Panama.

5. The interior of Hemingway's study above the carriage house behind the main residence at 907 Whitehead Street in Key West.

2

3

4

5

6

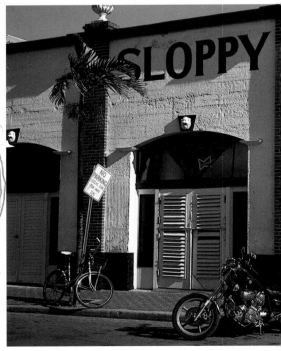

Calling Key West "the best place I've ever been any time anywhere," Ernest invited all his closest friends to come and join him in an exotic paradise that he found as conducive to work as to play. And so many of them accepted that the Hemingways soon found themselves holding something like a provincial court. The Murphys and the MacLeishes appeared, as did Max Perkins and the painters Waldo Peirce and Mike Strater. When French-speaking Bumby arrived from Paris, the poet Evan Shipman, Ernest's sidekick from the Closerie des Lilas days, joined the household as the boy's tutor. Surprisingly, the first visitors were Dr. Ed and Grace Hemingway, who by coincidence happened to be in Florida on an inspection tour of their real-estate investments. However, the most regular guests would be John Dos Passos and his bride Katy Smith, Ernest's childhood friend from Michigan summers and Pauline's former roommate in college. The Dos Passoses actually met one another in Key West, shortly after which the shy, introspective novelist and the quick-witted, outgoing, green-eyed Katy would become one of the most happily wed couples among contemporary writers.

Still, just as Hemingway, after Paris, would never again live in a large city, he would also never again so completely involve himself with a literary group as he had in the Montparnasse world of Stein, Pound, Joyce, Ford, and Fitzgerald. Hemingway seems always to have possessed the capacity to identify with the uncommon common man and to bring him to vivid life in fiction. In Key West he discovered many strong, simple, but colorful types, on the docks, at Sloppy Joe's, in Bimini, and elsewhere. Chief among them were the Bahamian-born Captain Bra Saunders, who taught the writer deep-sea fishing, thereby giving him a great subject, as well as a great metaphor, for his writing; Jim Sullivan, a boat repairman whom Hemingway asked to be godfather to his third son, Gregory, and to whom he codedicated *Green Hills of Africa*; and Joe Russell, the owner of Sloppy Joe's and a onetime smuggler who became a boon fish-

9

8

ing companion and served as the model for Henry Morgan in *To Have and Have Not*. However, his closest friend and fellow safarist would be the wealthy Charles Thompson, a local, native-born socialite educated in New York City and at Mt. Pleasant Military Academy whose fortune derived from family holdings in marine hardware, canneries, and a fleet of fishing vessels. Finding Ernest caught between rich sportsmen like Thompson and Tommy Shevlin and the proletarian "four-letter folk," Marjorie Kinnan Rawlings, a Florida resident and the author of *The Yearling*, published by Scribner's, commented on the risk that he ran by isolating himself in the kind of society afforded by Key West: "He must be afraid of laying bare before them the agony that tears the artist....They are the only people who would be pleased by the things in his work that distress all the rest of us."

6. Two of the men closest to Hemingway during his Key West years: Pauline's Uncle Gus Pfeiffer (right), the New York multimillionaire who paid for their house, and Charles Thompson (left), a local, very wealthy socialite who shared the writer's passion for hunting and fishing.

7. The Hemingways with Ernest's parents, who were the first to call on them after their arrival in Key West.

8. Sloppy Joe's, Key West's prohibition-era bar that became famous for the regular presence there of Ernest Hemingway, who spent long hours absorbing the stories of many a vivid character, from bootleggers and cigar-rollers to seamen, celebrities, and the cabin-cruiser set. In fact, Ernest became so fond of the roisterous, unpredictable atmosphere of Sloppy Joe's that he bought into the place. "I was the silent partner," he said. "We had gambling in the back and that's where the real money was. But getting good dice-changers was difficult because if he was so good you couldn't detect it yourself, you knew he would steal from you. The only big expense in a gambling operation, ours included, is police protection. We paid seventy-five hundred dollars to elect a sheriff who, in his second year in office, went God-happy on us and closed us down, so we closed down the sheriff. But Sloppy Joe's was a good, solid bar—one of the best."

9. Captain Bra Saunders, a familiar figure on the Key West waterfront who taught Hemingway deep-sea fishing.

FAR WEST: WYOMING

To escape the heat and humidity of summer in Key West, as well as the dangerous hurricane season, Ernest renewed the Hemingway tradition of repairing to northern wilderness as soon as the current work in progress would permit. And so very shortly after Pauline had been delivered of her first child, Patrick, born in late June 1928, the reluctant father packed up and drove northwest from Kansas City until he reached the Big Horn Mountains in Wyoming. Pauline soon joined him at a guest ranch near Sheridan, and thereafter, annually as long as he was in the United States, Hemingway would lead his entourage westward, staying in the early 1930s at the Nordquists' L-Bar-T Ranch on the far edge of Yellowstone National Park near the Montana state line. Here, in high, clear mountain air—a world of tall, green pines, silvery gray sagebrush, rushing, trout-rich streams, hearty breakfasts, and plenty of quiet in which to write or read—Ernest woke early, worked long hours at his desk, and then, in the afternoon, rode, fished, or hunted deer, elk, bighorn sheep, and bear, even grizzlies. In Wyoming he wrote parts of *A Farewell to Arms*, *Death in the Afternoon*, and *Winner Take Nothing*. As always, he avoided "phonies"—in this instance the dude cowboys and cowgirls from Eastern cities—and cultivated the "real" folk, such as the wranglers and professional outdoorsmen, who rewarded him with choice bits of authentic Americana. He, in turn, mesmerized them with his extraordinary gift for involving his listeners in anecdotes and reminiscences that he relayed with warmth and humor.

1. The cabin at the L-Bar-T Ranch, deep in the Montana-Wyoming woods, where the Hemingways spent late summer and autumn months throughout much of the 1930s. On the horizon loom Pilot and Index peaks in Yellowstone National Park.

2. A proud Hemingway in 1932, holding the gun he used to shoot the two Wyoming grizzlies whose silvery pelts hang in the background.

3. A cabin in which Ernest Hemingway did considerable writing and reading in the course of his long stays at the L-Bar-T Ranch in Wyoming.

4. Pauline in her jeans and fringed leather vest at the Nordquists' Wyoming ranch around 1932, with Bumby in the background.

1

DEATH IN THE AFTERNOON

The first book that Hemingway wrote following the publication of *A Farewell to Arms* was *Death in the Afternoon*, which Scribner's brought out in October 1932. It was also the author's first book-length work of nonfiction, a labor of love and scholarship celebrating "the modern Spanish bullfight" while also explaining it, "both emotionally and practically," for an uninformed, English-speaking audience. In one of his earliest letters to Max Perkins, written in 1925, less than two years after his first visit south of the Pyrenees, Ærnest had announced his hope of one day writing "a sort of Doughty's Arabia Deserta of the Bull Ring, a very big book with some wonderful pictures." And that is what he achieved with *Death in the Afternoon*, a lavishly illustrated technical and philosophical treatise which, even today, remains unsurpassed as an authoritative statement on the highly ritualized world of the corrida, from the breeding of the bull to the moment of truth in the *plaza de toros*.

To overcome the hostility and stimulate the interest of non-Latin readers, Ernest did more than offer clearly organized, well-written facts; indeed, he leavened his screed on tauromachy with elements of personal memoir, of anecdotes involving family and friends, of observations on Spanish character, culture, and climate, history and politics, vil-

lages, cities, plains, and forests, gypsies, dwarves, bootblacks, and beggars, wine, food, and fishing. Unfortunately he also made belittling and widely condemned asides about such fellow writers as William Faulkner, Aldous Huxley, André Gide, and Jean Cocteau, only to compensate for these lapses in freshly perceptive comments on Velázquez, El Greco, and Goya. Needless to say, the corrida also led him ever deeper into his constant preoccupation with bravery, war, suicide, and death, all seen, like bullfighting, as an occasion for self-discovery —for evincing "grace under pressure."

The faena *that takes a man out of himself and makes him feel immortal while it is proceeding, that gives him an ecstasy that is, while momentary, as profound as any religious ecstasy; moving all the people in the ring together and increasing in emotional intensity as it proceeds, carrying the bullfighter with it, he playing on the crowd through the bull and being moved as it responds in a growing ecstasy of ordered, formal, passionate, increasing disregard for death that leaves you, when it is over, and the death administered to the animal that has made it possible, as empty, as changed and as sad as any major emotion will leave you.*[1]

Death in the Afternoon opened with the éclat of a color frontispiece reproducing Juan Gris' painting entitled *The Torero*, a masterwork that Ernest had acquired during his 1931 sojourn in Spain. It progressed not only through the substantial text but also in extended, discursive, even didactic captions. Ernest made numerous digressions about writing that agglomerate as a personal artistic credo, making the book a treasure for every student of modern literature:

The individual, the great artist when he comes, uses everything that has been discovered or known about his art up to that point, being able to accept or reject in a time so short it seems that the knowledge was born with him, rather than that he takes instantly what it takes the ordinary man a lifetime to know, and then the great artist goes beyond what has been done or known and makes something of his own. But there is sometimes a long time between great ones and those that have known the former great ones rarely recognise the new ones when they come. They want the old, the way it was that they remember it. But the others, the contemporaries, recognise the new great ones because of their ability to know so quickly, and finally even the ones who remember the old do. They are

excused from not recognising at once because they, in the period of waiting, see so many false ones that they become so cautious that they cannot trust their feelings; only their memory. Memory, of course, is never true.[2]

Finally, *Death in the Afternoon* closes with a series of appendices, the first of which is a glossary with entries on pickpockets, "tarts about town," sodomites, sherry, and shellfish, right along with such orthodox bullring terms as *cojones, estocada, tienta,* and *veronica.* Next comes a list of his Anglo-Saxon circle's varied first reactions to the corrida, an encomium to the American matador Sidney Franklin ("the pride of Brooklyn"), and a calendar of bullfight dates and venues. There are also many insights into Spanish life:

If I could have made this enough of a book it would have had everything in it. The Prado, looking like some big American college building, with sprinklers watering the grass early in the bright Madrid summer morning; the bare white mud hills looking across toward Carabanchel; days on the train in August with the blinds pulled down on the side against the sun and the wind blowing them; chaff blown against the car in the wind from the hard earthen threshing floors; the odor of grain and the stone windmills.... If you could make the yellow flames of candles in the sun; that shines on steel of bayonets freshly oiled and yellow patent leather belts of those

2

3

4

who guard the Host; or hunt in pairs through scrub oak in the mountains for the ones who fell into the trap at Deva . . . and in the same town where Loyola got his wound that made him think, the bravest of those who were betrayed that year dove from the balcony onto the paving of the court, head first, because he had sworn they would not kill him; . . . if I could make him; make a bishop; make a Candido Tiebas and Toron; make clouds come fast in shadows moving over wheat and the small, careful stepping horses; the smell of olive oil; the feel of leather; rope soled shoes; the loops of twisted garlics; earthen pots; saddle bags carried across the shoulder; wine skins; the pitchforks made of natural wood (the tines were branches); the early morning smells; the cold mountain nights and long hot days of summer, with always trees and shade under the trees, then you would have a little of Navarra. But it's not in this book.[3]

Reviews of *Death in the Afternoon* were mixed at best. While his most favorable critic, Malcolm Cowley, characterized the book as a "Baedeker of bulls" as well as an "elegy to Spain and vanished youth," Max Eastman, the most damning of the commentators, entitled his *New Republic* piece "Bull in the Afternoon." After ridiculing the author's obsession with tragedy and ritual as "poppycock" suitable for "those Art nannies and pale-faced professors of poetry whom [he] above all men despises," Eastman concluded that "some circumstance seems to have laid upon Hemingway a continual sense of the obligation to put forth evidence of red-blooded masculinity. It must be made obvious not only in the swing of the big shoulders and the clothes he puts on, but in the stride of his prose style and the emotions he permits to come to the surface there. This trait of his character has . . . begotten a veritable school of fiction-writers—a literary style, you might say, of wearing false hair on his chest." Four years later, in August 1937, Hemingway could still rage at these remarks, which seemed to impugn his manhood, and when he hap-

pened to meet Eastman at Scribner's in New York there followed a tragi-comic scene that Max Perkins described in a letter to Scott Fitzgerald:

Ernest ripped open his shirt and exposed a chest which was certainly hairy enough for anybody. Max laughed, and then Ernest, quite good-naturedly, reached over and opened Max's shirt, revealing a chest which was as bare as a bald man's head. . . . Then suddenly Ernest became truculent and said "What do you mean accusing me of impotence?" Eastman denied that he had. . . . [Then Ernest] hit Eastman with an open book. Instantly, of course, Eastman rushed at him. I thought Ernest would begin fighting and would kill him, and ran round my desk to try to catch him from behind, with never any fear for anything that might happen to Ernest. At the same time, as they grappled, all the books and everything went off my desk to the floor, and by the time I got around, both men were on the ground . . . I looked down and there Ernest was on his back, with a broad smile on his face. . . .

As for those who attacked bullfighting itself, calling it immoral, Hemingway replied:

So far, about moral, I know only that what is moral is what you feel good after and what is immoral is what you feel bad after and judged by these moral standards, which I do not defend, the bullfight is very moral to me because I feel very fine while it is going on and have a feeling of life and death and mortality and immortality, and after it is over I feel very sad but very fine.

1. The jacket for the first edition of Hemingway's "Baedeker of bulls," published by Scribner's in late 1932.

2. The magnificent frontispiece to *Death in the Afternoon* was a full-color reproduction of Juan Gris' painting entitled *El Torero* (1913), a Cubist masterpiece that Hemingway added to his collection in 1931.

3. "Manolo Bienvenida, Domingo and Marcial Lalanda making the paseo in the ring at Aranjuez. . . ." *Death in the Afternoon.*

4. "The Seed bull. At twenty-two years the horns are splintered; the eyes are slow and all the weight has gone forward and away from where eight hundred and twenty-two sons came from to the ring so that in the end the hind quarters are light as a calf's but all the rest is built into the bull's own monument." *Death in the Afternoon.*

5. Max Eastman, whom Hemingway wrestled to the ground in Max Perkins' office at Scribner's after Eastman published "Bull in the Afternoon," a critique of *Death in the Afternoon* in which the author characterized Hemingway's manly life and literary style as one "of wearing false hair on his chest."

5

6

7

8

114

9

12

10

11

13

6. "Zurito, from Cordoba, one of the greatest picadors who ever lived, shooting the stick a little back of where it should go, having let the bull get the horn in so he may be well pegged. The style is perfect, the execution is cynical, and the horse, who will be dead very shortly (if you look closely you may assure yourself of this), is not panicky because those knees have convinced him that he is being properly ridden...." *Death in the Afternoon.*

7. "Veronica to the right made by Gitanillo de Triana. This is the second movement in the process of passing the bull by veronicas." *Death in the Afternoon.*

8. "...[Sidney] Franklin making a veronica in the ring at Cadiz." *Death in the Afternoon.*

9. "Vicente Barrera in a pase de pecho. This picture...show[s] the basis of the emotion in bull fighting. The emotion is given by the closeness with which the matador brings the bull past his body and it is prolonged by the slowness with which he can execute the pass." *Death in the Afternoon.*

10. "Maera in a pair of banderillas. Notice how the arms are raised and how straight the body is held. The straighter the body and the higher the arms the closer the bull's horn can come to the man." *Death in the Afternoon.*

11. Good killing. "Varelito has gone in over the horn, kept the bull's head down as he crossed with his left hand guiding the bull after the muleta and is coming out with the sword in and the bull already dead from the thrust." *Death in the Afternoon.*

12. Bad killing. "Manolo Bienvenida is coming out before he has ever gone in and is stabbing at the bull in passing without ever bringing his body within range of the horn." *Death in the Afternoon.*

13. "And finally El Gallo in one of the series of delicate formal compositions that the happier part of his life in the ring consisted of. The bull, as he should be, is dead. The man, as he should be, is alive and with a tendency to smile." *Death in the Afternoon.*

1

GREEN HILLS OF AFRICA

2

Financed by $25,000 from Pauline's Uncle Gus, the Hemingways, together with Charles Thompson, a Key West friend, sailed from Marseilles on November 22, 1933, aboard the SS *General Metzinger* bound for Suez and on to East Africa, where they disembarked at Mombasa, Kenya, to begin a safari that lasted until mid-February 1934. Their white hunter was Philip Percival, an Englishman who had hunted with Winston Churchill and Teddy Roosevelt and had long since earned fame as the best of his kind in East Africa. He and the Hemingways could scarcely have got along better, and, in *Green Hills of Africa*, Ernest paid Percival the compliment of viewing him through the smitten eyes of Pauline: "Pop [Percival] was her ideal of how a man should be, brave, gentle, comic, never losing his temper, never complaining except in a joke, tolerant, understanding, intelligent, drinking a little too much as a good man should, and, to her eyes, very handsome." Guided by this paragon, the Hemingway safari—complete with black drivers and gunbearers, a white assistant hunter, and two lorries as well as a doorless, high-clearance motor car—progressed through the Serengeti Plain under the snow-capped summit of Mt. Kilimanjaro. Along the way Ernest shot four lions; two leopards, thirty-five hyenas, cheetahs, a roan antelope, and numerous eland, waterbuck, and gazelles. Pauline, with Ernest's help, bagged the first lion, but most of the hunting evolved as an intense rivalry between Hemingway and his friend Thompson. Unfortunately for Ernest—certainly the more experienced and

better marksman—Charles came in for an unbroken string of good luck, which consistently brought him superior kills.

The rivalry abruptly ended, however, when Hemingway fell ill with amoebic dysentery so severe that he had to be evacuated by moth plane for treatment in Nairobi. Quickly put right with ementine injections, he rejoined the hunting cavalcade and then went on to nail not only the rhino but also sable and giant buffalo, one of which died bellowing like "a horn in the woods." After a dull interlude shooting zebra and oryx in the dusty Rift Valley, the hunters wound up in the park-like setting of Masai country, where they stalked the greater kudu, those splendid creatures with heart-shaped hoof tracks and backward spiraling horns that reminded Pauline of cathedral towers. Thompson's kills surpassed Hemingway's, but after a night of tormenting envy, Ernest decided to focus on his own achievements, prompting the philosophical Percival to comment: "We have very primitive emotions. It's impossible not to be competitive. Spoils everything, though."

During evenings around the campfire the group relaxed over whiskey and soda as each member relived the day's adventures. Percival, an expert raconteur, made a lasting impression on Ernest with his tale of a frozen

leopard found on the outer rim of Mt. Kilimanjaro's Kibo Peak. This poetic image would figure in the climax of "The Snows of Kilimanjaro." Africa also inspired much talk of courage and cowardice, and from these deliberations Hemingway wrote one of his most revealing and memorable passages in *Green Hills of Africa*:

I had gone through it myself until I figured it in my head. I knew what it was to be a coward and what it was to cease being a coward. Now, truly, in actual danger I felt a clean feeling as in a shower. Of course it was easy now. That was because I no longer cared what happened. I knew it was better to live it so that if you died you had done everything that you could do about your work and your enjoyment of life up to that minute, reconciling the two, which is very difficult.[1]

Hemingway left Africa "hungry" for more of it, not only the game but also the changing seasons, the people, their languages, traditions, and customs, which Ernest attempted to capture in *Green Hills of Africa*. His purpose, he said in the Foreword, was "to write an absolutely true book to see whether the shape of a country and the pattern of a month's action can, if truly presented, compete with a work of the imagination." As a result, *Green Hills of Africa* is much more than the account of a safari. With its odd mixture of description, narrative, literary commentary, and self-revelation, written in prose that, according to one reviewer, "sings like poetry without ever ceasing to be prose," the book is humorous and quite entertaining, especially about personalities. But it even soars once the author addresses the magnificent animals whose noble qualities he admires all the more for having ended their lives:

It was a huge, beautiful kudu bull, stone-dead, on his side, his horns in great dark spirals, widespread and unbelievable as he lay dead five yards from where we stood....I looked at him, big, long-legged, a smooth gray with the white stripes and the great curling, sweeping horns, brown as walnut meats, and ivory-pointed, at the big ears and the great, lovely heavy-maned neck the white chevron between his eyes and the white of his muzzle and I stooped over and touched him to try to believe it. He was lying on the side where the bullet had gone in and there was not a mark on him and he smelled sweet and lovely like the breath of cattle and the odor of thyme after rain.[2]

1. East Africa, the magnificent, and then unspoiled, world of wilderness and wild animals that Ernest and Pauline Hemingway—with their Key West friend Charles Thompson and the famous English white hunter Philip Percival—explored on safari from early December 1933 to mid-February 1934.

2. The Hemingway camp during the 1933–34 African safari.

3. Baron Bror von Blixen, the Danish aristocrat, onetime husband of the writer Isak Dinesen, and the director of Tanganyika Guides, Ltd., at the time of the Hemingways' safari. He joined the party at one point to hunt lions. A famous womanizer as well as white hunter, von Blixen, together with Philip Percival, would serve as models for Wilson in "The Short Happy Life of Francis Macomber," a masterpiece of a story that Hemingway created from his African experience.

4. Ernest Hemingway (far right) holding an oryx trophy, next to Philip Percival, the safari's brilliant white hunter, who holds a spectacular kudu trophy, the spiraling horns of which Pauline likened to cathedral towers. At the far left are Ben Fourie and Charles Thompson (slightly obscured by the forest of horns), at Kijungu Camp, Tanganyika, in February 1934.

5. The farmhouse in the Ngong Hills, Tanganyika, from which Isak Dinesen directed a coffee plantation during her marriage to Baron Bror von Blixen. Dinesen, whose African house the Hemingways visited, was one of the few writers Ernest never ceased to praise.

6. *Green Hills of Africa* (1935), the book-length account that Hemingway wrote of his 1933–34 safari to Kenya and Tanganyika.

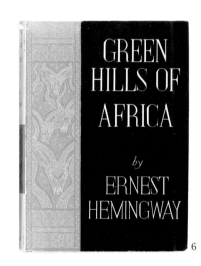

MACOMBER AND KILIMANJARO

In addition to *Green Hills of Africa*, Ernest's African adventure produced two nonpareil short stories: "The Short Happy Life of Francis Macomber" and "The Snows of Kilimanjaro." Based on a true story told to him by Percival, Ernest brought to "Macomber" all his powers of perception about Africa, the animals, and the people who hunted them. The story revolves around three characters on an East African safari: an embittered American couple, Francis and Margot Macomber, and their white hunter, the Englishman Wilson. The story opens in a dark mood, carried over from events of the preceding day and night, during which Macomber, a wealthy American "boy-man," disgraced himself by taking flight from a wounded and charging lion. Added to the torture of self-disgust are the scornful remarks of his beautiful but hardened wife, the silent contempt of Wilson, who had stepped in and gunned down the beast, and even the visible disdain of the African bearers. In the ultimate humiliation, Francis must endure his wife's decision to spend the night not with a coward but rather with the manly and heroic Wilson. Suddenly things change in the course of the new day's shoot, when Macomber, emboldened by his sense of having nothing further to lose, throws fear to the winds during a hot pursuit of three galloping buffalo, fired upon from the party's speeding car. As a result, Macomber bravely joins Wilson and enters the tall grass to finish off a wounded but still living bull. Francis stands firm as the animal charges; thrilled with his new-found self-esteem, he continues blasting away until the buffalo is almost on him—until, that is, he feels "a sudden white-hot, blinding flash explode inside his head and that was all he ever felt." Margot, firing from the open vehicle, "had hit her husband four inches up and a little to one side of the base of his skull."

Quite apart from the technical virtuosity with which Hemingway infused the struggle for a human soul with mounting, almost unendurable tension, "The Short Happy Life of Francis Macomber" offers the added virtue of an ambiguous conclusion. Almost twenty years after he had written the story, the author commented to an interviewer: "Francis' wife hates him because he's a coward. But when he gets his guts back, she fears him so much she has to kill him—shoots him in the back of the head." However, a line in the story itself suggests quite a different interpretation: "Mrs. Macomber, in the car, had shot at the buffalo with the 6.5 Mannlicher as it seemed about to gore Macomber." Had she wanted her husband to die, just as he was winning out in his test of courage, Margot needed only to have held rather than unleash her fire. Thus, the tragedy may lie in the disaster brought upon a man who confused moral strength with physical derring-do and personal, or even artistic, success with public approval.

Equally taut, if less action-packed, is "The Snows of Kilimanjaro," which explores the psychology of a dying man as he awaits transport, through the final afternoon and evening of his life, at a camp site in Tanganyika. Ravaged by gangrene, caused by a thorn scratch, a writer named Harry has time to quarrel with his wife, Helen, and reflect at length on his other, accumulated follies. Having married into money, he "destroyed his talent by not using it, by betrayals of himself and what he believed in, by drinking so much that he blunted the edge of his perceptions, by laziness, by sloth, and by snobbery, by pride and by prejudice, by hook and by crook." In the sheer eloquence of his flashback recollections and self-examination, Harry recovers his lost talent, which leaves him with the tragic realization that he "would never write the things that he had saved to write until he knew enough to write them well." Confronted with death, Harry is liberated from his lifelong obsession with it. He feels himself born aloft in a Puss Moth plane—like Hemingway during his dysentery attack—high above the huge vultures obscenely circling over the shady mimosa tree where he lay dying, higher and higher towards the greatest mountain in Africa, the snow-capped Kilimanjaro shining fantastically white in the sun.

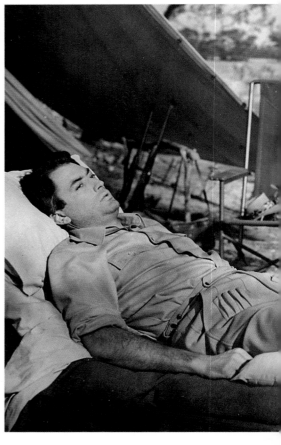

1. Mt. Kilimanjaro in northern Tanganyika, the snow-capped beauty of which took Ernest's breath away in late 1933 and inspired one of his most successful stories.

2. Gregory Peck and Susan Hayward in a scene from the Hollywood-made film *The Snows of Kilimanjaro*.

3. The August 1936 issue of *Esquire* in which Arnold Gingrich published "The Snows of Kilimanjaro."

4. The September 1936 issue of *Cosmopolitan* in which "Macomber" first appeared.

5. A poster for the 1946 film *The Macomber Affair*. Starring Joan Bennett and Robert Preston as the unhappy Margot and Francis Macomber and Gregory Peck as the virile white hunter Wilson, the movie based on "The Short Happy Life of Francis Macomber" was one of the best ever made by Hollywood from a Hemingway work.

OCEAN LINERS

1. Ernest, Pauline, and young Patrick Hemingway on the *Yorck* in April 1929, sailing from Havana to Boulogne.

For his first round trip across the Atlantic Hemingway traveled as a Red Cross volunteer on the French Line's *Chicago* in 1918, from New York to Bordeaux, and then the Italian Line's *Giuseppe Verdi* in 1919, from Genoa to New York. While both ships had probably been well-appointed passenger liners, Ernest knew them as little more than troop carriers fitted out like floating dormitories. The sustained love affair the writer would carry on with ocean liners began in mid-December 1921 when he and Hadley boarded the French steamer *Leopoldina* in New York and sailed for France. Carlos Baker described that momentous crossing:

Nothing could exceed Ernest's exuberance as he set forth on his second voyage to Europe. He danced and sang, shadow-boxed and shouted. Even seasickness did not keep him down for long. There was a French girl with a squalling infant traveling steerage. She had been deserted by her American husband, a veteran of the A.E.F., and her money had dwindled to ten francs. Ernest arranged a three-round exhibition boxing match as a benefit for the girl. His opponent was Henry Cuddy, an Italian fighter from Salt Lake City. They pushed back the tables in the dining salon and Hadley acted as her husband's second. Ernest outweighed his opponent and brought him to the verge of a knockout in the final minute.[1]

Thereafter, until the very end of his life, Ernest would cross the Atlantic by ship more than thirty times, in some years making as many as four voyages. Occasionally he chose an exotic route, as in 1928 when he and Pauline took the Royal Mail Steam Packet *Orita* from La Rochelle to Havana, or in 1929, when he led not only his wife but also his two elder sons and his sister Sunny aboard North German Lloyd's *Yorck* to sail from Havana to Boulogne. Then came the fabulous voyages on the rather filthy SS *General Metzinger*, which bore the Hemingways from Marseilles via the Suez Canal to Mombasa in East Africa, followed by a return journey on the Swedish Line's sparkling *Gripsholm*, which Ernest and Pauline shared with young Alfred Vanderbilt and Baron Bror von Blixen, the erstwhile husband of Isak Dinesen, one of the few writers whose work Ernest never failed to extol. This time he traveled first class, but in his early days and on at least one occasion in the thirties he made do in cabin class. Always,

however, Hemingway found great happiness in the short week it took to traverse the great ocean on a luxury liner offering a kind of pampered isolation that was not to be found anywhere else. The most indulgent and glamorous ship of them all was the colossal *Normandie*, which Ernest knew well from several crossings, but the vessel he preferred was the old *Île-de-France*. J.M. Brinnin evoked it in *The Sway of the Grand Saloon*:

Constructed by French workers in the St. Nazaire yards of Chantier de Penhoët, decorated by more than thirty different French firms, the Île-de-France *managed to absorb and integrate all influences. The result was something uneven in particulars, yet, on the whole, quintessentially Gallic. Neither new nor old, she possessed a warmth, a palpable sense of aristocratic reserve, a sort of laissez-faire grace that hid her touches of ugliness and mellowed the strains of the* brut *and the stridently modern that were evident throughout the length of her. Some things about her called forth the silly statistics and hyperbolic soufflés that new steamships had always evoked. Her "tremendous" main dining room was "twenty feet wider than the Church of the Madeleine"; the dance floor in the Salon de Conversation measured 516 square yards; the bar in the first-class lounge was "the longest afloat." Where other ships had their conventional garden lounges, she had a complete Parisian sidewalk café with awnings above, and saucers marked "six francs" on the tables; in her children's playroom there was a real carousel with painted ponies and proper music to go around by.*[2]

After years of shepherding passengers over the seas, the captain of the *Île-de-France* observed:

Crossing the Atlantic has taken on a sort of social significance. Thousands of persons, of no great consequence, have the self-satisfying experience of importance thrust upon them. They walk over the first-class gang-plank, are greeted by a band, are waited upon, deferred to, bowed to, coddled, and the rest, and each evening sit in a huge dining hall, wearing formal dinner dress, five nights in succession. This sort of thing becomes an annual pilgrimage into a small world where the ego is magnified and set to music. The North Atlantic deserves full credit for its uplift work among our prosperous nonentities.

Far from a nonentity, Ernest set off flashbulbs every time he approached the gangplank of an ocean liner.

2. The French Line's flagship *Normandie*, the most beautiful of all the great luxury liners of the 1930s. Hemingway boarded it for three different Atlantic crossings.

3. The first-class dining room on the *Normandie*. It was in a setting like this, albeit on the *Île-de-France*, that Hemingway, in March 1934, met Marlene Dietrich, who remained a close friend to the end of his life.

4. The *Île-de-France*, Ernest's favorite ocean liner on which the novelist made seven transatlantic voyages, beginning in 1931 and ending only in 1957.

1. Like Hemingway, Marlene Dietrich was a regular transatlantic commuter throughout the 1930s, and indeed it was on a westbound voyage, in late March 1934, that the two friends began their enduring relationship. Here, the beautiful star boards the *Normandie* in New York, only a year or two after she and Ernest first met over dinner on the French Line's *Île-de-France*.

2. In November 1938, at the end of his active involvement with the Spanish Civil War and on the eve of World War II, Hemingway once again crossed the Atlantic on a luxury liner that also carried "the Kraut." This time they traveled on the *Normandie*. As the book jacket she holds indicates, Dietrich liked Hemingway the writer as much as she liked Hemingway the man.

3. Dietrich could wear men's severely tailored clothes—pants, tie, and beret—and appear all the more erotic for it. Here, in her dark green glasses, the actress was caught arriving in Paris after a period of movie-making in Hollywood.

THE KRAUT

One of Hemingway's most enduring friendships was with Marlene Dietrich. They loved each other very much, and trusted one another with their most guarded secrets, but despite passionate feelings, they never, in the twenty-seven years of their relationship, had an affair.

Ernest and Marlene first met in 1934 during a transatlantic crossing, which Ernest once described to me:

Back in my broke days I was crossing cabin on the Île, but a pal of mine who was traveling first loaned me his reserve tux and smuggled me in for meals. One night we're having dinner in the salon, my pal and I, when there appears at the top of the staircase this unbelievable spectacle in white. The Kraut, of course. A long, tight white-beaded gown over that body; in the area of what is known as the Dramatic Pause, she can give lessons to anybody. So she gives it that Dramatic Pause on the staircase, then slowly slithers down the stairs and across the floor to where Jock Whitney was having a fawncy dinner party. Of course, nobody in that dining room has touched food to lips since her entrance. The Kraut gets to the table and all the men hop up and her chair is held at the ready, but she's counting. Twelve. Of course, she apologizes and backs off and says she's sorry but she is very superstitious about being thirteen at anything and with that she turns to go, but I have naturally risen to the occasion and grandly offer to save the party by being the fourteenth. That was how we met. Pretty romantic, eh?

As the years passed, Hem and the Kraut often spoke by long-distance phone, corre-

sponded regularly, and always dined together whenever they found themselves in the same town at the same time. Usually, this was New York and the 21 Club, but in Paris just after the Liberation they were in daily, even hourly, touch with one another at the Ritz, where both had rooms, as he reported the war for *Collier's* magazine and she—a German who had despised Hitler at first sight—rested up from her rounds of entertaining Allied troops.

Dietrich once told me:

The wonderful thing about Ernest is that he kneeled himself into his friends' problems. I know this is not good English, but I hope it conveys my feeling about his friendship. He was like a huge rock, off somewhere, a constant and steady thing. I honestly think that if more people had friends like Ernest was, there would be fewer analysts. Ernest found time to do the things most men only dream about. He had the courage, the initiative, the time, the enjoyment, to travel, to digest it all, to write, to create it, in a sense. He once said he never left any place except reluctantly, and I believe him. There was in him a sort of quiet rotation of seasons, with each of them passing overland and then going underground and reemerging in a kind of rhythm, refreshed and full of renewed vigor. He was gentle, as all real men are gentle; without tenderness, a man is uninteresting. Ernest Hemingway was the most positive life force I have ever encountered. I hate anything negative, and I hate waste. In Hemingway, nothing was wasted.

THE PILAR

Shortly before the Hemingways departed Key West for their African safari, Ernest heard about the wonders of marlin fishing some 100 miles away in Cuban waters. Eager to match the big game of Kenya and Tanganyika with the big fish of the Caribbean, Ernest had scarcely disembarked from the *Île-de-France* in early April 1934 when he took a taxi to the Wheeler Shipyard in Brooklyn and placed an order for a sleek, 38-foot diesel-powered boat that,

Hemingway would write many stories and articles, as well as invent many an unforgettable metaphor, from his experiences as skipper of the *Pilar*. They would also stir him, in whole or in part, to create such major, independent works as the novels *To Have and Have Not* (1937) and *The Old Man and the Sea* (1952), probably the most popular of all the author's books. Ernest, in fact, spent a portion of almost every day on the *Pilar*, as long as he was in Key West or Cuba; sometimes he remained aboard for days or weeks, writing, and proofreading as well as fishing. He brought up his three sons on the sea and taught them, along with numerous friends,

1

with its cruising range of 500 miles, would afford him an independence as well as an outdoor, sporting pleasure beyond anything he had known before. Named for the patron saint of Zaragoza, for the country this evoked—a country Ernest loved above all others—and, finally, for Pauline in her secret identity during courtship days, the *Pilar* drew 3½ feet of water, had a 12-foot beam, a green roof, a black body, and a varnished mahogany cockpit. The vessel also boasted two engines, of 75 and 40 horsepower, twin screws, double rudders, and a full-throttle speed of 16 knots; it held 300 gallons of petrol and could sleep six in the cabin as well as two in the cockpit. Ernest paid $7,500 for the *Pilar*—his prize possession—using $3,200 from personal savings and the remainder from an advance made to him by Arnold Gingrich against articles promised to *Esquire*.

the techniques and satisfactions of testing one's skill—one's moral fiber—against not only the open water and weather but also against the giants of the deep—tuna, marlin, and shark, even the occasional whale. During the 1930s the *Pilar* would provide a floating hideaway for the captain's extramarital romances with, first, the beautiful Jane Mason and, then, the brilliant fellow-writer Martha Gellhorn, whom he would marry in 1940. Shortly thereafter, Hemingway transformed the *Pilar* into an armed spy ship on the lookout for German U-boats, but that is a story for another chapter.

Meanwhile, with the *Pilar* under him, Hemingway became one of the great, innovative champions of deep-sea fishing, as the boat-builder and fishing authority John Rybovich, Jr., told Denis Brian in a recent interview:

3

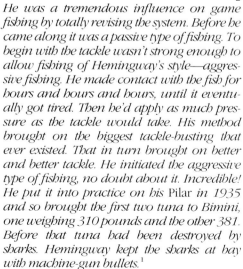

1. The *Pilar*, the 38-foot diesel-powered boat that Ernest Hemingway had built to his own specifications at the Wheeler Shipyard in Brooklyn. After its arrival in Key West on May 9, 1934, the *Pilar* would become the novelist's prize possession, a place for work, play, sport, good fellowship, and escape.

2. Ernest and his matador friend, the Brooklyn-born Sidney Franklin, on a Key West pier proudly displaying a marlin, the kind of giant fish the novelist hoped to go after in Cuban waters once he had command of the *Pilar*.

3. Ernest on Bimini with the largest marlin (500 pounds) ever caught in those waters. Unfortunately, it had been "apple-cored" by shark. It

He was a tremendous influence on game fishing by totally revising the system. Before he came along it was a passive type of fishing. To begin with the tackle wasn't strong enough to allow fishing of Hemingway's style—aggressive fishing. He made contact with the fish for hours and hours and hours, until it eventually got tired. Then he'd apply as much pressure as the tackle would take. His method brought on the biggest tackle-busting that ever existed. That in turn brought on better and better tackle. He initiated the aggressive type of fishing, no doubt about it. Incredible! He put it into practice on his Pilar *in 1935 and so brought the first two tuna to Bimini, one weighing 310 pounds and the other 381. Before that tuna had been destroyed by sharks. Hemingway kept the sharks at bay with machine-gun bullets.*[1]

had also been caught by Ernest's friend, the painter Henry Strater, and its resonance would one day be felt in *The Old Man and the Sea*.

4. A watercolor by Henry Strater, an old friend from Montparnasse days, showing Hemingway and company aboard the *Pilar*.

5. A frequent guest aboard the *Pilar* in the early 1930s, John Dos Passos posed here as if he were trying out for a part in *Jaws*.

6. Ernest often invited his friends to join him on the *Pilar* and "cavort in the deep." Here he would appear to be giving a demonstration of what he had in mind.

7. Ernest having a doze onboard the *Pilar*, with the ever-happy Jack at his knees and in his arms the machine gun he used to kill sharks trying to eat his big catches before he could bring them in, a technique the novelist innovated.

8. Hemingway would battle a marlin for hours, methodically working the line until he brought in the catch.

7

6

8

MAX PERKINS

The most prestigious editor of his time was Maxwell Perkins, a Vermonter who joined the New York publishing house of Charles Scribner's Sons in 1910, three years after his graduation from Harvard. In the course of his long and brilliant career, Perkins either discovered or decisively shaped an extraordinary number of major American talents—Ring Lardner, Scott Fitzgerald, Marjorie Kinnan Rawlings, Thomas Wolfe, and, finally, James Jones. Ernest Hemingway, whom Fitzgerald had recommended to Perkins in 1925 as "the real thing," became the brightest, most productive and enduring star in the entire Scribner's galaxy, which he joined in 1926 for the publication of, first, *The Torrents of Spring* and, shortly thereafter, *The Sun Also Rises*. Following the move from Paris to Key West in 1928, Perkins would become Hemingway's principal lifeline to the literary world, and after Dr. Ed Hemingway committed suicide in 1929, he evolved into more than an editor to Ernest—not only a good friend but also a father figure. Perkins advanced his most valuable author lavish sums of money, against future royalties that his faith in Hemingway assured him would be earned. Indeed Perkins' steadfast commitment to Ernest's work, throughout the relatively bad reviews that greeted almost everything the author produced in the 1930s, helped keep the Hemingway self-esteem intact until the genius it harbored could pull together and create *For Whom the Bell Tolls*, the masterpiece that Perkins published in 1940. Thanks to his innate tact, patience, and diplomacy—not to mention good literary judgment—Perkins emerged as one of the few close associates with whom Ernest never broke. And this despite the need that Perkins found to limit, if not altogether eliminate, the profanity and powerful four-letter Anglo-Saxonisms with which Hemingway loved to salt the pellucid purity of his language. As a result, Hemingway's books probably reached a much wider audience than they would have otherwise. A grateful Ernest forced the workaholic Perkins to visit him annually as long as he remained in Key West, taking the tired urbanite out to sea on the *Pilar*, where he had surprising success at pulling in some of the big ones from the deep. However, no relationship with the temperamental Hemingway could survive long without a few tense moments, one of which occurred in 1941 when Scribner's failed to have a stenographer record Sinclair Lewis' speech awarding Hemingway the Lim-

ited Editions Club's triennial Gold Medal. In a scorching letter to Perkins, a disappointed and outraged Ernest wrote.

Scribner's not haveing taken it down as I requested as a favour was the most careless, shiftless and callous action I have ever met in civil life. . . .

It is over and I'm fucked on that. Had driven all the way from Idaho to Arizona looking forward, like a dope, to reading it. . . . Now I never will and that something that could have had will never have. It was the only thing connected with writing I ever wanted to keep.

But when another crisis threatened to go out of control, Hemingway demanded that Perkins not fight with him—"because you are my trusted friend as well as my God damned publisher."

1. Max Perkins, the renowned Scribner's editor who worked on many of Hemingway's books from *The Sun Also Rises* to *For Whom the Bell Tolls*; he also edited Scott Fitzgerald, Ring Lardner, Marjorie Kinnan Rawlings, Thomas Wolfe, and James Jones. Even in Key West, where Ernest taught him to fish with the best, Perkins could not forgo his traditional tie and tight white collar.

2. Hemingway in Perkins' office at Scribner's, as he, Charles Scribner III, and the great editor listen to S.S. Van Dine, the author of the very successful Philo Vance mysteries.

3. Thomas Wolfe, the prodigiously gifted writer whom Perkins made into a great novelist by editing crates full of manuscript into a coherent, encompassable book. Finally, however, Wolfe could not bear the humiliation of his debt to Perkins and, after much anguish, left Scribner's for another house.

4. The Scribner's Building on Fifth Avenue. It was and remains one of the handsomest commercial structures in New York City.

PATRICK AND GREGORY

1. Ernest with his second-born, Patrick, at the age of five in Wyoming, where Papa had already begun to teach his boy the wilderness skills he had learned from his father.

2. Nine-year-old Gregory (Gigi), Hemingway's third and last child, feeding ducks and Canadian geese in Sun Valley.

Early in his marriage to Pauline Pfeiffer, Hemingway fathered two more sons, both of them—like Bumby, their elder half-brother—bright and extremely attractive youngsters. Ernest, however, found himself driven "bughouse" by the boys' infant squalling, and Pauline later admitted that she could not "*stand* horrid little children until they are five or six." Moreover, she was determined not to repeat Hadley's fatal mistake of appearing to neglect the father in favor of the son. As a result, Patrick, born in 1928, and Gregory, or "Gigi," born in 1931, grew up largely in the care of nursemaids while Ernest and Pauline spent weeks or even months away from home, in Spain, in Africa, in New York, and, later, in Havana. One long-term governess, unfortunately, proved to be a punishingly stern taskmistress who often made her charges scapegoats for her own emotional problems. One positive or counterbalancing influence was their half-brother Bumby or Jack, whom they saw when all three sons spent holidays with Ernest. Then Bumby, Patrick, and Gigi were brothers together, and Pauline so loved Ernest's firstborn, like one of her own, that she had Uncle Gus, the Sloan's Liniment tycoon in New York, establish a trust fund for

him at the same time that he was endowing the future of the two younger boys. Finally, as they emerged from infancy, the boys brought out the best in Ernest, especially his love of teaching and shaping, or reshaping, everyone in his own image. In a 1936 letter to his Pfeiffer mother-in-law, he said: "It is only this last year that I have gotten any sort of understanding or feeling about how anyone can feel about their children or what they can mean to them.... I was never a great child lover but these kids are really good company and are very funny and I think (though may be prejudiced) very smart."

If Hemingway honored Dr. Ed by imbuing all three of his own sons with a passion for and expertise in sports, hunting, fishing, and life in the wilderness, he stayed wide of Oak Park values in almost every other respect. A lenient parent, Ernest never spanked his offspring and frequently indulged them shamelessly, to the point of allowing ten-year-old Gigi to sample hard liquor until he "needed" a Bloody Mary to cure his hangover! Yet, as the boys approached manhood, Hemingway tended to regard them, as he did everybody else, as competitors, with rather disastrous results in the cases of both Patrick and Gregory. When Patrick suffered a major breakdown in 1947, following a tennis accident, he deliriously railed at all manner of fiends, one of whom appeared to be Ernest, the father who was devotedly nursing his boy, night and day, throughout three terrifying months. Once recovered, Patrick went on to graduate from Harvard, marry, and—with the help of Philip Percival and the fortune his mother left him at her death in 1952—become a white hunter in East Africa.

Gregory, perhaps the most intellectually gifted of the three boys, had manifold problems during the 1950s, beginning at St. John's College in Annapolis, Maryland, from which he unceremoniously withdrew to work in a Southern California factory and to suffer a drug bust, which occurred almost simultaneously with his mother's sudden demise at the age of fifty-seven. This in turn produced a violent, wounding row between Ernest and his youngest that never healed before Ernest himself perished in 1962. The two even accused one another of having "killed" Pauline. Meanwhile, Gigi, despite a decade of turmoil, pulled his life together, took a medical degree, married three times, and sired, in all, seven children. While he knew his father's dark, cruel side only too well, Gregory also remembered the multifaceted Ernest—the Ernest of his childhood and adolescence—as "kind, gentle, elemental in his vastness, tormented beyond endurance, and although we always called him papa, it was out of love not fear."

5

3

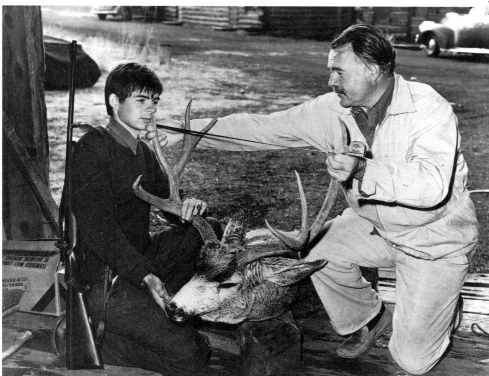

4

3. Ernest teaching ten-year-old Gigi the sporting skills he had already taught to Jack and Patrick. Gregory too would eventually hunt big game in Africa, but opted for medicine as a profession.

4. Eighteen-year-old Patrick with his first big game trophy, shot in 1946 near Ketchum, Idaho. Patrick would one day become a professional white hunter in East Africa.

5. Hemingway's three "chips" in 1940 at Sun Valley, Idaho: John (Jack, Bumby), seventeen; Patrick (Mouse), twelve; and Gregory (Gigi), nine. Looking at this picture, Ernest said: "...when I retire, we'll put the Bum in the movies, the Gigi in the prize ring, and the Mouse will *manage* all four of us—and good."

JANE MASON

During their New York-bound voyage on the *Île-de-France* in September 1931, Pauline and Ernest met Jane Mason, the immensely wealthy wife of a Pan American Airways official based in Havana. Breathtakingly beautiful, Jane would bewitch Ernest for the next five years, involving him in the longest of the few extramarital liaisons he ever risked. Quite apart from the film-star comeliness of her person—a wonderfully lithe but curvacious body supporting a perfectly oval face brightened by sapphire-blue eyes and strawberry-blond hair parted at the center—Jane Mason possessed a nimble wit, a deft and original pen, talent for songwriting and sculpture, and an insatiable sense of adventure. As if all this were not enough, she evinced an aristocratic manner along with a disconcertingly willful capacity to hold

her own in the masculine world of deep-sea fishing, pigeon-shooting, big-game hunting, drinking, swearing, reckless driving, and sexual aggressiveness. Unfortunately, Mrs. Mason also suffered from rapid and extreme manic-depressive mood swings, which made her quickly bored with almost everything and everyone she took up, including motherhood to two hapless, adopted sons. Although reared in Tuxedo Park, educated at Briarcliff and in Europe, and presented to society in a Washington, D.C. debut, Jane loved to rough it on both the high seas and in the wilderness, which made her all the more irresistible to Hemingway. Thus, it was for Jane that Ernest sought refuge, with increasing frequency, at the Ambos Mundos Hotel in Havana and in marlin-chasing off the Cuban coast. Jane, or Ernest's infatuation with her, may have been what most prompted Pauline to have Uncle Gus finance the African safari that kept the Hemingways absent from Key West for nine long months in 1933–34. Moreover, she may have been the all-important factor in Ernest's decision to buy the *Pilar* as soon as he had returned to American soil, a decision that liberated him to sail for Cuba whenever he wished.

While Pauline, more or less stoically, tolerated what was politely thought of as her husband's attempts to escape the growing numbers of Hemingway-watchers at Sloppy Joe's and on Whitehead Street, Grant Mason remained sufficiently absorbed in his work to be complaisant about his wife's affairs. This was not always easy, however, especially when, in 1933, Jane became so overwrought that she broke her back in a suicidal fall from a balcony on the Grants' lavish estate outside Havana. Finally, however, in 1936, the two

volatile lovers—Jane and Ernest—had a terminal row possibly over Colonel Cooper, an English white hunter whom Mrs. Mason had met in 1935 during her own safari in East Africa. As almost always in the aftermath of a once-valued relationship, Ernest turned bitter and portrayed Jane as the beautiful predatory wife in both "The Short Happy Life of Francis Macomber" and the anti-rich *To Have and Have Not* (1936), the only novel he published in the 1930s and the only one of all his novels with an overt social-activist theme. After ten years of unsuccessful marriage, the Masons divorced, which allowed Jane to take three more husbands, the last and most long-lasting one Arnold Gingrich, Hemingway's publisher at *Esquire*.

1. Jane Mason with her husband Grant and the two little English boys they adopted, at their palatial estate outside Havana.

2. Jane Kendall Mason in a 1936 portrait by Simon Elwes. President Coolidge pronounced Mrs. Mason the most beautiful woman who ever entered the White House. Certainly she was the most beautiful of all the women who became intimates of Ernest Hemingway.

3. Thanks to the *Pilar*, Hemingway could frequently escape Key West for journeys to Havana, where he and Jane Mason fished for marlin togther. Here, they display one of their catches on the *Pilar*. Ernest's affair with the gorgeous, shapely, manic-depressive Jane lasted from 1931 to 1936. In the bitter aftermath, the writer re-imagined her as the predatory wives in "Francis Macomber" and *To Have and Have Not*.

TO HAVE AND HAVE NOT

tung by Depression-spawned Leftist criticism of his writing as decadent because nonpolitical, and profoundly moved by the plight of the thirties' unemployed and impoverished—all the while that he himself lived among yacht-owning millionaires—Hemingway abandoned the "separate peace" themes of his greatest works, especially *A Farewell to Arms*, and wrote *To Have and Have Not*, the very title of which would seem to have announced a "new" socially aroused concern for the grotesque discrepancy between the rich and the poor in post-Crash America. In actual fact, Hemingway never wavered from his steadfast belief that the serious artist must write "books about the people you know, that you love and hate, not about the people you study up about. If you write them truly they will have all the economic implications a book can hold." As for political awareness, he had been astute enough—at the age of twenty-two—to recognize Mussolini's Fascism for the repressive, viciously totalitarian force it was when he saw it in Milan, on one of his first journalistic assignments in Europe. And for all his high living in the Caribbean, in Wyoming, in Africa, Madrid, Paris, and New York, Hemingway well knew the Dust Bowl world of highways thronged with the ragged dispossessed, encountered in annual cross-country trips as he drove his family, in a Model A Ford Coupe, from Key West to Piggott, Arkansas, across Kansas to cool, far-removed Yellowstone country. Jack Hemingway recalled those journeys in his memoirs:

It was the Depression and hard times were upon the land most of those years until the outbreak of World War II. . . . The parts of the Deep South through which we drove seemed to be populated only by undernourished-looking black families in run-down shanties, and I don't remember ever seeing much change in that regard until well after the war. . . . Whenever there was room, we would squeeze in some riders along the way who couldn't afford the price of a train ticket. They weren't called hitchhikers yet. Papa would always talk freely with them and get their story out of them. There were hard luck stories of every ilk and most with the ring of truth. For me it was learning that couldn't be duplicated elsewhere. There seemed always to be some humor and hope though, not matter how depressing the tale.[1]

Yet, owing to his sense of the artist as a creative loner and his romantic love of living like a rugged, self-sufficient frontiersman, Ernest

1

2

hated Roosevelt's New Deal as he saw it develop in Key West: "Some sort of Y.M.C.A. show. Starry-eyed bastards spending money that somebody will have to pay. Everybody in our town quit work to go on relief. Fishermen all turned carpenters. Reverse of the Bible." What did stir him to social activism, in the form of some of the period's best polemical writing, was the violent hurricane that wiped out a CCC camp on the Upper and Lower Matecumbe Keys. After rushing to the aid of the devastated community, Hemingway composed a blistering article for *The New Masses* in which he charged the federal bureaucracy with manslaughter:

1. Hemingway at the Matecumbe Keys in the wake of the historic 1935 hurricane that struck a defenseless CCC camp, killing hundreds of unemployed veterans assigned to work on a new highway from mainland Florida. After bringing medical supplies and helping to collect scores of dead bodies, Ernest published a scathing article entitled "Who Killed the Vets?" In the author's opinion, it was the Washington bureaucracy, which, despite early warnings from weather forecasters, had failed to evacuate the CCC camp.

2. A CCC tent camp in the mid-1930s.

3

Who sent nearly a thousand war veterans . . . to live in frame shacks on the Florida Keys in hurricane months? . . . Why were the men not evacuated . . . when it was known there was a possibility of a hurricane striking the Keys and evacuation was their only possible protection? . . . You could find them face down and face up in the mangroves. The biggest bunch of the dead were in the tangled, always green but now brown, mangroves behind the tank cars and water towers. They hung on there, in shelter, until the wind and the rising water carried them away. They didn't all let go at once but only when they could hold on no longer. Then further on you found them everywhere and in the sun all of them were beginning to be too big for their blue jeans and jackets that they could never fill when they were on the bum and hungry.[2]

If this convinced the Left that the most admired American novelist of his time appeared to have finally come into political maturity, so did *To Have and Have Not,* the long tale of Harry Morgan, an out-of-work owner of a cabin cruiser who, like the legendary Harry Morgan of an earlier era in the Keys, turns piratical in order to survive. When double-crossed by a Chinese crook, he robs the "Chink" and then kills him with his bare hands. Next, while ferrying bootleggers between Cuba and the Keys, Harry runs afoul the customs agent Frederick Harrison, an odious bureaucrat who calls himself "one of the three most important men in the United States." In the final episode Harry has had his boat impounded and his right arm amputated, both the consequences of a showdown with Harrison. But in a colorful monologue, his wife reveals that Harry still has his peerless manhood intact. Indeed, Harry's resourcefulness and enterprise appear all the more impressive by contrast with a trend-following novelist named Richard Gordon, corrupted not only by his literary and ideological opportunism but also by the rich whose company and favor he fauningly cultivates. While Gordon may be seen as an outrageous, and grossly unjust, parody of Dos Passos at the height of his critical success (with his portrait on the cover of *Time* four years before Hemingway achieved such eminence), his wealthy friends and flatterers Tommy and Hélène Bradley come forth as monstrous lampoons of Grant and Jane Mason, the one portrayed as impotent and the other as nymphomaniac. Meanwhile, Harry—the authentic but betrayed man—gains temporary possession of another boat, which allows him to take on revolutionaries for a clandestine voyage to Cuba. Listening to one of them explain how "the end is worth the means," as in Russia, where "Stalin was a sort of brigand for many years before the revolution," Harry realizes that he is sure to be murdered once he has served his purpose. Saying 'F— his revolution," Harry seizes a submachine gun and disposes of all four passengers, albeit not before one of them shoots him in the belly. As the Coast Guard cutter tows the blood-spattered boat towards a Key West pier, the mortally wounded Harry utters his last words: ". . . a man alone ain't got no bloody fucking chance." Not against the collective forces of bureaucracy, revolution, or the rich. In a powerful indictment of the latter, Hemingway wrote a virtuoso passage of satire, roll-calling the occupants of five yachts tied up at the pier as the dying Harry is brought in from the Gulf Stream: a pair of bickering homosexuals; a sixty-year-old grain broker worried about a call from the Internal Revenue Service; a dull but pleasant upright family secured by money "from selling something everybody uses by the millions of bottles, which costs three cents a quart to make, for a dollar a bottle in the large (pint) size, fifty cents in the medium, and a quarter in the small" (Sloan's Liniment, one of the sources of Pauline's large income?); and "two of the three hundred and twenty-four Esthonians who are sailing around in different parts of the world . . . sending back articles to the Esthonian newspaper" with each "Saga of the Our Intrepid Voyages" worth $1.30 a column; and, finally, "a professional son-in-law of the very rich and his mistress, named Dorothy," who masturbates in order to fall asleep:

I have to but what can you do? What can you do but go ahead and do it even though, even though, even anyway, oh, he is sweet, no he isn't, I'm sweet, yes you are, you're lovely, oh, you're so lovely, and I didn't want to, but I

132

3. A family of migrant fruit workers near Winter Haven, Florida, in July 1937. Although too much of an individual to appreciate the collectivism of Roosevelt's "alphabet" Depression-relief agencies, Hemingway took a warm-hearted interest in the destitute hobos and migrants that he and his family encountered along the dusty Southern and Midwestern highways as they drove from Key West to the cool, game-rich climes of Wyoming.

4. Walter Brennan, Lauren Bacall, and Humphrey Bogart, in a scene from the film version of *To Have and Have Not*, which transformed Bacall and Bogart not only into major screen stars but also into one of Hollywood's most romantic, long-wed couples.

5. Whatever the merits of the WPA, Hemingway thought that in Key West it was "some sort of Y.M.C.A. show": "Everybody . . . quit work to go on relief. Fishermen all turned carpenters. Reverse of the Bible."

6. *To Have and Have Not*, published in 1937, was Hemingway's only "proletarian" novel, as well as his only novel set in the United States.

7. A poster for the 1944 film version of *To Have and Have Not*. Although the novel is one of the least admired of Hemingway's works, it made a fabulously successful movie, possibly because of dialogue written by none other than William Faulkner. Ironically, the film's most famous line—"You know how to whistle, don't you? You just put your lips together and blow," spoken by Lauren Bacall to Humphrey Bogart—was contributed by the director, Howard Hawks.

am, now I am really, he is sweet, no he's not, he's not even here, I'm here, I'm always here and I'm the one that cannot go away, no, never. You sweet one. You lovely. Yes you are. You lovely, lovely, lovely. Oh, yes, lovely. And you're me. So that's it. So that's the way it is. So what about it always now and over now. All over now. All right. I don't care. What difference does it make? It isn't wrong if I don't feel badly. And I don't. I just feel sleepy now and if I wake I'll do it again before I'm really awake.[3]

Already deeply, even frenetically involved in reporting the Spanish Civil War, Hemingway ran out of time before he could get the various counterpoint elements of *To Have and Have Not* fully integrated. As a result, politically motivated critics found reason—thematic rather than aesthetic—to praise the novel, with Malcolm Cowley going so far as to see in Harry's collectivist valedictory Hemingway's "own free translation of Marx and Engels: 'Workers of the world, you have nothing to lose . . . ' " Most other critics, especially those who, like Edmund Wilson, had long regarded Hemingway as a great and universal artist, declared the work to be a relative failure. However, *To Have and Have Not* sold well, and when rewritten for the movies in 1944, by William Faulkner no less, it gave Humphrey Bogart and Lauren Bacall their most successful co-starring vehicle.

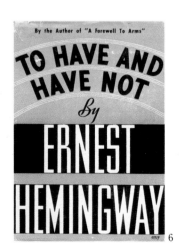

D SOBRE ESTAS LETRASHERMA
MORIR QUECONSENTIRTIRAM

THE
SPANISH
YEARS

———

MARTHA GELLHORN

On the rebound from his affair with Jane Mason and bored with his marriage to Pauline, the thirty-nine-year-old Hemingway felt his pulse quicken when a dazzling twenty-eight-year-old woman with lively eyes, a luxuriant fall of natural-blond hair, and long, elegant legs appeared at Sloppy Joe's in December 1936. This was Martha Gellhorn from St. Louis, on a family holiday, with her recently widowed mother and medical-student brother, that included a bus trip down the Keys to escape Miami, which none of the Gellhorns liked. As they soon discovered, Martha, or Marty, and Ernest had much in common, beginning with their parents, who on both sides had been suffragettes and obstetricians. Further, Martha and Ernest were established writers with a common interest in journalism as well as in fiction written with lean, clear, modern economy. Moreover, both had been certain enough of their literary vocations to leave school early—Ernest directly from Oak Park High without ever going to college and Martha from her junior year at Bryn Mawr, Hadley's alma mater. Afterwards, each had matured in France, Ernest among the expatriates of 1920s Montparnasse and Martha in the early 1930s among the politically alert French of her own age. During this time Martha had an affair with the Marquis Bertrand de Jouvenel, which lasted four years, and, one might say, made her the unofficial stepdaughter-in-law of Colette.

Ambitious to become a foreign correspondent, Martha did her first serious work in Paris, for *Vogue*, the United Press, and the *St. Louis Post-Dispatch*. Widely traveled on the Continent and well informed about its current problems, Martha wrote a novel entitled *What Mad Pursuit* (1934), the story of three American students who withdraw from their prestigious women's college to enrich their lives by immersing themselves in the dangerous waters of an intrawar Europe.

In the summer of 1936, Martha went to Germany to start work on another novel. The Nazis' brutality alarmed her, however, and the atmosphere was too ominous for writing. When war broke out in Spain and the Nazis mounted a campaign against the "red swine dogs" of the democratic Republic of Spain, Martha packed up and went there to try to warn the Spaniards of the Nazis' intentions. It was in the dining room of a Madrid hotel that Martha and Ernest met for the second time. At Hemingway's urging she began to write about the war itself, and submitted her pieces to *Collier's* magazine, which eventually hired her as their correspondent.

In early 1939, Martha and Ernest went to live in Havana, but it was not until 1940 that Pauline's divorce from Hemingway, on the grounds of desertion, became final. Ernest and Martha were married a couple of weeks later in Cheyenne, Wyoming, with a justice of the peace officiating. Robert Capa photographed the ceremony for *Life*.

After a trip to China, on which Hemingway went reluctantly, Martha flew to London to cover the start of World War II for *Collier's*. Ernest preferred to patrol the waters around Cuba, looking for U-boats, but Martha kept urging him to come to Europe. "You will feel deprived as a writer if this is all over and you have not had a share in it," she wrote. "The place is crying out for you, not for immediate stuff but for the record. I beg you to think this over very seriously, I say this not only because I miss you and want you here, but I hate not sharing it with you. It would be a terrible mistake to miss this, for both of us. I would never be able to tell you about it because I could never do the things that you can. You would be the one who would see for us." When Hemingway did finally go to London, *Collier's*

made him their leading correspondent, in place of Martha. This development spelled the end of their marriage, however, for Ernest met Mary and eventually sued for divorce on the grounds of desertion. It was granted in December of 1945. Under Cuban law, Ernest was entitled to keep all of Martha's possessions, including her clothes, books, swim suits, and even her typewriter. Such was the bitterness between them that he refused to send her any of her things. That bitterness was manifest in thinly veiled references to her in *Across the River and Into the Trees*, in which she is depicted as the third wife of Colonel Cantrell, who is the book's protagonist.

Ernest once told me:

Martha was the most ambitious woman who ever lived. She was always off to cover a tax-free war for Collier's. *She liked everything sanitary. Her father was a doctor, so she made our house look as much like a hospital as possible. No animal head, no matter how beautiful, because they were unsanitary. Her* Time *friends all came down to the* finca, *dressed in pressed flannels, to play impeccable, pitty-pat tennis. My pelota pals also played, but they played rough. They would*

1. Martha Gellhorn from St. Louis, the honey-blond novelist and essayist whom Hemingway met at Sloppy Joe's in late 1936 and married in November 1940, following two years together as fellow correspondents in war-torn Spain. In the beginning, Martha found great happiness with Ernest, as well as with his three sons, not only in Cuba, where she made a home for them at the Finca Vigía, but also in Sun Valley, Idaho. However, her rugged independence and their rival ambitions drove them apart in 1944, while they were reporting the European war on different fronts.

2. Hemingway not only dedicated *For Whom the Bell Tolls* to Martha Gellhorn; he also immortalized her in a loving, lyrical description of the novel's heroine, Maria: "Her skin and her eyes were the same golden tawny brown. She had high cheekbones, merry eyes and a straight mouth with full lips. Her hair was the golden brown of a grain field."

3. A compulsive leader, teacher, and big brother, Papa could hardly wait to instruct the beauteous Martha—as he had his two earlier wives, his sons, and virtually everyone else who came into his orbit—on hunting, fishing, and other outdoor activities, which he new so well.

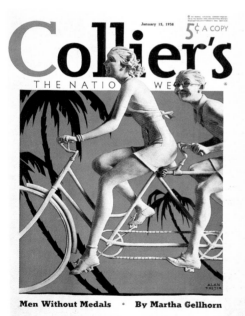

Men Without Medals • By Martha Gellhorn

4. *Collier's*, beginning in 1937, regularly published Martha Gellhorn's dispatches written at fronts ranging from Czechoslovakia to China. In this issue, "Men without Medals" was about the Abraham Lincoln Brigade, made up of idealistic American volunteers fighting for Loyalist Spain.

jump into the pool all sweated and without showering because they said only fairies took showers. They would often show up with a wagon full of ice blocks and dump them into the pool and then play water polo. That began the friction between Miss Martha and me—my pelota pals dirtying up her Time pals.

With the passage of time, however, that bitterness abated, and by 1953 Ernest was confessing to his friends that he had acted badly towards Martha and that he had indeed loved her very much.

In her wisdom, Gertrude Stein wryly summed up Ernest's marital problems: "Anyone who marries three girls from St. Louis hasn't learned much."

1. Hemingway at the Hotel Florida in Madrid writing a dispatch during his assignment as a NANA foreign correspondent covering the Spanish Civil War in 1937–38.

2. At the Battle of Teruel, which Hemingway covered in September 1937, Robert Capa made this photograph of the Loyalist stronghold in front of the Governor's Palace, the last bastion of Franco's Falangist or Nationalist forces. This was one of the few major battles won by the Loyalists, and Capa's depiction of it seems to foreshadow the vista of *For Whom the Bell Tolls*.

3. Hemingway interviewing Spanish guerrillas, prototypes of Pablo's band in *For Whom the Bell Tolls*.

4. Robert Capa's Spanish Civil War images resemble a 20th-century photographic update of Goya's *Los Desastres de la Guerra*.

THE SPANISH CIVIL WAR

No event in the 1930s so captivated and galvanized Western intellectuals as the Spanish Civil War, which broke out on July 17, 1936, when the army in Spanish Morocco, led by a cunning General Francisco Franco, mutinied against Madrid's Republican government, a Popular Front alliance that had assumed power in February with the support of less than half of Spain's voters. Trouble began as militants within the alliance got out of control and caused or allowed such atrocities as the burning of 160 churches, 260 political murders, the sacking of convents and newspaper offices, hundreds of general or partial strikes, the occupation and division of large estates by armed bands of peasants, and raging warfare between the country's two largest trade unions. Finally, what sparked the revolt in Morocco was the assassination of Calvo Sotelo, the far Rightist, or National Front, leader in the Spanish Parliament. Soon, the conflict in Spain took on the character of a stalking horse for the more universal showdown that many informed observers believed would come between Europe's Fascists, already in power in both Italy and Germany and actively assisting Franco's National forces, and their arch-enemy, the Soviet Union, which not only supported the Republican or Loyalist side in Spain but also maneuvered to infiltrate and

dominate them. Writers like Hemingway, Dos Passos, and MacLeish, André Malraux, and George Orwell, among many, many others, acknowledged the wholesale ruthlessness of Spain's anarchic Stalinists. But convinced, like Roberto in *To Have and Have Not*, that "the end is worth the means," they would cooperate with the Comintern and its surrogates, such as POUM (Partido Obrero de Unificación Marxista), as long as the common enemy appeared to be Fascism, which at the time loomed as the greatest of all threats to a free and just society.

Ernest overcame his distaste for politics, sided with the Loyalists, and accepted an offer to report the war for NANA (North American Newspaper Alliance). In departing New York in late February 1937, on the first of four trips he would make to embattled Iberia in 1937 and 1938, Hemingway was persuaded, as he wrote his mother-in-law, a devout Catholic

and thus pro-Franco like Pauline herself, that the "Reds may be as bad as they say," but "they are the people of the country," whose struggle was against "the absentee landlords, the moors, the Italians and the Germans."

Even before boarding the *Paris*, Hemingway helped the Loyalists by joining Dos Passos, MacLeish, and Lillian Hellman to create a corporation, Contemporary Historians, that would sponsor a documentary film on Spain by the Dutch director Joris Ivens. Once in Spain on March 16, he checked into the Hotel Florida, where he would soon be sharing a room with Martha. Here, as well as at Chicote's bar and the Hotel Gaylord, the Soviet-Communist headquarters, he met fellow correspondents Herbert Matthews (*New York*

4

Times) and Sefton Delmer (London *Express*); French novelists André Malraux and Antoine de Saint-Exupéry; the poets Pablo Neruda and Rafael Alberti; Russian correspondents Mikhail Koltzov and Ilya Ehrenburg; the crack photographer Robert Capa; the German novelist Gustav Regler, and the Hungarian General Lukács, and Dr. Werner Hielbaum, all of the Twelfth Brigade; and American Marxists Milton Wolff and Alvah Bessie of the Abraham Lincoln Brigade. Ernest, moreover, rediscovered such old Paris friends as the artist Luis Quintanilla and the composer Gustavo Durán, both of whom had become Generals in the Loyalist Army. A little-known but all-important acquaintance was Major Robert Merriman, a handsome California student of collective farming who abandoned his research in the Soviet Union to become a commander in the Abraham Lincoln Brigade, only to be killed in action during the final assault

on Belchite. In Merriman, Ernest found a model for Robert Jordan, the hero of *For Whom the Bell Tolls*.

Before completing the first two-month tour of duty in stricken Spain, Hemingway worked with Ivens on *The Spanish Earth*, covered the siege of Madrid, during which the Hotel Florida was regularly shelled, and reported the Loyalist victories over Italian troops at Guadalajara and Brihuega. As a correspondent, Hemingway impressed everyone as a great man at the peak of his form, courageous, unsparingly devoted to the Loyalists, and generous, sharing with others the many privileges that his fame brought him. Unfortunately, political inexperience cost him his friendship with Dos Passos, who broke with the Communists and turned against them when he learned that his translator, José Robles, a onetime professor of Spanish at Johns Hopkins University and then a Colonel in the Loyalist Army, had been secretly executed following a Moscow-like purge in which he was charged with espionage. Dos Passos proved to be right in believing Robles to have been innocent; in the meantime, however, Dos, a sophisticate in radical politics, was accused of political naïveté by Hemingway, who had, for the most part, accepted the Party line. Still, Ernest had no difficulty identifying two great villains within the Loyalist camp: André Marty, the psychopathic French commissar of the Communist Party, and Dolores Ibarruri, "La Passionaria" whose wildly emotional pro-Loyalist tirades over Madrid radio made the novelist want to "vomit."

Arriving back in New York aboard the *Normandie* on May 18, Hemingway briefly rejoined his family in Key West and Bimini, completed *To Have and Have Not*, and went with Martha and Ivens to show *The Spanish Earth* at the White House. Two days later, on June 4, 1937, he created a sensation with a speech delivered to a packed house at New York's Carnegie Hall during the League of American Authors Congress. The most prestigious writer there, and the last to become "politicized," Ernest declared:

Really good writers are always rewarded under almost any existing system of government that they can tolerate. There is only one form of government that cannot produce good writers, and that system is fascism. For fascism is a lie told by bullies. A writer who will not lie cannot live or work under fascism.

Hemingway then flew to Hollywood for a showing of *The Spanish Earth*, which raised almost $20,000 for ambulances to be shipped to Spain. Finally, back in New York, he stepped in, when Orson Welles' mellifluous voice and diction seemed too theatrical, and read his own script for the sound track of *The Spanish Earth*.

In early September 1937 Hemingway was in Spain for his second tour, which lasted until December, a time when the war was going badly for the Loyalists. However, Republican forces did prevail in the first battle of Teruel, where Ernest joined the troops for their triumphant entry into the city. Meanwhile, in his room at the Hotel Florida, he wrote his only play, *The Fifth Column*.

After celebrating Christmas in Barcelona with Martha, Hemingway traveled to Paris and found a desperately worried Pauline waiting for him. In January 1938 they returned to the United States together for a stressful two months in Key West before Hemingway boarded the *Île-de-France* on March 17 for his third NANA tour in Spain. There, during the siege of Barcelona he met an elderly Spaniard who inspired a new story entitled "The Old Man and the Bridge" and a young nurse named Maria, the "soul of serenity" albeit haunted by her memory of having been gang-raped by Nationalist soldiers early in the war. Both would figure large in *For Whom the Bell Tolls*. When Ernest left Spain in mid-May the Loyalists controlled nothing more than two cities: Barcelona and Madrid.

At the end of another unhappy period with Pauline, this time in Wyoming as well as in Key West, Ernest departed for his fourth and final NANA journey to Spain. On the way, he lingered two months in Paris with Martha, but by November he was on the banks of the

6. Bob Capa's photograph of refugees trudging across the barren, untilled fields of civil-war-torn Spain.

7. The playwright Lillian Hellman, a staunch Stalinist who collaborated with Hemingway, Dos Passos, and MacLeish to form Contemporary Historians, the purpose of which was to make a documentary film, *The Spanish Earth*, propagandizing the Loyalist side of the Spanish Civil War.

5. 8. André Malraux and George Orwell, two of the many foreign intellectuals who went to Spain, actively supported the Loyalist side against Franco's Falangists, and returned home,

Ebro, where his heroics were reported by Herbert Matthews in the *New York Times*:

It was during the Ebro battle in 1938; we had to take a rowboat to get over from the west to the east bank because the bridges had been bombed down. The current was swift and there were some nasty rapids a few hundred yards down the river, so the boat was being partly pulled across by a rope, which snapped. We started drifting swiftly toward the rapids. Hemingway quickly took the oars . . . and by an extraordinary exhibition of strength . . . got us safely across. He was a good man in a pinch.[1]

Muck them to hell together. . . . Muck every one of them to death to hell. Muck the whole treachery-ridden country. Muck their egotism and their selfishness and their selfishness and their egotism and their conceit and their treachery. Muck them to hell and always. Muck them before we die for them. Muck them after we die for them. Muck them to death and hell. . . . God pity the Spanish people. . . . Muck all the insane, egotistical treacherous swine that have always governed Spain and ruled her armies. Muck everybody but the people and then be damned careful what they turn into when they have power.[2]

5

6

like Hemingway, to write major books about the Iberian conflict. Malraux's *L'Espoir* (*Man's Hope*) appeared in 1938, the same year that also saw the publication of Orwell's *Homage to Catalonia*, written from the perspective of the war's victims. Orwell thought, as did Hemingway, that "the sin of all left-wingers from 1933 onwards is that they have wanted to be anti-fascist without being anti-totalitarian."

9. Hemingway in one of his more heroic moments, during the Ebro Battle of late 1938, when the rowboat ferrying him and other journalists across the Ebro River snapped its tow line and began to drift towards dangerous rapids a few hundred yards downstream. As *New York Times* correspondent Herbert Matthews wrote: "Hemingway quickly took the oars . . . and by an extraordinary exhibition of strength . . . got us safely across. He was a good man in a pinch."

Shortly thereafter NANA, no doubt believing the ultimate collapse of the Loyalists to be only a matter of time, canceled Ernest's contract, which left the novelist free to return home. Traveling with Marlene Dietrich on the *Normandie*, he arrived in New York on the 25th, just two months before the fall of Barcelona, the last Republican stronghold.

Soon after his return, Ernest began writing *For Whom the Bell Tolls*. In this passage an angry Robert Jordan gives vent to Hemingway's feelings about the war:

7

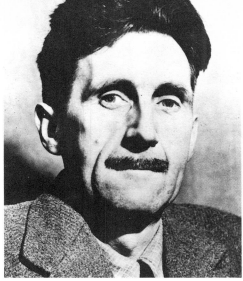

10, 11. *The Fifth Column* (1938), Hemingway's only play, written at the Hotel Florida in Madrid. The plot evolved around a secret fifth column operating within besieged Madrid while four of Franco's military columns were converging on the capital. When produced on Broadway in 1940, *The Fifth Column* was directed by Lee Strasberg and starred Franchot Tone, Lee J. Cobb, Lenore Ulric, and Katherine Locke.

12. One of the many propaganda posters created during the Spanish tragedy of 1936–39.

13. An edition of Spanish Civil War drawings by Luis Quintanilla, a Spanish artist Hemingway first met in 1922 in Montparnasse. In 1934, after Quintanilla was jailed in Madrid for revolution-

8

11

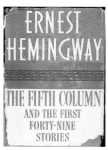

12

9

13

ary activity, Hemingway interceded with the President of Spain, organized an exhibition of Quintanilla's work at the Pierre Matisse Gallery in New York, paid all expenses for the show, and wrote an introduction to the catalogue. When finally released, with considerable help from Hemingway and Dos Passos, Quintanilla became a General in the Loyalist Army.

14. The book version of *The Spanish Earth*, a documentary film that Hemingway and Joris Ivens made in 1937, with the support of Contemporary Historians (Dos Passos, Archibald MacLeish, Lillian Hellman, and Hemingway), to propagandize the Loyalist cause in Spain, With Ernest reading his own script for the sound track, *The Spanish Earth* became one of the most admired and influential of all documentary films.

15. Hemingway in 1937 at work in Spain filming *The Spanish Earth*.

14

THE PLAYBILL
FOR · THE · ALVIN · THEATRE

10

15

FOR WHOM THE BELL TOLLS

For his second great war novel, Hemingway did not allow himself the ten-year gestation that elapsed before he wrote *A Farewell to Arms*. Convinced that the Spanish Civil War was a mere prelude to a much vaster and more prolonged global conflict, Ernest made haste to capture its significance in the novel that he began to write on March 1, 1939, just weeks after Barcelona had fallen in late January and exactly six months before Nazi Germany invaded Poland on September 1, thereby unleashing World War II. Consistent with his sense of universal disaster in the making, he also enlarged his conception from the private war and the "separate peace" made by Frederic

Europe *is the lesse, as well as if a* Promontorie *were, as well as if a* Mannor *of thy* friends, *or of* thine owne *were; any mans* death *diminishes me, because I am involved in* Mankinde; *And therefore never send to know for whom the* bell *tolls; It tolls for* thee.

The particular island on which Hemingway's characters would, in the concentrated span of less than three days in late May 1937, confront a crisis symptomatic of the entire Spanish struggle was a Loyalist guerrilla sanctuary high in the Sierra de Guadarrama northwest of Madrid. There, well behind the Fascist lines, Robert Jordan is to use his acquired expertise in demolition to blow a steel bridge over a deep gorge and coordinate the destruction with a surprise attack by Loyalist troops under the command of his friend General Golz. While Robert may represent

the benefits according as they have striven for them. And those who have fought against us should be educated to their error." Meanwhile, virtually dominating the scene is Pilar, a raw-boned, vulgar, outspoken, but wise Gypsy whose fierce loyalty to the mission stands in shaming contrast to the cowardly defeatism of her husband, Pablo. In one of her great, aria-like soliloquies, she recounts Pablo's slaughter of the Nationalist leaders in the cliff-top village near Avila:

"I hit him hard with my elbow and said, 'Cabron! Drunkard! Let me see' [while struggling with a brutish lout for a chair on which to stand].

"Then he put both his hands on my head to push me down and so he might see better and leaned all his weight on my head and went on shouting, 'Club them! that's it. Club them!'

Henry in the 1929 novel. Now his hero, Robert Jordan, a young American professor of Spanish from Montana, would be willing to sacrifice personal love and life itself for the sake of being "involved in Mankinde." As the archaic spelling here would suggest, the author once again searched among classic sources for a poetically succinct expression of his theme. This time it was provided by John Donne, in whose little 17th-century meditation on the interdependency and tragedy of the human condition Hemingway found both the title of his new novel and its eloquent epigraph:

No man is an Iland, *intire of itselfe; every man is a peece of the* Continent, *a part of the* maine; *if a Clod be washed away by the* Sea,

the engaged but objective liberal who, out of devotion to the Spanish people, could work for the Communist-dominated Loyalists without losing sight of their mistakes, he is surrounded by a guerrilla band composed of sharply individualized characters evincing a whole range of political and moral values so conflicted as to end by ruining their common cause. At one extreme stands the blood-thirsty Pablo, whose earlier massacre of a village's Fascist leaders foreshadows his craven theft of Robert's ex-plosives. At another extreme is Anselmo, Robert's sixty-eight-year-old guide who seems to exemplify normal human decency, crying out: "... we should win the war and shoot nobody.... we should govern justly and ... all should participate in

" 'Club yourself,' I said and I hit him hard where it would hurt him and it hurt him and he dropped his hands from my head and grabbed himself and said, 'No hay derecho,

4   5

THE NEW NOVEL BY HEMINGWAY
"For Whom the Bell Tolls" Is the Best Book He Has Written

FOR WHOM THE BELL TOLLS. By Ernest Hemingway. 471 pp. New York: Charles Scribner's Sons. $2.75.

By J. DONALD ADAMS

THIS is the best book Ernest Hemingway has written, the fullest, the deepest, the truest. It will, I think, be one of the major novels in American literature.

There were those of us who felt, when "To Have and Have Not" was published, that Hemingway was through as a creative writer. That is always a dangerous assumption to make regarding any writer of much innate ability, but it did seem that Hemingway was blocked off from further development. We were badly mistaken. Technical skill he had long ago acquired; the doubt lay in where and how he could apply it, and that doubt he has now sweepingly erased. The skill is even further sharpened than it was, but with it has come an inner growth, a deeper and surer feeling for life, than he has previously displayed. Whatever brought about this growth—whether his experience of the Spanish war, out of which this novel was made, or something else, it is plainly to be seen in this book, from beginning to end. There are no traces of adolescence in the Hemingway of "For Whom the Bell Tolls." This is the work of a mature artist, of a mature mind.

The title derives from John Donne. The passage from which it comes faces the book's first page:

No man is an *Iland*, intire of it selfe; every man is a peece of the *Continent*, a part of the *maine*; if a *Clod* bee washed away by the *Sea*, *Europe* is the lesse, as well as if a *Promontorie* were, as well as if a *Mannor* of thy *friends* or of *thine owne* were; any mans *death* diminishes *me*, because I am involved in *Mankinde*; And therefore never send to know for whom the *bell* tolls; it tolls for *thee*.

It is a fine title, and an apt one, for this is a book filled with the imminence of death, and the manner of man's meeting it. That is as it should be; this is a story of the Spanish war. But in it Hemingway has struck universal chords, and he has struck them vibrantly. Perhaps it conveys something of the measure of "For Whom the Bell Tolls" to say that with that theme, it is not a depressing but an uplifting book. It has the purging quality that lies in the presenting of tragic but profound truth. Hemingway has freed himself from the negation that held him in his other novels. As Robert Jordan lay facing death he looked down the hill slope and thought: "I have fought for what I believed in for a year now. If we win here we will win everywhere. The world is a fine place and worth the fighting

for and I hate very much to leave it." The frame of the story is a minor incident in the horror that was the war in Spain. Robert Jordan is a young American in the Loyalist ranks who has been detailed to the blowing up of a bridge which the General Staff wants destroyed

Ernest Hemingway.

to prevent the bringing up of enemy reinforcements. His mission carried him into hill country where he must seek the aid of guerrilla bands. Jordan destroys the bridge, but while he is escaping with his companions his horse is knocked from under him by an exploding shell, and we leave him lying on the hillside, his leg crushed by the animal's fall. He sends his companions on and waits, with a submachine gun beside him, for the enemy's approach.

Those who leave him are, with Jordan,

the main figures in the story. Among them is the girl Maria, whom Jordan, in the four-day span of the story's action, has met and loved. And as "For Whom the Bell Tolls" is a better story of action than "A Farewell to Arms," so too is this a finer love story than that of Lieutenant

Henry and Catherine Barkley. That is saying a good deal, but it is true. I know of no love scenes in American fiction, few in any other to compare with those of "For Whom the Bell Tolls" in depth and sincerity of feeling. They are unerringly right, and as much beyond those of "A Farewell to Arms" as the latter were beyond the casual couplings of "The Sun Also Rises."

The book holds, I think, the best character drawing that Hemingway has done. Robert Jordan is a fine portrait of a fight-

ing idealist, and the Spanish figures are superbly done, in particular the woman Pilar, who should take her place among the memorable women of fiction—earthy and strong, tender, hard, wise, a woman who, as she said of herself, would have been a good man, and yet was a woman made for men. The brutal, unstable Pablo, in whom strength and evil were combined, the good and brave old man Anselmo—these and others are warmly living in this heroic story.

I wrote once that Ernest Hemingway can see and describe with a precision and a vividness unmatched, since Kipling first displayed his great visual gift. There are scenes in this book finer than any he has done. The telling of how the Civil Guard was shot in Pablo's town and how the fascists were beaten to death between rows of men armed with flails and hurled over a cliff into the river 300 feet below, how the fascists walked out one by one from their prayers in the City Hall and severally met their deaths, has the thrust and power of one of the more terrible of Goya's pictures.

In all that goes to make a good novel "For Whom the Bell Tolls" is an advance beyond Hemingway's previous work. It is much more full-bodied in its drawing of character, visually more brilliant, and incomparably richer in content. Hemingway's style, too, has changed for the better. It was extraordinarily effective at times before, but it is shed now of the artificialities that clung to it. There is nothing obtrusive about the manner in which this book is written; the style is a part of the whole; there is no artifice to halt the eye. It has simplicity and power, delicacy and strength.

This is Hemingway's longest novel, and it could be, I think, as most books can, a little shorter, and with benefit. It seems to me that some of the long passages in which Robert Jordan's mind turns back to his days in Madrid retard the narrative unnecessarily and could well have been omitted. If there are other flaws in this fine performance, I have not yet found them. A very good novel it unquestionably is, and I am not at all sure that it may not

prove to be a great one. That is not something to determine on a first reading. But this much more is certain: that Hemingway is now a writer of real stature, not merely a writer of abundant talents whose work does not measure up to his equipment. "For Whom the Bell Tolls" is the book of a man who knows what life is about, and who can convey his knowledge. Hemingway has found bigger game than the kudu and the lion. The hunter is home from the hill.

6

---

1. *For Whom the Bell Tolls* (published on October 21, 1940), the masterful novel that Hemingway extracted not only from his two years of covering the Spanish Civil War for NANA but also from his many years of visiting, studying, and loving Spain.

2. The pine-forested terrain in the Guadarrama Mountains north of Madrid in which Hemingway set his 1940 novel *For Whom the Bell Tolls*. Down the road to the left is the all-important bridge on which the book's essential plot turns.

3. Tawny-blond and beautiful Martha Gellhorn, the *Collier's* foreign correspondent with whom Hemingway fell in love during the Spanish Civil War, and Captain (later Major) Robert Hale Merriman, the highest-ranking American in the International Brigades. When Hemingway wrote *For Whom the Bell Tolls* he took Merriman and Gellhorn as partial models for Robert Jordan and Maria.

4. Dolores Ibarruri, famous as "La Passionaria" for the violent rhetoric of her tirades over Madrid Radio on behalf of the Loyalist cause. Hemingway said she made him want to "vomit," and he parodied her in *For Whom the Bell Tolls*.

5. André Marty, the paranoid French Communist Commissar of the International Bridges who appears as his own treacherous self in *For Whom the Bell Tolls*.

6. J. Donald Adams' front-page review in *The New York Times Book Review*, which helped launch *For Whom the Bell Tolls* into orbit as the best-selling novel since *Gone With the Wind*. Not only did Adams call the book Hemingway's best written, fullest, deepest, and truest work to date, but he also knew "of no love scenes in American fiction and few in any other to compare with those of 'For Whom the Bell Tolls' in depth and sincerity of feeling."

7. Sam Wood directing Ingrid Bergman and Gary Cooper in the sleeping-bag scene, based on this passage from the novel: "Then there was the smell of heather crushed and the roughness of the bent stalks under her head and the sun bright on her closed eyes and all his life he would remember the curve of her throat with her head pushed back into the heather roots and her lips that moved smally and by themselves and the fluttering of the lashes on the eyes tight closed against the sun and against everything, and for her everything was red, orange, gold-red from the sun on the closed eyes, and it was that color, all of it, the filling, the possessing, the having, all of that color, all in a blindness of that color. For him it was a dark passage which led to nowhere, then to nowhere,

7

then again to nowhere, once again to nowhere, always and forever to nowhere, heavy on the elbows in the earth to nowhere, dark, never any end to nowhere, hung on all time always to unknowing nowhere, this time and again for always to nowhere, now not to be borne once again always and to nowhere, now beyond all bearing up, up, up and into nowhere, suddenly, scaldingly, holdingly all nowhere gone and time absolutely still and they were both there, time having stopped and he felt the earth move out and away from under them. . . . "

8. The Loyalist guerrilla mountain sanctuary in *For Whom the Bell Tolls*, with its full cast of characters as assembled by Paramount Pictures for the smash-hit movie. At the center are the rebellious Pablo, played by Akim Tamiroff, and his indomitable wife, the strong, earthy, and wise Pilar, brought to life unforgettably by the Greek actress Katina Paxinou. Clinging to the cliffside at their left are the lovers: the savaged but serene Maria, in the person of Ingrid Bergman, and Robert Jordan, the young American Spanish scholar-cum-demolition expert whose role Gary Cooper, a longtime Hemingway friend, undertook.

a fire. And I saw the priest with his skirts tucked up scrambling over a bench and those after him were chopping at him with the sickles and the reaping hooks and then some one had hold of his robe and there was another scream and another scream and I saw two men chopping into his back with sickles while a third man held the skirt of his robe and the priest's arms were up and he was clinging to the back of a chair and then the chair I was standing on broke and the drunkard and I were on the pavement that smelled of spilled wine and vomit. . . .

After all the bodies of the murdered Fascists had been thrown over the cliff at the edge of the town square, Pilar continued:

"That night I slept with Pablo. I should not say this to you, guapa, but on the other hand, it is good for you to know everything and at least what I tell you is true. Listen to this, Inglés. It is very curious.

"As I say, that night we ate and it was very curious. It was as after a storm or a flood or a battle and every one was tired and no one spoke much. I, myself, felt hollow and not well and I was full of shame and a sense of wrongdoing and I had a great feeling of oppression and of bad to come, as this morning after the planes. And certainly, bad came within three days. . . ."[1]

In the midst of Pablo's ruthlessness and Pilar's rough integrity shines the luminous figure of young Maria, a refugee from a Fascist attack that left her starved, tortured, gangraped, and shaven-headed. Her mutilated innocence touches the heart of Robert, who by his very tenderness towards Maria both heals her wounds and complicates, while enriching, his knowledge that only a powerful capacity for life makes one truly willing to kill or risk being killed in the course of realizing that capacity to the fullest. Responding to Robert, Maria joins the Inglés in his sleeping bag, where, at the climax of one of the most effective scenes in Hemingway's fiction, the lovers "felt the earth move out and away from under them." No longer coldly committed, but now emotionally entangled, Robert forgives, even while despising, Pablo after he steals the dynamite, making it necessary to blow the bridge by a more dangerous means—hand grenades. The technique works, but the explosion kills Anselmo. While escaping on horses that Pablo acquired by another mass murder—this time of a rival partisan band—Pablo, Pilar, and Maria make it through the Nationalists' gunfire, but Robert suffers a broken thighbone when an enemy bullet sends his big gray horse rolling over him. Ordering the distraught Maria to leave

9. Ingrid Bergman saying goodbye to the Hemingways after their luncheon together at Jack's in San Francisco, where they discussed with Bergman the possibility of her playing Maria in For Whom the Bell Tolls.

10. Hemingway and Ingrid Bergman during their discussion of her role as Maria in the movie version of For Whom the Bell Tolls.

11. Poster for the film that Paramount Pictures made from Hemingway's For Whom the Bell Tolls.

mujer. This, woman, you have no right to do.' And in that moment, looking through the bars, I saw the hall full of men flailing away with clubs and striking with flails, and poking and striking and pushing and heaving against people with the white wooden pitchforks that now were red and with their tines broken, and this was going on all over the room while Pablo sat in the big chair with his shotgun on his knees, watching, and they were shouting and clubbing and stabbing and men were screaming as horses scream in with the others, for "we both go in thee now," Robert settles under the trees and, with a submachine gun cradled in the crook of his left arm, fights pain and unconsciousness while debating with himself whether to commit suicide, thus avoiding capture and interrogation under torture. Or should he wait until the Fascist cavalrymen appear and then engage them so that they have no choice but to shoot him? Either way, Robert prepares himself for the momentous event of his own death: "I have fought for what I believed in for a year now. If we win here we will win everywhere. The world is a fine place and worth the fighting for and I hate very much to leave it." Like Pilar, who considered herself lucky to have been knocked out of seeing the whole of Pablo's massacre, Robert counts his good

luck that just as he feels "completely integrated," while taking a long look at the big white clouds in the sky, Nationalist Lieutenant Berrendo rides into the sunlit place where the first trees of the pine forest join the green slope of the meadow. In an echo of the opening line of the entire narrative, the novel ends with dramatic simplicity: "He could feel his heart beating against the pine needle floor of the forest."

The novel gains in richness and truth from the mixture of pure fictional characters (the guerrilla band), those inspired by actual people (Maria, for instance, whose golden hair and skin recall Martha Gellhorn and whose sordid history and serene soul Hemingway borrowed from a nurse he had met in war-torn Barcelona), and the real people—

mostly political figures—who perform as themselves (La Passionaria, Gustavo Durán, and André Marty, the treacherous, Stalin-like French commissar of the International Brigades). Moreover, *For Whom the Bell Tolls* abounds in the kind of verisimilitude that only a writer long familiar with Spain and its Civil War could have provided. The physical setting was inspired, in part, by the deep El Tajo gorge that cuts through the Andalusian town of Ronda, where Ernest went on his first bullfight tour in 1923, and where a political massacre like the one led by Pablo did actually occur early in the Civil War.

Marxist critics scorned *For Whom the Bell Tolls*, because in his concern for truth and humanity, rather than politics, Hemingway felt compelled to expose the Left, as well as the

11

Right. Closer to the consensus was the New York *Times* review by J. Donald Adams, who called *For Whom the Bell Tolls* "the best book Ernest Hemingway has written, the fullest, the deepest, the truest. It will, I think, be one of the major novels of American literature." Years later, Carlos Baker would call the work "a study of the betrayal of the Spanish people—both by what lay within them and what had been thrust upon them—and it is presented with that special combination of sympathetic involvement and hard-headed detachment which is the mark of the genuine artist."

After selection by the Book-of-the-Month Club, *For Whom the Bell Tolls* (published on October 21, 1940) became the biggest bestseller since *Gone With the Wind*. Thanks to the movie version starring Ingrid Bergman and Gary Cooper—a tremendous box-office draw—the book went on selling well right through 1944, earning for its author the first big money he had ever received from his writing.

10

1 9 4 1

WORLD
WAR II AND
HEMINGWAY
WAR III

———

1 9 4 4

1. The old, rambling stucco farm house at the Finca Vigía, the 15-acre estate near Havana that became Hemingway's home base from April 1939 until 1960 when Castro's anti-Americanism compelled him to leave.

2. Sun Valley Lodge, Idaho, nestled in the bossom of the magnificent Sawtooth Mountains, where, beginning in September 1939, Hemingway and his entourage found refuge every fall.

3. The Sawtooth Range with Little Redfish Lake, where Papa and his sons spent many happy hours fishing and hunting.

CALM BETWEEN THE STORMS

By the time *For Whom the Bell Tolls* appeared on October 21, 1940, the Second World War that Hemingway had long predicted was in full, destructive swing, but before he once again got swept up in global conflict, Ernest could enjoy a brief interlude of basking in the glow of major work not only well done but also acknowledged with near universal acclaim.

In April 1939 Martha had found the Finca Vigía, a "Lookout Farm" near the village of

the swimming pool and tennis court, the groves of mango trees, royal palms, and bougainvillea alive with hummingbirds. Recruiting a carpenter to restore the house and a staff to run the place (butler, Chinese chef, two maids, three gardeners, a chauffeur), the Hemingways—Martha mainly—created a luxuriant haven where they could write in peace or entertain their friends in style. For a change of scene or pace, there was always the *Pilar* anchored nearby, or Havana's baseball teams, jai-alai games, cock fights, and night life. For shooting, Ernest could go to the Club de Cazadores or to the Cuban countryside

4. Papa loved Havana's Floridita quite as much as he did Sloppy Joe's in Key West, but he also enjoyed checking out low dives like this one, also in old Havana.

5. Lindy's on Broadway in New York's theater district, where during an intermission of *Hellzapoppin*, playing across the street at the Winter Garden, Hemingway received a $100,000 check from Paramount Pictures.

San Francisco de Paula some dozen miles southeast of Havana, and it was here that Ernest established a new home. Although rather overgrown and broken down, the 15-acre estate had many virtues: the breeze-cooled hill on which the rambling one-story Spanish-colonial house stood, the structure's high-ceilinged 50-foot living room with its distant view of the capital and the sea beyond, rustling with wild duck, quail, and pheasant. And there was the Floridita in Havana's aged quarter near Moro Castle, a relaxed, old-fashioned restaurant with ceiling fans, a roving trio, and a bar that attracted characters as colorful and varied as those at Sloppy Joe's in Key West. Even more than Martha, who was often away on foreign assignments for *Collier's*, Ernest and his three sons loved the Finca and the *dolce far niente* it encouraged, and it remained Ernest's home until Castro-induced animosity towards Americans forced Papa to leave.

Coincident with his move to Cuba, Ernest decided to move farther West for his annual retreat from the rigors of tropical summer, even more severe in Cuba than in Key West. The place he chose was Sun Valley, Idaho, where Averell Harriman, as director of the Union Pacific Railroad, had been developing an unusual rustic lodge for skiing in winter and fishing or hunting at other times. To promote the resort, Harriman offered free accommodations to certain celebrities from Hollywood, New York, and elsewhere, among them the Gary Coopers, Claudette Colbert, Ingrid Bergman, Dorothy Parker, and Ernest Hemingway. Delighted with the

picturesque Swiss-style lodge and the splenderous environs, lorded over by the Sawtooth Mountains and host to a teeming population of wild game, Ernest gathered about him Martha and the three Hemingway sons. Martha integrated nicely into the group, developing genuine affection for the boys, especially fifteen-year-old Bumby. She wrote to Hadley that she didn't "see how a woman could produce a better or more beautiful boy."

Even New York, where Ernest always felt, as he once said, like "a blind sardine in a processing factory," proved exhilarating when

5

he and his bride arrived there in November 1940 and again in January 1941. As a bestselling novelist with a New York publisher, a frequent transatlantic commuter on ocean liners berthed at the Hudson River piers, and an avid follower of big-time sports, Hemingway spent many days and nights in New York City, for various short durations, especially when two of his wives—Pauline and then Mary Welsh—took apartments there. Still, Gotham, for him, seemed little more than a necessary evil, except in the satisfying aftermath of *For Whom the Bell Tolls*' triumphant publication. One such moment was described by Carlos Baker:

He was levitated and joyous. Donald Friede approached him one night when he and [Gustavo] Duran were attending a performance of Olsen and Johnson's Hellzapoppin *at the Winter Garden, and handed him a check for $100,000 [from Paramount Pictures for the right to film* For Whom the Bell

4

Tolls]. It was the most money he had ever seen in one lump, and they went into Lindy's Bar to celebrate. When he flourished the check under the bartender's nose, the word quickly spread, and the company was electrified. Congratulatory hands whacked his broad shoulders and the sweaty good will of Hell-zapoppin blossomed along the bar.[1]

The uniquely popular Lindy's—a place with room for everyone, from theatrical greats, leading politicians, and sports heroes to anonymous starry-eyed folk from the hinterlands—is long gone, and so too the intimate, human scale and relatively innocent, fun-loving spirit of prewar New York that contributed so much to the euphoria of Ernest's feverish, all-too-brief calm between the storms of love and war.

6. The Hemingway gang in the fall of 1940, complete with Martha Gellhorn, Ernest's three sons, and the family's longtime chauffeur, jacket-clad Toby Bruce.

7. The Hemingways on a wing shoot near Sun Valley, Idaho, with Gary and Rocky Cooper, among others.

7

10

8. Après-ski at the Sun Valley Lodge, with Martha surrounded by Taylor "Beartracks" Williams, Ray Milland, Tillie Arnold, and Rocky Cooper.

9. Claudette Colbert, one of the many ski-loving stars lured to Idaho by Averell Harriman, the developer of Sun Valley Lodge.

10. Ernest and Martha Hemingway in New York in late 1940 or early 1941, celebrating the simultaneous publication of his novel *For Whom the Bell Tolls* and her novel *A Stricken Field*. After covering the Spanish Civil War together, throughout 1937 and 1938, they had just been married on November 20, 1940, in Cheyenne, Wy.

8

THE WAR IN CHINA

In late January 1941, Hemingway joined Martha and departed for China, where she was being sent by *Collier's* to report on the long, drawn-out struggle with Japan. Martha had already seen action, first in Czechoslovakia early in 1939 and then, a few months later, in Finland. Here she arrived just as the Russians launched their frustrated offensive. Back in Sun Valley, Ernest good-humoredly grumbled: "What old Indian likes to lose his squaw with a hard winter coming on?" Now, Martha would take him with her, just as she had done at the outset of their experience in Spain. Protesting that his new wife's idea of fun was to honeymoon on the Burma Road, Ernest signed a contract with *PM*, a serious independent New York news-

Then, by plane, an antique Chris-Craft, truck, car, boat, and horse, the Hemingways visited the front in several parts of Canton, encountering conditions that Martha called an "agony to watch and a horror to share." Appalled at the squalor, she wrote: "The pond water was rotting garbage and mud rather

2

than water, pigs rooted in the muck, flies swarmed, and over all the villages hung the smell of China's night soil, the deadly national manure." Flying 770 miles into the interior, they reached Chungking, China's wartime capital, and had lunch with General and Mme Chiang Kai-shek, whose fear of the Chinese Communists—greater than of the Japanese—made it a risky thing when they went underground for a secret meeting with Chou En-lai. Next, they flew south over the Burma Road to Laschio before continuing by car to Mandalay and by train to Rangoon. After a sweltering pre-monsoonal week in the Burmese capital, Martha left for Singapore and Java while Ernest returned to Hong Kong, where, during his final week in China, he boasted of having made do as best he could overnight with three beautiful Chinese girls, supposedly a gift from an Asian friend. On May 6 Heming-

way flew to Manila on the first leg of a tedious nine-day island-hopping journey to Los Angeles.

However desultory his seven dispatches for *PM*, Hemingway did conclude that, in his opinion, the United States might soon find itself at war with Japan. As always, he was at his best in critical circumstances, and Martha generously praised the stoicism, humor, adaptability, and courtesy with which he endured not only the boredom and discomfort of the China trip but also her chronic complaints. Meanwhile, to *Collier's* readers, Ernest praised the dispatches his wife sent from China: "The things that happen to her people really happen, and you feel it as though it were you and you were there. . . . She gets to the place, gets the story, writes it and comes home." Then he added: "That last part is the best." Unfortunately for their marriage, Mar-

1

paper, to write articles assessing how the Far Eastern turmoil might affect American commercial, military, and naval interests around the Pacific rim. Perhaps the couple hoped to recapture the romantic camaraderie of their years covering the Spanish Civil War, but China offered quite a different kind of challenge—grim and exhausting as anything in Spain but totally unrelieved by the purposeful involvement that the Hemingways had known in Madrid.

Of course, there was Hong Kong, which Ernest and Martha reached by crossing to Honolulu on the SS *Matsonia* and then flying by way of Guam. Once there, they spent a month in Kowloon's Peninsula Hotel, enjoying Chinese cuisine, shooting, and the racetrack, while Ernest quickly mastered coolie English and collected his usual entourage of miscellaneous cronies and admirers.

tha Gellhorn Hemingway would come home less and less as the expanding global war beckoned with ever-greater urgency.

Very shortly after the Hemingways left Asia, Hong Kong and Rangoon both fell to the Japanese, and six months following Ernest's flight from Honolulu to Los Angeles the Japanese attacked Pearl Harbor. Although China and its people impressed Hemingway, they did not stir his imagination enough to become material for new fiction, either stories or a novel. In Washington he and Martha predicted that the Communists would dominate China after the war.

1. The recently married Hemingways preparing to disembark the SS *Matsonia* on their arrival in Honolulu, the first leg of a long journey made in early 1941 to report the China-Japan War.

2. Hemingway examining maps with a British officer in Hong Kong.

3. Ernest and Martha Hemingway near the front in China in early 1941, when they covered the struggle being waged by Chiang Kai-shek not only against Japan but also against the Chinese Communists.

4. Papa dining with Chinese military officers. At one such occasion the novelist drank fourteen of his hosts under the table.

5. During their 30,000-mile journey to China, then over the Burma Road to Rangoon and back, Martha and Ernest traveled by horse, boat, an

ancient Chris-Craft, truck, and plane, always under conditions that he bore stoically while she openly expressed unmitigated horror.

6. Chinese troops threading their way through rice paddies and polluted ponds. Observing scenes like this, Martha wrote: "...over all the villages hung the smell of China's night soil, the deadly national manure."

7. In Chungking the Hemingways interviewed Mme Chiang Kai-shek at the table where she wrote outside her husband's bomb shelter.

by a German sub so that once a boarding party had assembled on the deck, the *Pilar* hardies could drill them with machine-gun fire and then destroy the vessel itself by blasting it with bazookas and tossing hand grenades down the conning tower. Although Captain Hemingway never got a chance to carry out this bold and imaginative plan, the *Pilar* operation did report useful gen on U-boat movements, making it possible for the Navy to bomb and presumably sink several of the subs that for a while held Cuba under blockade. Subsequently, Papa said:

I explained to the crew the dangers involved, since Pilar *was no match for any U-boat that wanted to blast it. Despite the dangers, Gregorio, who was boat-mate to me, was very happy to go out because we were insured ten thousand dollars a man and Gregorio had never figured he was worth that much. The quarters were very cramped, but the crew got along fine. No fights. On one tour we stayed out fifty-seven days.*

Finally, Hemingway acceded to the urgings of his wife, Martha—who from the start regarded the Crook Factory and sub-hunting as little better than a Keystone Cops farce—and decided to go to Europe to cover the war. But, for whatever reason, Ernest passed up other offers to accept a proposal from *Collier's* that he take over from Martha as their correspondent. Martha naturally resented the loss of her *Collier's* credentials, but she continued to cover the war. Understandably, she was not very sympathetic when, upon her arrival in London, she found Ernest in St. George's Hospital with a concussion, suffered in an automobile crash while returning through

WORLD WAR II AND WIFE IV

Discouraged by the fatigue and frustration of the China trip—the censorship and propaganda that made war correspondence difficult at best—Hemingway resisted Martha's insistence that, for the world's greater good, he must cover the action in Europe as only he, with his unique talent, experience, and prestige, could do it. Ernest preferred, however, to let his wife undertake journalistic assignments all round the Caribbean and then in besieged Britain, North Africa, and Italy, while he concentrated his war effort on the home front. This meant Cuba, where his proposal of two rather far-fetched anti-Nazi schemes received an enthusiastic response from the new American Ambassador, Spruille Braden, who in turn won approval from the Cuban government permitting Ernest to set up a counter-intelligence operation. In this first of his undercover ventures, Papa established the "Crook Factory" in the Finca's guest house, where he quickly organized six full-time operatives and twenty secret agents, recruiting them from the ranks of fishermen, jai-alai players, pimps and their whores, refugee grandees, and, for good measure, one Basque priest. Hemingway even persuaded Gustavo Durán, a Spanish friend from Mont-

parnasse days who had abandoned his career in music composition for the sake of serving as a General in the Loyalist Army, to travel all the way from New York and take charge of the Finca spooks. The spy ring went into effect in May 1942, and before disbanding it in April 1943, Ernest and his "crooks" had indeed kept an eye on the thousands of pro-Franco, pro-Hitler Falangists in Cuba. Meanwhile, they had also reported a quantity of unverifiable rumors, enjoyed a good many picturesque adventures, and won for the spy master himself a generous allotment of scarce gasoline from the American Embassy's private store.

Hardly had Ernest got the Crook Factory under way when he received authorization and materiel that enabled him to arm the *Pilar* and transform it into a spy ship for the purpose of foiling German U-boat activity in the Caribbean. Accordingly, the cabin cruiser set forth camouflaged as a marine research vessel but, in actuality, equipped with government-issue bazookas, explosives, .50-caliber machine guns, and radio equipment. This time the personnel would be an eight-man crew that included Winston Guest, a Churchill relative and Phipps heir; a Basque sailor named Francisco Paxtchi Ibarlucia; and the *Pilar's* longtime mate Gregorio Fuentes. While cruising in open waters off the northern coast of Cuba, Ernest hoped to be halted

3

4

5

1. By the time Martha Gellhorn Hemingway risked the wrath of her husband and arrived in London in late October 1943, the British capital had already been thoroughly blitzed, as here at the height of the German bombing in July 1941.

2. Gustavo Durán, called "my hero" by Papa while covering the Spanish Civil War. A Hemingway friend from Montparnasse days, Durán gave up music composition to become a General in the Loyalist Army. After that cause failed, Ernest invited Durán to Cuba and placed him in charge of the Crook Factory. As an intelligent, well-educated, attractive Spaniard with Rockefeller connections (through marriage), Durán soon found important work to do at the American Embassy in Havana, before joining the United Nations in 1946. However, his lack of interest in the Crook Factory cost him his relationship with Hemingway.

3. A bearded Papa, with Wing Commander Alan Lyn, at an RAF aerodrome in late June 1944, preparing to take off for a bombing raid on a German V–1 launching pad. In Britain, Hemingway had a special commission from the RAF to report its readiness for the invasion of German-occupied France, as well as his correspondent's credentials from *Collier's*.

4. Mary Welsh with three of her colleagues at Time, Inc., in London during the early 1940s. On the rebound from his marital quarrels with Martha, Ernest proposed marriage to Mary almost immediately after they met, which was within days of his arrival in the British capital in May 1944. At the far left in the photograph is Bill Walton, the brilliant *Time* correspondent with whom Ernest bunked during their coverage of the Allied push across France and into Germany.

5. General Eisenhower addressing a group of para-troopers just before D-Day.

6. American troops preparing to cross the English Channel for the D-Day landing on the Normandy beaches.

6

7. An autographed snapshot from General R.O. Barton, commander of the First Army's Fourth Infantry Division. It was this group, particularly the 22nd Regiment led by Colonel Buck Lanham, that Hemingway followed all across France to the Liberation of Paris and on to the storming of the Siegfried Line in September-December 1944.

8. Papa at the the head of the table in the Hôtel de la Mère Poularde on Mont Saint-Michel in April 1944, during a two-day rest he took following his second concussion in little more than two months. Around the table, from left to right, are *Time* correspondent Bill Walton, Mme Chevalier, Ernest, an Army Signal Corp photographer, M. Chevalier, and *Life* photographer Bob Capa.

9. Beautiful sea-girt Mont Saint-Michel, the monastic Romanesque-Gothic pile towering above the little hotel where Hemingway and pals rested a couple of days in early August 1944.

7

10. The triumphant march of General Leclerc's Free French forces down the Champs-Élysées on August 25, 1944.

11. In Paris, Hemingway quickly renewed contact with old friends from Montparnasse days, particularly Sylvia Beach. Here, at Deux Magots, he reads to Janet Flanner, longtime Paris correspondent for *The New Yorker*. The manuscript he holds is probably that of the many-stanzaed poem he wrote for Mary Welsh, the *Time* correspondent who was replacing Martha Gellhorn in his affections.

blacked-out streets to his hotel from a late-night party given by *Life* photographer Robert Capa. Martha showed little sympathy for Ernest's plight, and, in fact, took a separate room at the Dorchester and went about her London life without him. To compensate, Ernest had found a new source of sympathy and comfort in the person of Mary Welsh, a *Time*

8

9

correspondent with a good figure, a piquant if not pretty face, and a crafty, eager way with men.

On the military side of things, Hemingway disregarded the seriousness of his injury and took to the air with the RAF. On June 6, just two weeks after his accident, he even boarded an attack transport to observe the D-Day landing below the Normandy cliffs on what was called Omaha Beach. Martha, meanwhile, further exasperated Ernest by actually going ashore with the troops, thanks to her intrepid act of stowing away on a hospital ship. By mid-July, however, Ernest too was in France following the advance of the 22nd

Regiment of the First Army's Fourth Infantry Division, whose regimental commander, Colonel "Buck" Lanham, would become his World War II buddy and a cherished friend to the end of his life. Buck and Papa stuck together as the 22nd's brave troops spearheaded the Normandy breakout, entered Paris, attacked the Siegfried Line, and held a key position in the Battle of the Bulge. Early in the long campaign, however, Ernest concussed his poor battered head yet again, this time by diving into a ditch, on top of Capa, to avoid fire from a German anti-tank gun as the two of them raced forward on a motorcycle. After two days of rest at Mont Saint-Michel, he overlooked dizziness, double vision, chronic headaches, ringing ears, verbal slurring, and memory loss to become, with the blessing of OSS Colonel David Bruce, an ad hoc military governor of Rambouillet some 30 miles from Paris. There, in his most famous and contro-

versial exploit during this war, Hemingway used his fluent French, commanding personality, and instinct for strategy, to calm the populace, hold the town for several days, interrogate prisoners, and direct intelligence-gathering about enemy defenses on the road to Paris. He also amassed an arsenal, removed his correspondent's insignia, and bore arms, which so annoyed fellow correspondents that he barely escaped being sent home after an official inquiry caught up with him two months later.

As the Fourth Infantry Division approached and eventually breached the massively fortified Siegfried Line, Papa made

extended sorties to the front. At one point he stunned all present in Lanham's mess by calmly continuing to cut and consume his meat while everyone else headed for the potato cellar when a bomb exploded outside. For Hemingway, the war climaxed at the savage, decimating Battle of Hürtgenwald that raged from November 15 to early December. To gain a single mile through freezing rain, snow, pillboxes, land mines, relentless shelling, and "dense, dank woods straight out of German folk tales," the 22nd Regiment suffered more than 300 casualties, among the 24,000 Americans killed, wounded, or captured. Before it was over, Ernest defied the Geneva Convention, took up arms, and fired on the enemy as German troops penetrated close enough to threaten Lanham's headquarters. Meanwhile, he also worried about Lieutenant John Hemingway, his eldest son Jack or Bumby, an OSS officer who, after par-

10

11

achuting into Occupied France, was taken prisoner by the Germans on October 28.

Finally, Hemingway covered the Battle of the Bulge in Belgium and Luxembourg, but weakened by pneumonia, he missed the main action. Here, the biggest battle was with Martha, who joined him for Christmas in Rodenburg outside Luxembourg City. Almost two months after she had written him for a divorce, they went through a terminal quarrel and spent their last night together. On March 6, 1945, following two months in Paris court-

12

13

ing Mary Welsh, Papa flew back to New York and told Max Perkins of his intention to write a great trilogy of war novels. He then went on to Key West to collect Gregory and Patrick and take them with him to the Finca. Mary Welsh arrived there on May 2, the same day that Lieutenant John Hemingway was released from a German prison camp.

Ernest's war exploits elicited mixed reviews: British Air Marshal Peter Wykeham, who flew Hemingway, at his request, on a foolhardy pursuit of V-1 rockets, wrote in the London *Times*:

He impressed me as the sort of man who spends his whole life proving that he is not scared. . . . [The RAF public relations officer— actually, the poet John Pudney—in charge of the American novelist felt] like a gentle man who's accidentally found himself leading a rampaging bull. He got into more and more drunken parties, fights, and wrangles, being thrown into fountains, ejected from hotels and locked in people's rooms.[1]

On the other hand, *Time* correspondent Bill Walton bunked with Ernest at the front and thought him at the very top of his spectacular form. Moreover, David Bruce, the OSS officer who authorized Hemingway's "governorship" at Rambouillet, would later write:

I entertain a great admiration for [Ernest], not only as an artist and friend, but as a cool, resourceful, imaginative, military tactician and strategist. He unites, from what I saw of him, that rare combination of advised reck-

14

160

THE G.I. AND THE GENERAL
by Ernest Hemingway

15

16

12. Hemingway with Colonel Buck Lanham inspecting German artillery after the 22nd Infantry Regiment had breached the Siegfried Line in September 1944.

13. Papa inspecting the dense fortifications and forest that made the Siegfried Line a formidable obstacle to the Allied advance into Germany proper.

14. Marlene Dietrich, the German-born Hollywood star who tirelessly entertained Allied troops during their campaign to free Europe from German occupation. Like her old friend Hemingway, Dietrich stayed at the Ritz in between sorties to the front. When both happened to be in residence, she is reputed to have sung to him sitting on the edge of his bathtub while he shaved.

15. One of the dispatches that Hemingway cabled from France for publication in *Collier's*.

16. On June 16, 1947, at the American Embassy in Havana, Ernest Hemingway received the Bronze Star medal from the US Military Attaché in recognition of his meritorious service as a foreign correspondent with the Allied forces in Europe during World War II.

17. Hemingway in snowbound Luxembourg in December during the Battle of the Bulge, the last military campaign he would ever cover.

lessness and caution that knows how properly to seize upon a favorable opportunity which, once lost, is gone forever. He was a born leader of men, and, in spite of his strong independence of character, impressed me as a highly disciplined individual.[2]

As for Papa, he found himself in his element once he got going with the 22nd Infantry Regiment. To Mary he wrote from Normandy: "We have a very jolly and gay life, full of deads, German loot, much shooting, much fighting." Later in life, on reflection, Ernest looked upon his seven-month involvement with the Liberation of France and the invasion of Germany as dangerous and intense but brief, irregular, full of excitement, comradely, and lucky.

17

LIBERATING THE RITZ

Ernest always claimed that he and his band of "irregulars" (stragglers assembled from various military units) entered Paris in advance of Leclerc's Allied forces. Papa said that he zoomed down the Champs-Élysées in his jeep and headed straight for the Ritz, which he "liberated" by invading the bar and ordering champagne for everyone. But the euphoric mood had begun at the first sight of Paris, from the high road over which Leclerc's tanks would advance. "I had a funny choke in my throat and I had to clean my glasses," Ernest wrote, "because there now, below us, gray and always beautiful, was spread the city I have loved best in all the world."

For Hemingway, Paris was the Ritz Hotel, and vice-versa. In the early days, of course, when he was poor and struggling, Ernest lived in furnished rooms on the Left Bank, but even then his good friends, Scott Fitzgerald and others, were staying at the Ritz, and Ernest went there often to visit them. With the success of *The Sun Also Rises* and *A Farewell to Arms*, both partially written in Paris, Papa was able to make the Ritz his home, and from then on he never lived anywhere else when he came to the French capital. "When in Paris," he once told me, "the only reason not to stay at the Ritz is if you can't afford it." In fact, he wrote:

When I dream of afterlife in heaven, the action always takes place in the Paris Ritz. It's a fine summer night. I knock back a couple of martinis in the bar, Cambon side. Then there's a wonderful dinner under a flowering chestnut tree in what's called "Le Petit Jardin." That's the little garden that faces the Grill.

After a few brandies I wander up to my room and slip into one of those huge Ritz beds. They are all made of brass. There's a bolster for my head the size of the Graf Zeppelin and four square pillows filled with real goose feathers—two for me, and two for my quite heavenly companion.

The Ritz bathrooms have a dimension and a marbled elegance all their own. One of their features is the king-size bathtub, invented by César Ritz after the corpulent King Edward VII, who delighted in bathing with young lovelies, got stuck in an ordinary tub. Ritz also invented the king-size bed, indirect lighting, and closets that are illuminated as the door opens. Moreover, he established the basic, now universal, raiment for the dining room: white tie for the waiter, black tie for the maître d'hôtel. And it was Ritz who put brass buttons on the bellhop.

The bar on the Rue Cambon side, presided over by the legendary Georges, became a focal point of Paris visitors, especially the fabled figures of the Belle Époque and the years between the two World Wars. There was President Teddy Roosevelt, laughing, big-voiced, and robust, back from an African hunting expedition, surrounded by enthralled friends. The Maharajahs of Cooch-Behar and Jaipur could often be found drinking champagne together. On one occasion, when Hemingway was having drinks with Scott Fitzgerald, Scott table-hopped by swinging from a chandelier. Graham Greene constantly complained that his martinis were not dry enough. The Duchess of Windsor routinely had cocktails with the playboy Jimmy Donohue, before going off to join the Duke for dinner. At lunch, the following day she frequently arrived without the Duke, who had not yet recovered from the night's revels. "I married David for better, for worse," the Duchess remarked, "but not for lunch." King Alfonso of Spain, another regular, would automatically be served his special drink—a quart of Dom Perignon champagne liberally laced with cognac and a dozen strawberries. Another Ritz habitué was Cole Porter, who, over drinks one evening wrote the immortal lyrics: "The world admits/Even bears in pits do it/Even pekineses in the Ritz do it/Let's do it, let's fall in love."

Noël Coward at his special table, Douglas Fairbanks, Sr., and Mary Pickford holding hands, Winston Churchill and Duff Cooper drinking scotch, Rockefeller and Woolworth, J. Pierpont Morgan and Major Hodge, Andrew Carnegie, Tommy Manville and his wife of the moment, Wallace Beery with his booming frog-voice and his infinite capacity for drink and companionship, Dietrich but never in pants—all contributed to the heady atmosphere of the Ritz' Cambon bar.

Also adding to the legend of the place was an incident that occurred one evening in the 1920s when Hemingway was having drinks with Scott Fitzgerald. After a rather decadent-looking Englishman came in with a young lady whose dazzling beauty excited Scott, the latter asked Georges to send out a groom to fetch a box of orchids, which Scott promptly sent to the beauty's table with a note suggesting that they meet at a later time. The young lady just as promptly rejected the box and sent it back to Fitzgerald, who opened it up, and, in his misery, ate the orchids, petal by petal. "The amazing part of it," Ernest said, "was that it worked and Scott got his way with that beauty. Afterwards, I always referred to such ruses and maneuvers as the Orchid Ploy."

The Ritz' most celebrated regulars were Coco Chanel and Marcel Proust. In 1934, the beautiful and fabulously wealthy couturière gave up her mansion in the Rue du Faubourg Saint-Honoré and moved into a suite at the Ritz, directly across the street from her salon in the Rue Cambon. Despite having a luxurious flat above the salon, she remained at the Ritz, right through the Occupation, until her death in 1971. For Proust, who maintained an apartment in the Rue Hamelin, the Ritz was a refuge, a spiritual home. According to George Painter, Proust biographer:

The great hotel became his second home, a substitute for the palaces of Cabourg, Venice and Evian which he would never see again. At the Ritz he found again the movement and enigmas of a miniature world, the comfort and security of family life, the satisfaction of his lifelong craving for reciprocal service and gratitude. He wrote in his cork-lined bedroom, but went to the Ritz to live.[1]

Even at the end, Proust thought of the Ritz, sending his chauffeur Odilon, to the hotel for a bottle of his favorite beer, always kept on ice for him. As he neared death he feared the beer would not make it in time, but it did, and after the dying Proust took a final satisfying sip, his last words were: "Thank you, my dear Odilon, for getting me the Ritz beer."

Charles Ritz, César's only child, would become one of Ernest's oldest and closest friends. They loved to talk fishing and hunting and honestly admired each other. I was present on the day Charley Ritz discovered that Ernest had left a trunk in the hotel's basement, where it had gone unnoticed for twenty years. We opened the trunk, and in it was a treasure trove of manuscripts, in fact some of the material that later was to constitute a major part of one of Hemingway's most successful books, *A Moveable Feast*, the posthumously published memoir of the author's early life in Paris.

4

1. The entrance to the Paris Ritz from the Place Vendôme, through which Ernest Hemingway passed when he "liberated" the great hotel on the evening of August 25, 1944.

2. The modestly scaled but exquisitely appointed reception salon at the Paris Ritz.

3. The Ritz Grill and Petit Jardin in the time of Marcel Proust, a regular at dinner, if not a resident, whose presence and legend still haunt the hotel. Ernest acknowledged Proust's abiding spirit while taking "a wonderful dinner under a flowering chestnut tree in what's called 'Le Petiti Jardin.'... the little garden that faces the Grill."

4. Ernest thought Heaven might be somewhat like the Ritz, where, "after a few brandies I wander up to my room and slip into one of those huge Ritz beds. They are made of brass. There's a bolster for my head the size of the Graf Zeppelin and four square pillows filled with real goose feathers—two for me, and two for my quite heavenly companion."

5. When *Life* photographer Bob Capa arrived at the Ritz late on Liberation Day in Paris he was greeted at the entrance by Hemingway's GI chauffeur, who announced: "Papa took good hotel. Plenty stuff in cellar. You go up quick."

5

THE
CUBAN
AND
VENETIAN
YEARS

———

MARY WELSH

Mary Welsh became Ernest's fourth wife and the one to whom he was married the longest. She came from Bemidji, Minnesota, where she was born in 1908. She attended Northwestern University's School of Journalism, but left school for a job on the staff of *The American Florist*, a magazine written for the nation's florists. She had other odd journalistic jobs before she was able to land on the staff of London's *Daily Express*, thanks to her introduction to Lord Beaverbrook who owned the paper. While in London she met and married an Australian journalist named Noel Monks

1. Mary Welsh, the *Time* reporter whom Hemingway met shortly after his arrival in wartime London in May 1944. A year later Mary would be in Cuba to become the mistress of the Finca Vigía and the fourth as well as the last Mrs. Ernest Hemingway. As this photograph would suggest, her interest in animals, both wild and domestic, was as keen as her husband's.

2. Immediately upon her arrival at the Finca, Mary was introduced to the favorites among Ernest's large family of cats and dogs. Fortunately, she won their approval; otherwise, her pending marriage to the master would have been in serious jeopardy. Meanwhile, the Finca's "deep and delicious" swimming pool would meet with Mary's enthusiastic approval.

3. The Hemingways at ease in their 50-foot living room at the Finca. Sharing the walls with Ernest's trophy heads were paintings by an old friend, Waldo Peirce, and the Spanish master Juan Gris.

4. Mary and Ernest Hemingway strolling through their 15-acre estate known as the Finca Vigía and located some 11 miles outside Havana.

(she had had a brief previous marriage to a student she had met in college). Monks was traveling a great deal covering the Spanish Civil War and other events for his paper. As a consequence he and Mary did not see much of one another.

Mary eventually left the *Daily Express* to join the staff of *Time* magazine's London bu-

reau. Not long after her arrival in London, she met Irwin Shaw, the novelist, with whom she had an affair, and it was through Shaw that Mary met Hemingway who had asked Irwin to introduce him.

It didn't take Ernest very long to lure her away from Shaw, and to persuade her to divorce Monks and marry him. While the two of them waited for their divorces to become final, Ernest took Mary back to Cuba where they were married in 1946.

Mary shared Ernest's enthusiasm for fishing, spending days at a time on the *Pilar*, for skiing and hunting and prowling the streets of Paris and Venice. She enjoyed drinking as much as Ernest did, and she became an accomplished cook and hostess. But their married life was far from tranquil. Their quarrels were frequent and noisily vitriolic, often accompanied by objects hurled around in anger. These outbursts were followed by long periods of noncommunication, and, on a few occasions, by stormy separations.

On one such occasion, when Mary found out that Ernest had entertained a lady of questionable virtue at the Finca while Mary had been back in the States visiting her parents, the resulting confrontation was volcanic. Eventually Mary relented, however, because, as Ernest told me, "the thing that actually got me out of the doghouse is that I love Miss Mary truly. She knows this and it helps her to forgive me when I am in the wrong. She ended that incident by telling me that I was not taking life seriously. Someday I might take it seriously and a lot of characters will hang by their necks until dead."

In 1954, after their plane crashed in the jungle in Africa, the Hemingways again had a period of combativeness, accusing each other of behaving badly under pressure. Hemingway told me:

Mary was lovely the first four months on safari, really wonderful and most of the time quite brave. But after the first crash, when we were down in the jungle with the elephants pretty thick, she got a little testy—refused to believe I could tell the males from the females by the smell. Her other failings were that she never really considered lions dangerous and that the really bad fight we had with a leopard—when I had to crawl on my face into bush thicker than mangrove swamp and kill him with a shotgun—was stunting. Leopard was hurt bad and very dangerous, and I had a piece of shoulder bone in my mouth to keep my morale up. I had to fire at the roar because it was too thick to see. So that was stunting. Actually, what I'm saying is not against

her because she was in a state of shock from the crashes, but she doesn't know about shock nor believe in it and she thinks when I am removing impacted feces from a busted sphincter, I am dogging it. But mostly she is loving and wonderful. And, as I say, very brave. But I wish she had some Jewish blood so she would know that other people hurt. But you can't have everything and I married a women who is one-half Kraut and one-half Irish and that makes a merciless cross but a lovely woman. She is my pocket Rubens.

Despite these manifestations of incompatibility, there was also a strong interdependency that became more pronounced as Ernest's physical and psychological problems overwhelmed him during the last years of his life.

The last time I saw Ernest, at the Mayo Clinic, he was very concerned about Mary because he had been difficult and had given her a hard time when she had come to see him. He was anxious that I understand his true feelings for her. We had gone for a drive, and, feeling good about this brief respite from the hospital's confinement, he said:

Mary is wonderful. Always and now. Wonderful. She's been so damn brave and good. She is all that is left to be glad for. I love her. I truly love her. You remember I told you once she did not know about other people's hurts. Well, I was wrong. She knows. She knows how I hurt and she suffers trying to help me—I wish to Christ I could spare her that.

Whatever their periods of domestic turbulence, I think Ernest's description of Mary, as it appeared in *Look* magazine in 1956, would probably be the assessment of her that he would like to leave to posterity:

Miss Mary is durable. She is also brave, charming, witty, exciting to look at, a pleasure to be with and a good wife. She is an excellent fisherwoman, a fair wing shot, a strong swimmer, a really good cook, a good judge of wine, an excellent gardener, an amateur astronomer, a student of art, political economy, Swahili, French and Italian and can run a boat or a household in Spanish.

THE FINCA VIGÍA

In early 1939, at the conclusion of the Spanish Civil War, Ernest and Martha settled in Cuba, at the Finca Vigía a few miles outside Havana. The village of San Francisco de Paula, where "Lookout Farm" was located, was itself a poverty-stricken shambles. But the Hemingway property, which Papa bought at the very end of 1940 for $12,500, was fence-enclosed and consisted of 15 acres of flower and vegetable gardens, a cow pasture with a half-dozen cows, fruit trees, a defunct tennis court, a large swimming pool, and a low, once-white limestone villa that was a bit crumbled but dignified. Eighteen kinds of mangoes grew on the long slope from the main gate up to the house that Ernest called his "charming ruin." Immediately in front of the house was a giant ceiba tree, sacred in voodoo rites, orchids growing from its grizzled trunk, its massive roots upheaving the tiled terrace and splitting the interior of the house itself. But Ernest's fondness for the tree was such that despite its havoc, he would not permit the roots to be touched. A short distance from the main house was a white frame guest house. Behind the main house, to one side, was a new white gleaming three-storied square tower with an outside winding staircase.

The walls of the dining room and the nearly 50-foot living room of the main house were populated with splendidly horned animal heads, and there were several well-trod animal skins on the tiled floors. The furniture was old, comfortable, and undistinguished. Inside the front doors was an enormous magazine rack that held an unceasing deluge of American and foreign-language periodicals. A large library off the living room was crammed with books that lined the walls from the floor to the high ceiling. Ernest's bedroom, where he worked, was also walled with books; there were over five thousand volumes on the premises. On the wall over his bed was one of his favorite paintings, Juan Gris' *Guitar Player*. Another Gris, Miró's *Farm*, several Massons, a Klee, a Braque, and Waldo Peirce's portrait of Ernest as a young man were among the paintings in the living room.

In Ernest's room there was a large desk covered with stacks of letters, newspapers, and magazine clippings, a small sack of carnivores' teeth, two unwound clocks, shoehorns, an unfilled pen in an onyx holder, a wood-carved zebra, wart hog, rhino, and lion in single file, and a wide assortment of souvenirs, mementos and good-luck charms.

1

Papa never worked at the desk. Instead, he used a stand-up work place he had fashioned out of the top of a bookcase near his bed. His portable typewriter was snugged in there, and papers were spread along the top of the bookcase on either side of it. He used a reading board for longhand writing. There were some animal heads on the bedroom walls, too, and a worn, cracked skin of a lesser kudu decorated the tiled floor.

Hemingway's bathroom was large and cluttered with medicines and medical paraphernalia, which bulged out of the cabinet and onto all surfaces. The room was badly in need of paint, but painting was impossible because the walls were covered with inked records, written in Ernest's careful hand, of dated blood-pressure counts, weights, prescription numbers, and other medical and pharmaceutical intelligence.

The staff for the Finca normally consisted of the houseboy René, the chauffeur Juan, a Chinese cook, three gardeners, a carpenter, two maids, and the keeper of the fighting cocks. Mary built a white tower in back of the house in an effort to get the complement of thirty cats out of the house, and to provide Ernest with a place more becoming to work in than his makeshift quarters in his bedroom. It worked with the cats, but not with Ernest. The ground floor of the tower was the cats' quarters, with special sleeping, eating, and maternity accommodations, and they all lived there with the exception of a few favorites like Crazy Christian, Friendless' Brother, and Ecstasy, who were allowed house privileges. The top floor of the tower, which had a

2

sweeping view of palm tops and green hillocks clear to the sea, had been furnished with an imposing desk befitting an Author of High Status, bookcases, and comfortable reading chairs, but Ernest rarely wrote a line there—except when he occasionally corrected a set of galleys.

The dinner regulars at the Finca were Roberto Herrera, a bald, deaf, powerful, unprepossessing, gentle, devoted Spaniard, in his late thirties, who, according to Ernest, had had five years of medicine in Spain and who had come to Cuba after having been impris-

168

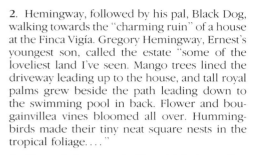

1. The foyer to the Finca's main house, with its view into the dining room and its magazine rack loaded with periodicals from all over the world.

2. Hemingway, followed by his pal, Black Dog, walking towards the "charming ruin" of a house at the Finca Vigía. Gregory Hemingway, Ernest's youngest son, called the estate "some of the loveliest land I've seen. Mango trees lined the driveway leading up to the house, and tall royal palms grew beside the path leading down to the swimming pool in back. Flower and bougainvillea vines bloomed all over. Hummingbirds made their tiny neat square nests in the tropical foliage...."

3. The main house at the Finca Vigía. According to Gregory Hemingway, "the rambing, one-story Spanish colonial house was perched on the highest point of land in the area, and had a wonderful view of the lights of Havana."

4. The library at the Finca with some of Ernest's 5,000 books.

5. Hemingway, with Black Dog at his feet, working in the master bedroom, where he preferred to be rather than in the study that Mary arranged for him at the top of the white tower she had built behind the main house. Although Ernest sometimes read proof there, he felt lonely so far removed from the household sounds.

6. Ernest and Mary Hemingway presiding over lunch attended by a group of the master's regular cronies.

oned for fighting on the Republican side in the Civil War; Sinsky Duñabeitia, a salty, roaring, boozing, fun-loving Basque sea captain who manned a freighter run from the States to Cuba and was a constant at the Finca whenever his ship was in port; Father Don Andrés, called "Black Priest," a Basque who had been in the Bilbao Cathedral when the Civil War broke out. Don Andrés had climbed into the pulpit, exhorting all the parishioners to get their guns and fill the streets and shoot what they could and the hell with spending their time in church. After that, he enrolled as a machine-gunner in the Republican army. Of course, when the war ended he was kicked out of Spain. He sought refuge in Cuba, but the Church there took a dim view of his past behavior and assigned him the poorest parish in the worst section. Thus, the name Black Priest. Ernest had befriended him, as he befriended scores of Franco refugees, and Black Priest, wearing a brightly colored sport shirt, would come to the Finca on his days away from his parish and devote himself to eating, drinking, swimming in the pool, and exchanging reminiscences with Ernest and Robert.

Mondays to Thursdays I try to maintain quiet. But the weekends are always on the

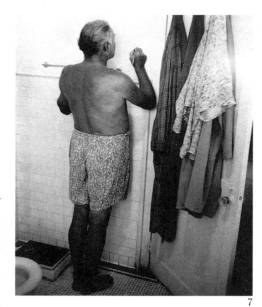

7

8

verge of uproar, and sometimes over the verge. Papa doesn't like to go to other people's houses because he says he can't trust the food and drink. The last time he accepted a dinner invitation was about a year ago. They served sweet champagne which he had to drink to be polite, and he said it took ten days for him to get it out of his system.

7. Ernest's bathroom could never be painted because of the health records—dated blood-pressure counts, weight changes, prescription numbers—written on the walls.

8. Papa with his fighting cocks and their trainer.

9. In the winter of 1950–51 Gary Cooper, an old friend from Sun Valley and the star of two Hemingway movies, visited the Finca.

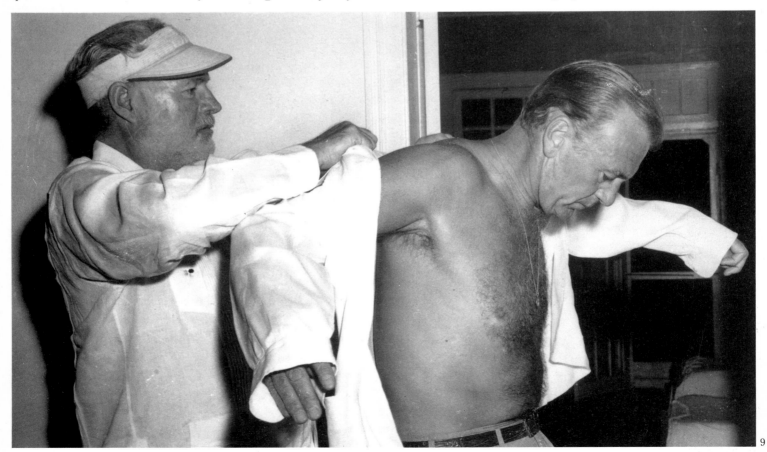

9

170

1

2

3

He would always arrive on time for
*   breakfast,*
Scamper on your feet and chase the ball;
He was faster than any polo pony,
He never worried a minute at all.
His tail was a plume that scampered with him,
He was black as night and as fast as light
So the bad cats killed him in the fall.

1, 3. In Cuba, Ernest developed a great fondness for cats and kept a horde of them at the Finca Vigía. He allowed the catsies to roam wherever they wished, even on the dining table or over his typewriter and desk while he worked.

2. Two of Papa's favorite cats.

CATS OF THE FINCA

Hemingway had an abiding fondness of animals, especially dogs, bears, owls, fighting cocks, and cats. Wherever Ernest went, even for a brief time, he wound up with a cat in his household. At the Finca there were cats everywhere, inside and outside the house; at the base of the white tower there were permanent quarters for some twenty or thirty of the Finca cats.

Each of the cats had a name, and Ernest doted on them, even to the extent of feeding them an array of vitamin tablets every morning which he dispensed from the dining-room table. On one occasion when I was at the Finca, a feline tragedy occurred, and Ernest commemorated the event with this poem:

There was a cat named Crazy Christian
Who never lived long enough to screw,
He was gay-hearted, young and handsome,
And all the secrets of life he knew.

ADRIANA IVANCICH

It was on an earlier visit to Venice in 1948 that Ernest had met those Venetians who were destined to be the principal characters in what would be his next novel, *Across the River and Into the Trees*. It was at the insistence of Count Federico Kechler that Ernest and Mary by-passed Portofino, where they had planned to spend the winter, and went to Venice instead. It was Count Kechler who chose the Gritti Palace for them, and who introduced them to the society in which he moved. Of the Venetians whom he met, Ernest particularly liked the members of the Franchetti clan. Baron Franchetti shared Ernest's love for hunting and invited him to the Franchetti hunting preserve in Latisana. It was there that Ernest met Adriana Ivancich, a tall, eighteen-year-old aristocratic beauty with long black hair and a curiously shaped but not unattractive nose that Ernest described as "pure Byzantine."

Adriana was descended from along line of distinguished Venetians, a family of ship owners and captains who plied the seas during the glory days of the Doges. Generations of Ivanciches had lived in the ancestral palazzo

in the Calle de Remedio, which had been constructed in the 16th century from architectural plans drawn up by one of Italy's greatest architects, Palladio. The family also owned a country estate outside San Michele.

Adriana was born in Venice in 1930 and enjoyed a privileged life until the start of World War II, which drastically worsened the Ivancich fortunes. Adriana was only ten years old at the time. The Ivancich country villa at San Michele fell victim to Allied bombing, and towards the end of the war her father was found brutally murdered in an alleyway in San Michele.

After the war, Adriana's mother, Dora, a staunch patrician, managed to hold the family together, and Adriana received traditional schooling at the Liceo Classico, and a formal society debut when she turned eighteen. At

the time Adriana met Hemingway, she had just returned from Switzerland where she had gone to study French, and had been invited to join the Franchettis for that hunting weekend at their Latisana lodge, which was adjacent to the Ivancich estate.

Before the weekend was over, it was clear that Ernest was quite captivated with the young beauty, and he invited her to have dinner at Harry's Bar later in the week, ostensibly to meet Mary. As it turned out, Ernest saw Adriana almost every day during his sojourn in Venice, and when I accompanied him to Venice a few years later, she was again constantly in our company. By then, Ernest had written his new novel, *Across the River and Into the Trees*, which, in true Hemingway tradition, was a romanticized version of reality, a projection that allowed his involvement with Ad-

riana to resolve itself in his imagination.

In the novel, the protagonist, an American Colonel, aged fifty, has an affair with an adoring Venetian Contessa named Renata, whose age and description match those of Adriana. Hemingway did not allow the book to be published in Italy when it originally came out in the States, but when it was finally published in Italy, an article appeared in the weekly magazine *Epoca* that boldly pronounced, over Adriana's prominent by-line: "I am Hemingway's Renata." The article told about the first meeting between Adriana and Ernest, and then went on to relate how they saw each other day after day. "At first I was a bit bored with this man," Adriana confessed, "so much older and more experienced than I, who spoke slowly and whom I did not always understand. But I felt that he liked having me near him and liked to talk and talk." Adriana then recounted how their relationship grew, but that she didn't suspect that Mary was worried about her until Mary told her so one day. However, after their talk, Adriana said, Mary understood that her affection would never be transformed into love and that not only was she not a danger but was in fact a help.

Her helpfulness was, Adriana said, in restoring Ernest's writing vigor.

Hemingway told me that he had fallen ill while writing Across the River and Into the Trees *and had had to put it aside because he could no longer write, but after having met me he felt a new energy travel from me into him. "You have given me back the possibility*

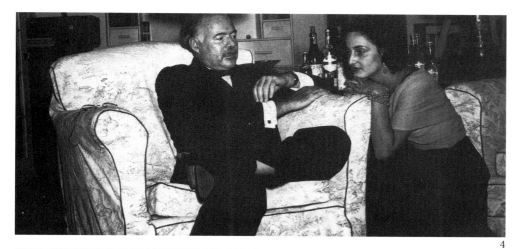

eral of his novels had begun as short stories—and Ernest thought that the magazine might consider running the novel in three installments when it was finished. That's exactly what happened, and Ernest only returned to Italy after completing the manuscript, taking me with him, to check on the accuracy of his depiction of some of the places he had written about.

I was often with Adriana, sometimes when Hemingway was with her, often alone with her when Hemingway had social obligations with Mary. There was a time she arrived in New York with her mother on their way to visit the Hemingways in Cuba, and for a week or two Adriana and I went out every evening. We knew each other very well. I'm sure that she had had no sexual involvement with Ernest, but she was completely captivated by his personality, by his wisdom, and by his celebrity; he had cast a spell over her which she was never able to dispel.

Adriana was first unhappily married for three years to a jealous Greek, thereafter marrying an indigent German Count with whom she was equally unhappy. She wrote an autobiography, which she entitled *The White Tower* (a reference to the white tower at the Finca), but it did not generate the income or attention she had hoped for. As a result, Adriana became depressed and withdrawn, drank heavily, and in 1983 hanged herself from a tree on her farm north of Rome. She was cut down while still alive but died shortly afterwards in a hospital.

1. Cortina d'Ampezzo, where the Hemingways spent Christmas and a good part of the winter of 1948–49.

2. Mary walking up the path from the Hemingways' chalet in Cortina.

3. Adriana Ivancich, the eighteen-year-old Venetian aristocrat whose dark beauty completely captivated Ernest Hemingway when, in November 1948, he came upon her combing her long wet hair before an open fire late one rainy afternoon at a hunting lodge in Latisana. Here she stands on a bridge over a canal in Venice, the city whose romantic qualities were inextricably linked with Ernest's feelings for Adriana.

4. It is surely a measure of the love Hemingway felt for Adriana that he would don a tux, the garment he most hated in all the world.

5. Ernest seemed not to be content until he had fallen in love with two women at once, in this instance his blond, middle-aged wife Mary and the eighteen-year-old, darkly beautiful Adriana Ivancich. Though passionate, Ernest's affair with the Venetian girl remained chaste. It would also end tragically, with Adriana so eternally obsessed with Hemingway that twenty-two years after his suicide she too commited suicide by hanging herself.

of writing again, and I shall be grateful to you for it always. I have been able to finish my book and I have given your face to the protagonist. Now I will write another book for you, and it will be my most beautiful book. It will be about an old man and the sea."

The curious part of this recitative is that Adriana confesses that when she read the novel she told Ernest that she did not find the dialogue very interesting and that, "as for Renata, no, a girl with that grace and family tradition, and so young as well, does not sneak out of the house to have amorous rendezvous and gulp one martini after another, as if they were cherries. No, she was full of contradictions. She was not real." Adriana says Ernest then told her: "You are too different to understand, but I assure you that girls like that do exist. What is more, in Renata there is not one

woman only, but four different women whom I have actually met."

In point of fact, most of Adriana's account is a figment of her romantic imagination, for I have firsthand knowledge of the genesis of *Across the River*. I first met Hemingway in 1948 when I was dispatched to Cuba by the magazine for which I worked, to ask him to write an article on the future of literature. Predictably, that article never came to pass, but Ernest suggested that he might write a short story instead, for the same amount of money the magazine had offered for the article. In subsequent conversations with him, he informed me that the short story was beginning to develop into something longer and suggested that I return to Cuba to discuss it. That's how I learned that the short story would likely be a novel—he told me that sev-

THE STONES OF VENICE

Hmingway never went to Venice in the summer, at least not in the years that I knew him. He explained it thus:

The stones of Venice are not responsive to the sun. The gray Adriatic winters bring a light that paints the city properly. Only in winter will you see the true Venice. The narrow, tight calles *are intended to shelter you against the whipping Adriatic wind. The paving stones of St. Mark's are meant to glisten in the rain. The black clouds that roll in from the sea give the Grand Canal a brooding canopy that makes it truly dramatic. And being in an enclosed gondola as it pitches and tosses its way across the canals in the winter water, that is Venice.*

It was my good fortune to have Hemingway as my guide on my initial visit there in January 1950. A motor launch dispatched from the Gritti Palace Hotel was waiting for us when we arrived. The uniformed boatman took our bags and stowed them aboard. "This is one boat ride you'll never forget," Ernest said. "No one ever forgets his first ride down the canals of Venice."

There was a slight drizzle, but Ernest stood on the stern deck of the launch instead of going inside the cabin, and I stood beside him as we went under a series of bridges. We passed a black iron fretwork bridge on a canal that led into the Rio Nuovo, then slowed down as we approached the imposing lantern that marks the entrance to the Grand Canal, where the launch picked up speed.

My breath caught as the sudden sweep of the Grand Canal appeared before us. The launch was straining against a strong wind off the mountains. We passed along the symmetrical line of palazzi, which stood like elegant soldiers. Ernest pointed to one palazzo that had a garden in front and several trees. "Lord Byron lived there. It's owned by an old contessa, friend of mine. She allows no one to sleep in Byron's bed."

And then Ernest pointed to a small, homely villa screened by a ragged edge of vegetation. "That's where the great Italian poet d'Annunzio lived," he said. "One of my all-time heroes." We passed before a serenely beautiful church, which Ernest identified as the Santa Maria del Giglio, swung sharply across from it and tied up at the wooden dock of the Gritti, the only place Ernest stayed while in Venice. "This was once the palace of a great Venetian Doge, Andrea Gritti," he said. "Now it is simply the finest hotel in Venice—that is, if you like to be surrounded by comfort and beauty without being fawned on or over-attended."

The hotel still looked like the residence of a Prince rather than a hotel. The lobby was brief and to the point, and no two rooms were alike. The marbled floors were occasionally covered by faded Oriental rugs probably brought back by some expeditionary fleet in the long ago days when the Venetians dominated the seas. Ernest and Mary Hemingway occupied a huge room on a third-floor corner where the Grand Canal veered sharply, thus wrapping itself round their high, gothic windows. I had a small, tapestried room on the floor above.

Papa suggested we go to Harry's Bar for lunch, "so Hotch can get a proper look at St. Mark's." Mary, being fatigued, stayed behind. As we left the Gritti, Ernest called a greeting to the gondoliers huddled in the lee of the hotel to escape the biting wind. When we turned a corner and suddenly came upon the magnificence of St. Mark's, Ernest said: *That's the second thing you will never forget, and you're seeing it at its best, wintertime. No*

3

vendors selling pigeon corn, no portrait photographers snapping tourists, no lines waiting to get into the church or off-key bands playing for the hordes of thirsty Germans at the outdoor cafes. Even the goddam pigeons have gone and we are two Venetian boys come home from a long sea voyage.

We passed a food shop with Parmesan cheeses and hams from San Daniele, and succulent sausages whose aromas seemed to seep through the display window. Ernest went in and bought an eighth of a kilo of a smoky, black pepper-corned salami, which he said had the true flavor of meat from hogs that ate mountain acorns. We nibbled the sausage as we continued our walk. We passed a cutlery shop, an antiques store with ancient maps and faded prints, which Ernest inspected, nodding in approval, and a restaurant that he said was rife with pretentious sauces.

Continuing to walk, we climbed the steps of bridges that led us across feeder canals. We stopped in front of a jeweler's, Cogdognato & Company, and Ernest spent some time studying a tray of small Moor heads carved in ebony and gold and decorated with diamonds, emeralds, and rubies. The protagonist of *Across the River* gave one of these to the young Contessa whom he loved, and a few minutes later, when we entered Harry's Bar, a small, nondescript room on the canal, there was a girl waiting for Ernest who resembled the one in the novel. Her name was Adriana Ivancich, a tall, 19-year-old aristocratic beauty with long black hair and sensuous eyes, and she was wearing one of those Moor pins on the lapel of her jacket.

1, 2. Venice, the Queen of the Adriatic, captivated Hemingway's imagination in the postwar years quite as thoroughly as Paris and Pamplona had in the early 1920s. However, it was "only in winter," he insisted, "will you see the true Venice.... The paving stones of St. Mark's are meant to glisten in the rain. The black clouds that roll in from the sea give the Grand Canal a brooding canopy that makes it truly dramatic." I took the picture in Fig. 2 while standing on the Hemingways' balcony at the Gritti Palace.

3. Ernest and Mary Hemingway in Venice in the winter of 1948–49, rather enjoying the rain. "The stones of Venice are not responsive to the sun," Papa explained. "The gray Adriatic winters bring a light that paints the city properly."

4

4. In Venice, Hemingway made friends with this butcher whose shop windows near the Gritti he admired for their inviting displays of calves' heads, trotters, and joints. On one occasion the butcher filled Ernest's order for ground beef so that I could cook hamburgers for the Ivancich family in the kitchen of their palazzo.

5. The Gritti Palace, where the Hemingways found "comfort and beauty without being fawned on or over-attended."

6. In Venice, Hemingway said, "the narrow, tight *calles* are intended to shelter you against the whipping Adriatic wind."

5

The following morning, Ernest took me on one of his favorite excursions, which began with a ride across the Grand Canal in a gondola ferry, all of us standing in a tight group in the well of the gondola. We walked across countless bridges, crisscrossing in and out of very narrow streets, Ernest commenting on the houses, the piazzas, the shops, the trattorias where he had eaten remembered meals, and the old palaces we passed, many of them in disrepair. Our destination was the far side of the city where it fronted on the Adriatic, and where the fish market was located.

I had never seen a market so heavily stocked with fish—gray-green lobsters in rope-handled boxes, spilling mounds of small soles, albacore, and bonito. Eels alive and wriggling in huge containers of water, splendid prawns, gray and opalescent shrimp destined to be spitted and broiled, clams of many sizes and many fish I had never seen before. Ernest asked a clam seller to open a dozen for us, and we ate them from the shell while taking sips of the vodka Ernest carried in a silver flask that he took from the inside pocket of his Hong Kong jacket.

On subsequent trips to Venice, Ernest took me on a tour of his favorite Venetian art—the Titians and Tintorettos and, in particular, a Veronese painting in the Doge's palace: *An Old Man with a Young Woman*. And at the Teatro La Fenice we attended a thrilling performance of Beethoven's *Fidelio*.

When it came time to leave, Ernest rode the Gritti launch with me back to the head of the canal where the trains arrived. "Before you come the next time," he said, "get hold of John Ruskin's *The Stones of Venice*. There's more there than you'll want to know, but it's the best work on Venice ever written."

ACROSS THE RIVER AND INTO THE TREES

The novel that Adriana and her ancient Adriatic city inspired became Hemingway's own personal *Death in Venice* or *Winter's Tale*. Published on September 7, 1950, *Across the River and Into the Trees* is a prose poem essentially devoid of action but rich in meditative discourse, between eighteen-year-old Countess Renata and battle-scarred, fifty-year-old American Colonel (ex-General) Richard Cantwell, on the courage and equanimity, toughness and resilience, the interconnectedness and distance of youth and old age. But elegiac as the mood of *Across the River* may be, the tension mounts—in a vintage Hemingway manner—along with the increasing evidence that this may be the hero's final weekend of life, a time when the themes taken up by the protagonists circle about and finally settle on "How much of all that is good here can survive the onslaughts of evil without being spoiled?" The darkly beautiful Renata, whose name translates as "reborn," has all the bloom, wise innocence, and brave sense of immortality that Cantwell did when he, at her exact age, spilled blood in defense of the Veneto against Austrian attacks and thus became an honorary Venetian for life. In magical evocations of the great lagoon in winter—the marshy, bird-populated environs, the rain-soaked and windswept Piazza San Marco, the wintry urban canals, "sighing" bridges, and *gondolieri*, the Gritti Palace and Harry's Bar—Hemingway set the scene for his story of a gallant old career soldier who, after being scapegoated for failed campaigns ordered by stupid, bureaucratic superiors, has finally rediscovered and come to terms with an earlier, idealistic self. That he finds renewal and comfort in Renata and she in him arises as much from her own fresh sorrow—the loss of father and ancestral villa to the violence of World War II—as from his chivalry, hard-won insight, and ardent love of her and life, both of which he intends to experience strenuously, wholeheartedly to the very end.

A central image is the young Countess' heirloom emeralds—the stones of Venice. Square-cut long ago by mastercraftsmen and handed down from mother to daughter throughout generations, they are something durable as well as wonderful that brings the past—glittering, intensely colored, valuable—into present and onrushing time. Renata insists that Cantwell have them for the weekend. "Put your hand in your right-hand pocket and feel very rich," she says, "I am rich," replies the Colonel. In the end, however, he returns the gems, a gesture signifying perhaps that life itself has merely been lent, that its flame, like the fire in the green stones, must pass to youth. For Cantwell, what survives in the flame—the life that remains unspoiled by murderous experience—and makes it worth passing on are courage, love, a chivalric code, generosity, a sense of beauty and of the ridiculous, and the capacity for soundly based belief.

By its very May-December theme, as well as its northern Italian setting, *Across the River and Into the Trees* invited comparison with the incomparable *A Farewell to Arms*, and given this competition, the novel struck almost every serious critic as a grave disap-

pointment. The letdown proved doubly hard since Hemingway's vast readership had waited a full decade for a new novel. A representative reaction came from Maxwell Geismar in *Saturday Review of Literature*:

This is an unfortunate novel and unpleasant to review for anyone who respects Hemingway's talent and achievement. It is not only Hemingway's worst novel; it is a synthesis of everything that is bad in his previous work and throws a doubtful light on the future. It is so dreadful, in fact, that it begins to have its own morbid fascination. . . .

Indeed, the critical gang-up on *Across the River* became so extreme that it took Evelyn Waugh—who did complete a great trilogy of war novels—to point out the absurdity of the mass attack. Writing in *Commonweal*, he said:

[The critics] have been smug, condescending and derisive [and they] all are agreed that there is a great failure to celebrate. . . . Why do they all hate [Hemingway] so? I believe the truth is that they have detected in him something they find quite unforgivable—Decent Feeling. Behind all the bluster and cursing and fisticuffs he has an elementary sense of

chivalry—respect for women, pity for the weak, love of honor—which keeps breaking in. There is a form of high supercilious caddishness which is all the rage nowadays in literary circles. That is what the critics seek in vain in this book, and that is why their complaints are so loud and confident.

1. Harry's Bar in Venice, a restaurant that Hemingway helped to immortalize in *Across the River and Into the Trees*:

"As Colonel Cantwell stepped out of the door of the Gritti Palace Hotel he came out into the last sunlight of that day. There was still sunlight on the opposite side of the square but the gondoliers preferred to be sheltered from the cold wind by lounging in the lee of the Gritti, than to use the last remaining heat of the sun on the wind-swept side of the square.

"After noting this, the Colonel turned to the right and walked along the square to the paved street which turned off on the right. As he turned, he stopped for a moment and looked at the Church of Santa Maria del Giglio.

"Coming down the other side, he saw two lovely looking girls. They were beautiful and hatless and poorly but chicly dressed, and they were talking very fast to each other and the wind was blowing their hair as they climbed with their long, easy-striding Venetian legs and the Colonel said to himself, I'd better quit window-gazing along this street and make that next bridge, and two squares afterwards you turn due right and keep along it till you are in Harry's.

"He did just that . . . walking with his same old stride and only seeing, quickly, the people that he passed. There's a lot of oxygen in this air, he thought, as he faced into the wind and breathed deeply.

"Then he was pulling open the door of Harry's Bar and was inside and he had made it again, and was at home."

2. Hemingway enjoyed a marvelous season of duck-hunting in the marshes and canals near Torcello in the Venetian Lagoon during November 1948. From this experience he created the brilliant opening chapter of *Across the River*.

3. *Across the River and Into the Trees* (1950), Hemingway's first postwar novel, his last on the theme of love and war, and a work that took the author back to the most primary sources of his inspiration, the Veneto in northeastern Italy. The hero resembles the author of *A Farewell to Arms* who, as a fifty-year-old US Colonel, deliberates on youth and old age while falling in love with a girl of the old Venetian aristocracy. Her age, it so happens, is the same as that of the eighteen-year-old Ernest at the time he was wounded at Fossalta while involved in the defense of Venice against the Austrian Army.

THE OLD MAN AND THE SEA

I was visiting Hemingway at his Finca in Cuba in 1951, when late one night he came into my room, carrying a clip board which had a sizable sheaf of manuscript trapped in its metal jaw. Ernest seemed tentative, almost ill at ease as he said: *Wanted you to read something. Mary read it all one night and in the morning said she forgave me for anything I'd ever done and showed me the real goose flesh on her arms. So have been granted a sort of general am-*

nesty as a writer. Hope I am not fool enough to think something is wonderful because someone under my own roof likes it. So you read it—and level with me in the morning.

He put the clip board down on my bed table and left abruptly. I got into bed, turned on the lamp, and picked up the manuscript. The title was written in ink: *The Old Man and the Sea*. Night bugs popped against the screen, huge brilliant moths buzzed insistently, sounds drifted up from the village below, but I was in the nearby port-town of Cojímar and then out to sea, having one of the most overwhelming reading experiences of my life. It was the basic life battle that had always intrigued Ernest: A brave, simple man struggling unsuccessfully against an unconquerable element. It was also a religious poem, if absolute reverence for the Creator of such early wonders as the sea, a splendid fish, and an old man's courage can be accepted as religious.

poon. A catch so large could not be brought aboard the skiff; thus, Santiago lashes it to the vessel and then sets the small, patched sail for home now many miles away. Little by little, the old man loses the contest he fought so hard to win, as first one shark, then two, and finally whole rapacious packs move in and devour the prize trophy. Upon arriving in Cojímar, Santiago has nothing left of his catch but its skeleton, the bony head, and the once proud, sail-like tail.

Published in the September 1, 1952, issue of *Life* and in book form by Scribner's a week later, selected by the Book-of-the-Month Club, and praised by almost every critic who reviewed it, *The Old Man and the Sea* became, by a wide margin, the best-selling and most popular of all Hemingway's books. Bernard Berenson, the noted art historian, seemed to speak for most of his fellow critics when he observed:

... The Old Man and the Sea *is an idyll of the sea as sea, as un-Byronic and un-Melvillian as Homer himself, and communicated in a prose as calm and compelling as Homer's verse. No real artist symbolizes or allegorizes—and Hemingway is a real artist—but every real work of art exhales symbols and allegories. So does this short but not small masterpiece.*

1. Gregorio Fuentes, the second *Pilar* mate, who, together with his predecessor, Carlos Gutiérrez, served as the model for Santiago in *The Old Man and the Sea.*

2. Carlos Gutiérrez, the first *Pilar* mate. In 1936 Gutiérrez told Hemingway the story of the old fisherman who, after a long streak of rotten luck, caught a great marlin while fishing from a skiff, only to have the catch devoured by sharks before it could be brought in.

3. Cojímar, the Cuban fishing port where Hemingway moored the Pilar between voyages. Papa made it the setting for *The Old Man and the Sea.*

4. *The Old Man and the Sea*, Hemingway's most popular and enduringly profitable book. Published in September 1952 by Scribner's, the 27,000-word novella was simultaneously copublished by *Life* in its September 1 issue, which sold 5,300,000 copies in two days. It would also be selected by the Book-of-the-Month Club, win the Pulitzer Prize, prove decisive in the minds of the Swedish Academy, and remain on the best-seller list for six months.

5. Translated into many different languages, including Arabic, *The Old Man and the Sea* continues to earn well over $100,000 a year in foreign royalties.

Ernest said that at the heart of the book is "the oldest double *dicho* I know."

"What's a double *dicho?*" I asked.

"It's a saying that makes a statement forward or backward. Now this *dicho* is: Man can be destroyed but not defeated."

"Man can be defeated but not destroyed."

"Yes, that's its inversion, but I've always preferred to believe that man is undefeated."

The Old Man and the Sea is set in Cojímar, a fishing village seven miles east of Havana where Hemingway kept the *Pilar.* The book records the epic struggle of an elderly fisherman named Santiago who, after months of terrible fishing luck, rows alone into the Gulf Stream. Towards high noon Santiago hooks a gigantic marlin that for two days and two nights pulls him far out in the ocean as he hangs on for dear life, maneuvering to keep the fish on his hook. On the third day, again near noon, he finally manages to bring the fish alongside and there kills it with his har-

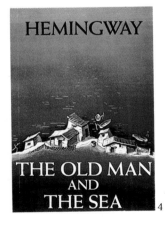

6. Hemingway at work with the film crew for *The Old Man and the Sea*. Not only did the author edit the filmscript; he also served as technical adviser during the on-location scenes shot in Cuban and Peruvian waters.

7. Santiago (Spencer Tracy) and Manolo in a scene from the film version of *The Old Man and the Sea*.

8. Papa with the 800-pound marlin he caught while helping the Hollywood crew shoot sequences at Cojímar, in the Gulf Stream, and off the Peruvian coast for the movie based on *The Old Man and the Sea*.

HEMINGWAY AND HOLLYWOOD

The history of Hemingway's involvement with Hollywood began with Paramount's 1933 production of *A Farewell to Arms* starring Helen Hayes and Gary Cooper. Virtually all of Ernest's major novels and short stories were made into movies, but, with one exception, he disliked all of them. That exception was *The Killers* (1947), which starred Burt Lancaster and Ava Gardner, but, ironically, it was a film that was virtually unrelated to the story itself. Other movies—*The Snows of Kilimanjaro* (Gregory Peck), *The Macomber Affair* (Robert Preston), *For Whom the Bell Tolls*

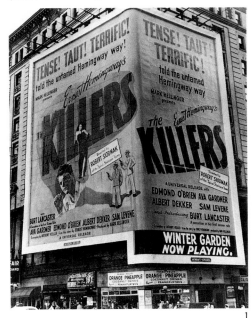

(Gary Cooper, Ingrid Bergman), *My Old Man* (renamed *Under My Skin*)—he felt lacked authenticity. After he saw Rock Hudson and Jennifer Jones in a 1958 remake of *A Farewell to Arms*, he said: "You know, you write a book like that that you're fond of over the years, then you see that happen to it, and it's like pissing in your father's beer."

1,2. *The Killers*, produced by Mark Hellinger and starring Ava Gardner, Burt Lancaster, and Edmond O'Brien, was the only film made from his fiction that Hemingway liked. Released in 1947, it launched Lancaster on one of the most distinguished careers in film history.

3. The sultry Ava Gardner in a cheesecake still for *The Killers.* She would star in two more Hemingway films and come to know the author quite well in both Spain and Cuba.

I went with Ernest to see *The Sun Also Rises* the day before the start of the 1957 World Series, for which Ernest had made a special trip to New York. When Mary asked him how he liked it, he said: "Any picture in which Errol Flynn is the best actor is its own worst enemy."

The only movie that Ernest himself had anything to do with was *The Old Man and The Sea*. He edited the script and then spent weeks with a camera crew off the coast of Peru, catching large marlins that never got hooked at the right hour for the Technicolor cameras; so like all movie marlins, they wound up being sponge-rubber fish in a Culver City tank. Ernest sat through *all* of that movie, numb. "Spencer Tracy looked like a fat, very rich actor playing a fisherman," was his only comment.

For the most part, Ernest approved of my television adaptations of such works of his as "The Snows of Kilimanjaro," "The Battler," "Fifty Grand," "The Light of the World," "The Gambler, the Nun and the Radio," and *For Whom the Bell Tolls*, as well as my adaptation of his only play, *The Fifth Column*, which had a stellar cast headed by Richard Burton, Maximillian Schell, and Sally Ann Howes.

4,5. Preliminary production sketches for *The Old Man and the Sea.*

6. Ernest and Mary Hemingway with the producer Leland Hayward (far right) and his wife Slim (second from the right), Spencer Tracy (center), and George Brown (between the Hemingways), Ernest's professional sparring partner from New York, in early April 1953. The Hollywood contingent had just arrived to confer about the projected filming of *The Old Man and the Sea.*

THE OLD MAN — AS HE RAISES THE HARPOON — — —

SC. 266

THE NOBEL PRIZE

On October 28, 1954, the Swedish Academy announced that the Nobel Prize for literature would be awarded to Ernest Hemingway:

For his powerful style-forming mastery of the art of modern narration, as most recently evinced in The Old Man and the Sea. . . . *Hemingway's earlier writings displayed brutal, cynical, and callous signs which may be considered at variance with the Nobel Prize requirements for a work of ideal tendencies. But on the other hand he also possesses a heroic pathos which forms the basic element of his awareness of life, a manly love of danger and adventure, with a natural admiration of every individual who fights the good fight in a world of reality overshadowed by violence and death.*

Hemingway excused himself from attending the ceremonies in Stockholm, giving as the reason the unhealed injuries he had suffered in airplane crashes during his second African safari, made in the winter of 1953–54. But even if he had been in the best of health he probably would not have gone. Ernest made very few public appearances in his lifetime, attributable to his intense shyness and his smoldering hatred of The Tuxedo. "Wearing underwear is as formal as I ever hope to get," he once said. But he did send an acceptance message, which was read for him at the ceremonies in Stockholm by the United States Ambassador, John M. Cabot:

Members of the Swedish Academy, Ladies and Gentlemen: Having no facility for speechmaking nor any domination of rhetoric, I wish to thank the administrators of the generosity of Alfred Nobel for this prize. No writer who knows the great writers who did not receive the prize can accept it other than with humility. There is no need to list these writers. Everyone here may make his own list according to his knowledge and his conscience. It would be impossible for me to ask the Ambassador of my country to read a speech in which a writer said all of the things which are in his heart. Things may not be immediately discernible in what a man writes, and in this sometimes he is fortunate; but eventually they are quite clear and by these and the degree of alchemy that he possesses he will endure or be forgotten. Writing, at its best, is a lonely life. Organizations for writers palliate the writer's loneliness but I doubt if they improve his writing. He grows in public stature as he sheds his loneliness and often his work deteriorates. For he does his work alone and if he is a good enough writer he must face eternity, or the lack of it, each day. For a true writer each book should be a new beginning where he tries again for something that is beyond attainment. He should always try for something that has never been done or that others have tried and failed. Then sometimes, with great luck, he will succeed. How simple the writing of literature would be if it were only necessary to write in another way what has been well written. It is because we have had such great writers in the past that a writer is driven far out past where he can go, out to where no one can help him. I have spoken too long for a writer. A writer should write what he has to say and not speak it. Again I thank you.

1. Hemingway receiving the press at the Finca on October 28, 1954, the day the Swedish Academy announced in Stockholm that he had been awarded the Nobel Prize for literature.

THE
DANGEROUS
YEARS

---

1 9 5 4

1 9 6 1

AFRICA REVISITED

Hemingway once said: "I love Africa, and I find it's another home, and anytime a man can feel that, not counting where he's born, is where he's meant to go." It was in that mood of poetic optimism that Ernest and Mary set out, in the summer of 1953, from Marseilles to Mombasa, there to hunt with the renowned Philip Percival, who came out of retirement for the event, and to visit with Patrick, himself now a white hunter in Tanganyika. Joining them on the safari, this time financed by *Look* rather than Pauline's Uncle Gus, was the Hemingways' old friend from Cuba, Mario Menocal. After a splendid start near Percival's beautiful farm outside Machakos, the safari ran into trouble when Hemingway grew as anxiously competitive with Menocal as he had been with Charles Thompson in 1932. But after the rival departed, Papa quieted down and, instead of shooting animals, contented himself

with admiring them, while also enjoying the fabulous landscape and whatever book he happened to be carrying. To get a better look at Africa's wonders, the Hemingways hired a pilot to take them up in a Cessna 180 to view the Ngorongoro Crater, the Mountains of the Moon in Ruandi-Urundi, and Murchison Falls in Uganda, where the Nile cascades down in one cataract after another on its way to the fertile valley of the Sudan and Egypt. While making his third pass over the falls, the pilot dipped to avoid a flight of ibis, whereupon the plane struck a telegraph wire suspended above the gorge and then crash-landed in heavy brush. Miraculously, the pilot walked away unhurt, and the only injuries suffered by his passengers were Mary's two broken ribs and Papa's shoulder sprain.

After a night dozing by a fire that Hemingway built in the jungle, near a herd of elephants, the party managed to hail a passing riverboat, which turned out to be the one used in filming *The African Queen*. Upon their arrival at Butiaba the Hemingways found themselves awaited by a policeman

and a bush pilot, both of whom had been searching for their bodies after a BOAC pilot flying over Murchison Falls spotted the wrecked Cessna but no sign of survivors. Thus, the world already believed that the great American writer Ernest Hemingway, recent Pulitzer Prize winner for the critically acclaimed best-seller *The Old Man and the Sea*, had died in a plane crash in East Africa. Later, Ernest would enjoy reading the premature reports of his demise and numerous full-

length obituaries. Meanwhile, he announced "my luck, she is running good" to the astounded press, which promptly mythologized the occasion by reporting that Papa had come out of the jungle flourishing a bunch of bananas and a bottle of gin.

A few hours later, though, his luck had run not so good. A rescue plane, a de Havilland Rapide, had been sent to fly the Hemingways back to their base in Kenya, but it crashed on take-off and burst into flames, and this was the crash that left its marks on Ernest. He said that when the second plane crashed and burned, he suffered a ruptured kidney and other internal injuries, a concussion and double vision.

Still, Hemingway refused to give up, and after resting in Nairobi and dictating his piece for *Look*, he flew with Percival to join Patrick for deep-sea fishing near a beach camp on the Kenyan coast. When a brush fire broke out nearby, Ernest tried to help fight the blaze, only to go dizzy and tumble into the flames. Although quickly pulled clear, Papa had nonetheless sustained burns on his face, and most of his hair was singed off.

Ernest went by boat from Africa to Venice,

1. Uganda's Victoria Nile in its spectacular, 400-foot plunge down a step-like series of cataracts known as Murchinson Falls before continuing on course through the Sudan to Egypt and finally the Mediterranean. It was while viewing this wonder of the East African Rift that the Hemingways suffered the first of the two plane crashes that brought an end to their 1953–54 African safari.

2. Ernest stalking a furious rhino wounded by another hunter and left to charge anyone who happened to pass by.

3. The Hemingways going by the cookbook as they prepare game for the safari pot.

4, 5. Shampooing away the red dust stirred up by the safari vehicle cruising through the East African brush.

6. To hold down his weight and keep in shape, Papa boxed all his life and everywhere, even in his fifties and on safari.

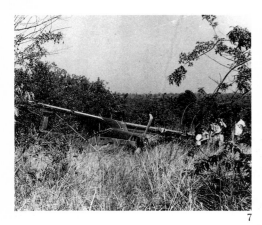

and I joined him soon after he arrived at the Gritti. Papa did not seem as bad off as I had feared, but some of the aura of massiveness did appear to have gone out of him. He told me:

When I picked myself up off the floor of the second plane, I felt busted inside. The rear door was bent and jammed. My right arm and shoulder were dislocated but I used my left shoulder and my head and had good pushing room to get it open. Roy Marsh, the pilot, was up front with Miss Mary. I yelled to him, "I have it open here. Miss Mary okay?" Was glad to see Miss Mary without a scratch on her and carrying her vanity case. Never been in a crisis yet that a woman forgot her jewels.

7.   The Cessna 180 after it crashed in the brush near Murchinson Falls with Ernest and Mary Hemingway on board.

8. Papa with his beautiful leopard trophy.

9. Hemingway keeping up with his African journals.

10. Around the camp fire with two great white hunters, Philip Percival and his son Richard.

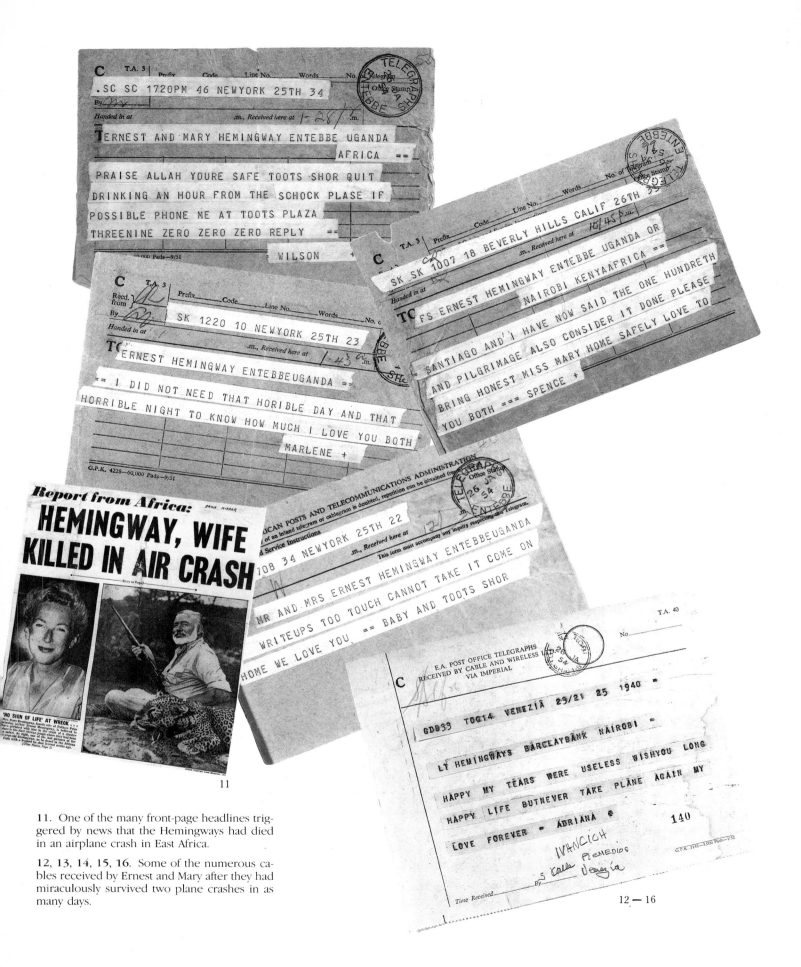

C T.A. 3   Prefix   Code   Line No.   Words   No. of Telegram

.SC SC 1720PM 46 NEWYORK 25TH 34

By

Handed in at   .m., *Received here at* 1·28

ERNEST AND MARY HEMINGWAY ENTEBBE UGANDA

AFRICA ==

PRAISE ALLAH YOURE SAFE TOOTS SHOR QUIT

DRINKING AN HOUR FROM THE SCHOCK PLASE IF

POSSIBLE PHONE ME AT TOOTS PLAZA

THREENINE ZERO ZERO ZERO REPLY ==

WILSON

C T.A. 3   Prefix   Code   Line No.   Words   No. of Telegram

SK SK 1007 18 BEVERLY HILLS CALIF 26TH

Received here at 10/45

FS ERNEST HEMINGWAY ENTEBBE UGANDA OR

NAIROBI KENYAAFRICA ==

SANTIAGO AND I HAVE NOW SAID THE ONE HUNDRETH

AND PILGRIMAGE ALSO CONSIDER IT DONE PLEASE

BRING HONEST MISS MARY HOME SAFELY LOVE TO

YOU BOTH === SPENCE +

C T.A. 3   Prefix   Code   Line No.   Words   No.

Recd. from

By

SK 1220 10 NEWYORK 25TH 23

Handed in at   .m., *Received here at* 1·43

ERNEST HEMINGWAY ENTEBBEUGANDA

== I DID NOT NEED THAT HORIBLE DAY AND THAT

HORRIBLE NIGHT TO KNOW HOW MUCH I LOVE YOU BOTH

MARLENE +

G.P.K. 4228—60,000 Pads—9/51

Report from Africa:
HEMINGWAY, WIFE KILLED IN AIR CRASH

'NO SIGN OF LIFE' AT WRECK

AFRICAN POSTS AND TELECOMMUNICATIONS ADMINISTRATION

108 34 NEWYORK 25TH 22

Received here at

MR AND MRS ERNEST HEMINGWAY ENTEBBEUGANDA

WRITEUPS TOO TOUCH CANNOT TAKE IT COME ON

HOME WE LOVE YOU == BABY AND TOOTS SHOR

T.A. 40

E.A. POST OFFICE TELEGRAPHS
RECEIVED BY CABLE AND WIRELESS LTD
VIA IMPERIAL

No.

C

GD839 TOG14 VENEZIA 29/21 25 1940 =

LT HEMINGWAYS BARCLAYBANK NAIROBI =

HAPPY MY TEARS WERE USELESS WISHYOU LONG

HAPPY LIFE BUTNEVER TAKE PLANE AGAIN MY

LOVE FOREVER - ADRIANA #   140

IVANCICH
REMEDIOS
Calle Venezia

G.P.K. 3145—3,000 Pads—1/52

Time Received   By

11

11. One of the many front-page headlines triggered by news that the Hemingways had died in an airplane crash in East Africa.

12, 13, 14, 15, 16. Some of the numerous cables received by Ernest and Mary after they had miraculously survived two plane crashes in as many days.

12 — 16

MANO A MANO

In the summer of 1959, Spain's two great matadors—proud men, the one married to the other's beautiful sister, a certain animosity between them—were about to engage in a series of deadly combats known as *mano a manos*. True *mano a manos* are rare, for only once in a generation, if that, are there two great matadors concurrently fighting. The difference in procedure

1

between a *mano a mano* and a regular bullfight is that ordinarily there are three matadors on a card, fighting two bulls each, while in the hand-to-hand combat two matadors split six brother bulls by lot, and the one who cuts the most ears and tails plainly triumphs.

Ernest explained that although every bullfight involves some rivalry, when two great matadors square off, that rivalry becomes deadly. This is so, he said, because when one of them does something that is not a trick, but classic and exquisitely dangerous, compounded of perfect nerves, judgment, courage and art, then the other is forced to equal it or surpass it, and if in so doing he has any temporary failure of nerves or judgment, he will be seriously wounded or killed.

In addition to the exciting rarity of a truly great *mano a mano*, there was for Ernest the added factor that both Luis Miguel Dominguín and Antonio Ordóñez were his good friends, and he greatly admired both of them as men and as matadors. But it was Ernest's judgment that Antonio was the greater matador, for Ernest felt he had achieved perfection in all three categories: the cape, the *muleta*, and the kill.

Ernest and Mary had gone to Spain in May of 1959, and I had joined them in June in Alicante. Mary preferred to stay in Málaga at the villa of Bill Davis, an American expatriate who was an old Hemingway friend long resident in Spain. Meanwhile, all that summer, Ernest, Bill Davis, and I followed Antonio Ordóñez' bullfighting schedule, going from Barcelona to Burgos then down to Madrid, then back up to Burgos and then Vitória, along the way Ernest delighting in the sounds, sights, tastes, and aromas of his beloved Spain. Papa intended to use this experience to update *Death in the Afternoon*, and to write an account of the *mano a manos* for *Life*.

When we reached Pamplona, Mary joined us for *La Fería de San Fermín*, seven days and seven nights melted into one 168-hour day. For Hemingway, this was a reacquaintance with the riau-riau of his youth. At noon two rocket-bombs exploded in the hot bright sky, and the town erupted, right before our eyes without our seeing it happen. One minute the deserted square, the next minute a com-

pact mass of revelers, pipes, fifes, and drums playing the riau-riau music, men and boys all red and white, arms high, dancing and singing to the music, then crouching down, then up again, arms around, bobbing to the pounding rhythm. For seven days and nights, the streets never empty.

The cafés were jammed, but the Chöko maintained for Ernest the table he had staked out. It was easy to tell the tourists by their costumes, which were as distinctive as the white duck pants, white shirts, red scarves, and berets of the Navarre men. The twenty-five thousand tourists were mainly American college kids, and their costumes consisted of tight chino pants and T-shirts.

Each day of the Fería, in the early morning, the bulls for that day's corrida were released from the pens at one end of town to run along a street leading towards the bull ring. It is traditional for the intrepid to join the group of men and boys who race down the street in front of the onrushing bulls. Front runners get a big head start, middle runners keep a modest distance ahead, and then the brave ones or crazies, depending on one's point of view, try to stay as close to the bull pack as possible without getting gored. Ernest ran with the bulls in the old days, but now his legs were too unreliable; still, he enjoyed the daily scramble of the runners trying to elude the bulls.

Just to the northeast of Pamplona lie the Irati River and its forests, which were such an integral part of *The Sun Also Rises*. Papa feared they might have been completely ruined, but his worry proved unfounded. For four afternoons we picnicked at various places along the river, going higher and higher up the mountain, leaving at noon, getting back just in time for the bullfight. We traveled in three cars, each car responsible for part of the picnic, which flourished with squabs, cheeses, and cold, smoked trout, Navarre black grapes and brown-speckled pears, eggplant and pimientos in a succulent juice, unshelled shrimps and fresh anchovies. The wine was kept cold in the clear Irati water, and each day we swam up the river, which flowed through a gorge between the high-rising walls of the beech-covered mountain. It was miraculous to leave the wild tumult of the Fería and a half-hour later to be in the midst of this primitive, quiet beauty.

Ernest sat with his back against a beech trunk, his lips pleasurably parted, his old eyeglasses in his lap, patting an itinerant hound dog who had sought him out, and it was obvious that this was not the enjoyment of memory, but the enjoyment of experiencing. This summer he was not revisiting the windswept

2

slopes of the Escorial to see the vestiges of *For Whom the Bell Tolls,* or driving slowly along the circuitous Left Bank route he used to take from his unheated room to the Jardin du Luxembourg to avoid the tantalizing restaurant smells. This summer, unlike so many others in his late life, was young.

1. Plaza de Toros in Madrid.

2. A flier for Madrid's San Isidor Festival bullfights in May 1954.

3. A *tienta* on a ranch in the Escorial in the lee of the Guadarrama Mountains, with Luis Miguel Domínguin, the greatest matador of his time, trying his skill with the *muleta* in preparation for a return to the bullring after retirement caused by a serious goring. As Hemingway defined it in *Death in the Afternoon,* a *tienta* is "the testing of calves for bravery on a bull-breeding ranch."

4. A convivial lunch in the aftermath of the *tienta,* attended by Domínguin, his current amour Ava Gardner, and the Hemingways, among others.

5. Papa and Mary at one of his favorite bars in Madrid during the "dangerous summer." Annie and Bill Davis stand at extreme left and right, with Rupert Belleville just behind Annie.

6. Antonio Ordóñez meditating prior to a corrida in the *mano a mano* series he fought with Luis Miguel Domínguin in the summer of 1959.

Such halcyon moments were in marked contrast to the *mano a manos*, the peculiar dramatics of which Papa explained as follows: *Luis Miguel claims to be Number One, so he must substantiate that claim every time he appears now, but he has the handicap of having become rich. The daylight between a matador's groin and the bull's passing horns increases as his wealth increases. But I will say for Luis Miguel that he truly loves to fight when his stuff is going for him, and on those days he seems to forget he is rich. But Antonio does not forget it, ever—Miguel's wealth, that is—and that's where the gimlets get sharpened. Miguel has demanded more money than Antonio for these* mano a manos, *and he is getting it, but this has rancored Antonio, who is out to prove that Miguel does not deserve it. No one has a fiercer pride than Antonio, and that's the deadliness of this combat. Antonio considers it an insult that Miguel does not treat him as an equal, and I can tell you that before this summer is over, Antonio will impale Miguel on the horns of his pride and destroy him. It is tragic but like all tragedy, preordained.*

Ernest predicted correctly. In Bilbao, the *mano a manos* ended abruptly and for keeps when the mounting pressure from Antonio finally caught up with Dominguín. It happened while Luis Miguel was placing the bull for the picador. It is one of the most elementary moves in bullfighting, and every matador does it thousands of times. But Luis Miguel inexplicably moved into the bull instead of away, and its horn caught him in the groin and slammed him against the horse. The picador drove his lance into the bull as Dominguín was tossed into the air, but the bull disregarded the lance and caught the matador again as he came down and chopped at him several times on the sand before they made the *quite* and ran him to the infirmary.

Ernest went to see him in the hospital that evening. Dominguín was suffering very much from the penetration of the horn, which had ripped up into his abdomen and very nearly taken his life. Papa talked to him for a short while in a low voice, and Luis Miguel nodded and smiled a little.

Afterward, walking back to the hotel, Hemingway said: "He's a brave man and a beautiful matador. Why the hell do the good and brave have to die before everyone else?" He did not mean die as in death, for Dominguín was going to survive, but what was important to his living had died. I remember Ernest once telling me: "The worst death for anyone is to lose the center of his being, the thing he really is. Retirement is the filthiest word in the language. Whether by choice or by fate, to re-

tire from what you do—and what you do makes you what you are—is to back up into the grave."

During his travels that summer, Ernest was approached by an eighteen-year-old Irish girl named Valerie Danby-Smith. Valerie presented herself as a stringer assigned to interviewing Ernest for a Dublin newspaper. She had no apparent journalistic skills, but she worshiped Ernest's every word and simply latched onto us when we continued our journey. Ernest eventually appointed her his secretary, and she stayed with him for the rest of his life, returning to Cuba with him, and then, after his death, serving as secretarial functionary for Mary.

7.

7. Dominguín and Ordóñez preparing to enter the bullring for their *mano a mano* at Ciudad Real in August 1959, with the *sobre saliente*, A. E. Hotchner, masquerading as a matador named El Pecas ("The Freckled One").

8. Papa receiving the ovation accorded him at every bullring he entered during the Dominguín-Ordóñez *mano a manos*.

9. Ready for the kill, Ordóñez carefully sights along his sword before making the final thrust over the horns.

10. Dominguín in agony and comforted by his brother after a bad *cornado*—goring—in the stomach during the *mano a mano* at Bilbao.

11. Ordóñez executing a low pass with the *muleta* to lead the bull around him during the *faena*.

12. Ordóñez surrounded by concerned friends, including Ernest Hemingway, after he had received a slight wound in his battle with a bull.

8.

9.

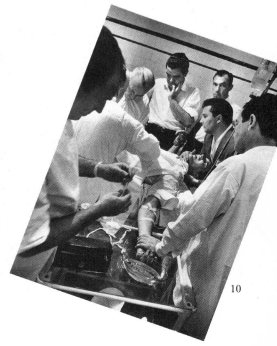

10.

11

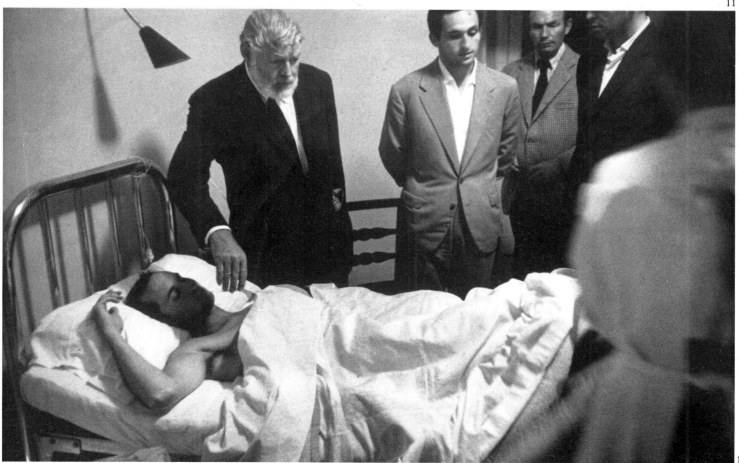

12

195

THE LAST BIRTHDAY PARTY

When Ernest's sixtieth birthday came round on July 21, 1959, the Hemingways and I were in the midst of the *mano a manos*, intermittently staying with Bill Davis at his magnificent villa, La Consula, in Churriana on the southern coast of Spain. Here Mary threw a grand, unforgettable party that she had been planning for more than two months. La Consula, set in the midst of a huge, elegantly gardened estate, was a colonnaded mansion of delicate mien that looked like the palace of a junior Doge. Protected by outer and inner gates, both manned, it had furnishings handmade, for the most part, by Spanish artisans working from Davis' designs, and the art inside complemented the exterior. Floors and balustrades, stairs and tabletops, bathrooms and porticos were all marble, and marble enveloped the swimming pool.

Mary felt that Ernest's birthdays, because of his lack of cooperation, had always been observed with a pause rather than a celebration, and this time she was determined to make up for all the lost parties. She succeeded.

Mary had ordered champagne from Paris, Chinese foods from London, and from Madrid bacalao, a dried codfish that is the basic ingredient for the highly seasoned Bacalao Vizcayina, one of her specialities. She had hired a shooting booth from a traveling carnival, a fireworks expert from Valencia, the citadel of fireworks, flamenco dancers from Málaga, musicians from Torremolinos, and waiters, barmen, and cooks from all over.

The Davis house slept only twenty-five; so Mary had taken over a couple of floors at a new skyscraper hotel, the Pez Espada, on the beach in nearby Torremolinos. The invitees came from every direction, and they began arriving on the 20th: the Maharajah of Jaipur with his Maharanee and son; the Maharajah of Cooch Behar with his Maharanee; General C.T. "Buck" Lanham from Washington, D.C.; Ambassador and Mrs. David Bruce, who flew down from Bonn; various Madrid notables; several of Ernest's old Paris pals; thirty friends of Antonio's; and Gianfranco Ivancich, Adriana's brother, who arrived from Venice with his wife, driving a new Barrata Lancia that Ernest had bought with his Italian royalties.

The party started at noon, July 21st, and ended at noon, July 22nd, and Ernest called it the best party that ever was. He danced, popped champagne, proposing marvelously funny toasts to his guests, and shot cigarettes from the lips of Antonio and the Maharajah of Cooch Behar. When the orchestra, which

played on the upper veranda, struck up the fiesta music of Pamplona, Antonio and Ernest led all the guests in a riau-riau that snaked all over the grounds. The one sober moment of the evening occurred at the end of the dinner when David Bruce, who in August 1944 had authorized Ernest's "governorship" of Rambouillet, proposed a simple and affectionate toast. Ernest bowed his head against his chest and was visibly touched.

The firecracker wizard from Valencia put on a lavish and noisy display, but one of a salvo of giant rockets unfortunately lodged in the top of a royal palm tree near the house and set the treetop on fire. Attempts by some of the guests to climb a 60-foot ladder and attack the blaze with a garden hose were perilously abortive; so the fire department was eventually summoned from Málaga.

The hook and ladder that arrived were straight out of Mack Sennett—and so were

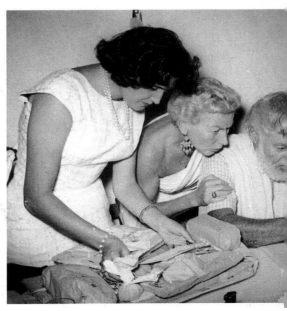

the firemen. But they fought the blaze courageously, saving the tree, the house, and the
night. The firemen were immediately assimi-
lated by the party, and so were their uniforms
and their fire engine, which Antonio, wearing
the fire chief's helmet and raincoat, raced
around the garden with the siren wide open.

After breakfast the guests started to depart,
but it was not until noon that the last of them
had retired. The Churriana sun was up hot by
now, and Ernest had a swim before going to
bed.

1. La Consula, the home of Bill Davis on the
southern coast of Spain, where Mary staged a
fabulous party to celebrate Ernest's sixtieth
birthday.

2. A few of the thirty-four guests who came
from all over for the big birthday party at La
Consula.

3. Papa refreshing himself with a swim after the
grand all-night party that Mary threw at La Consula in Spain to celebrate her husband's sixtieth
birthday.

4. Carmen Ordóñez and Mary helping Papa
open the many presents he received at his sixtieth birthday party.

5. Watched by General Buck Lanham, Ernest
shoots cigarettes from Ordóñez' mouth, using
a rickety carnival air gun loaded with pellets.
The shooting booth, hired from a traveling carnival, was just one of the many diversions that
Mary arranged for the birthday party at La
Consula.

6. When the Málaga hook-and-ladder company
arrived to extinguish a fire started by a rocket,
we took over their equipment. Here, Hemingway and Ordóñez watch me ham it up with the
actress Beverly Bentley, then in Málaga making
a Smell-O-Vision movie, later to become one of
the many Mrs. Norman Mailers.

KETCHUM

Ernest did not return to the West for ten years, during which time he and Mary traveled abroad—to Venice, Africa, and Spain, as well as back to the Ritz in Paris—but events in Cuba finally forced Papa to return to Idaho. At first he and Mary simply rented a house, but after Castro came to power, setting off a wave of anti-Americanism in Cuba, Ernest permanently abandoned his beloved Finca, with all its priceless possessions, and sought a substitute home in the West. As Papa told me when I was in Cuba in 1960 helping him edit *The Dangerous Summer*, the account of the *mano a manos*, for *Life*:

Castro doesn't bother me personally. I'm good publicity for him, so maybe he'd never bother me and let me live on here as always, but I am an American above everything else and my country is being vilified. I guess I knew it was all over for me here the night they killed Black Dog. A Batista search party, looking for guns, came barreling in here in the middle of the night and poor Black Dog, old and half blind, tried to stand guard at the door of the Finca, but a soldier clubbed him to death with the butt of his rifle. Poor old Black Dog. I miss him. In the early morning when I work, he's not there on the kudu skin beside the typewriter; and in the afternoon when I swim, he's not hunting lizards beside

E ager to renew his prewar routine of spending the late summer and autumn months in the Far West, Hemingway in April 1946 gathered up Mary, summoned his three sons from California, and set out for Sun Valley, Idaho, the scene of the Hemingways' "calm between the storms" in 1939–41. The journey went well until Ernest and Mary reached Casper, Wyoming, where she went into deep shock from a fallopian tube ruptured by an ectopic pregnancy. With the local surgeon away on a fishing trip, Mary would have died except for Ernest, who boldly forced a hospital intern to transfuse the patient until her pulse revived. Thereafter, the grateful Mary never ceased to proclaim her husband "a good man to have around in a crisis." Meanwhile, Papa lost several good friends during his Western sojourns in 1946 and 1947, foremost among them Max Perkins, dead of pneumonia at the age of sixty-four, and Katy Dos Passos, decapitated in a catastrophic automobile accident caused by the sun suddenly blinding Dos as he drove along a Cape Cod road.

Despite these losses, Ernest did have a robust circle of old friends in Sun Valley—the Gary Coopers, Ingrid Bergman, Slim Hawks, Lloyd and Tillie Arnold, and Taylor "Beartracks" Williams. And, as always, Ernest's spirits were uplifted when he was again surrounded by the majestic Sawtooth Mountains and its wilderness world full of doves, Hungarian partridge, pheasant, mallard, wild geese, hare, deer, and bear.

the pool; and in the evenings when I sit in my chair to read, his chin isn't resting on my foot. I miss Black Dog as much as I miss any friend I ever lost. And now I lose the Finca—there's no sense kidding myself—I know I must leave it all and go. But how can you measure that loss? Everything I have is here. My pictures, my books, my good work place and good memories.

As a consequence, in May 1959, Hemingway bought a house near Ketchum, 1 mile from Sun Valley, from the millionaire sportsman Bob Topping for $50,000. Although charmless in its concrete, bunker-like four-squareness, the Ketchum retreat did offer privacy on 17 acres surrounded by glorious mountains and overlooking the lively, meandering Big Wood River.

This was the refuge to which the Hemingways came in November 1960, direct from the aftermath of a desperate, flying trip that

Papa made to Spain, to verify details of his *Life* article and stand by Ordóñez, who he insisted needed him in order to do his best. While on that trip to Madrid, and before that at his Finca, researching and writing *The Dangerous Summer*, his persona had begun to undergo a profound change. He became cantankerous and suspicious, magnifying trivial and routine occurrences beyond reality. For instance, Ernest angrily denounced a photograph of Antonio performing in the bullring as it appeared in *Life*, which ran installments of the manuscript: Papa claimed that it was so faulty an illustration that its appearance would "ruin" him and make him "a laughing stock among the experts who really knew about bullfighting." When Ernest attempted to apologize to Antonio for having used that photo, Antonio interrupted to say that he thought it was a splendid picture that seemed perfectly okay to him.

Ernest's personality problems steadily worsened. His usually vigorous sense of humor became moribund. He avoided the friends whose company he had most enjoyed. He fretted about his writing, complaining that he couldn't get things straight in his head nor find the right words with which to express himself. After spending months agonizing over how to cut *The Dangerous Summer* for *Life*, he turned his attention to trying to write the concluding paragraphs for what was to become *A Moveable Feast*. Week after week he spent long, painful hours trying to write the conclusion, but his mind could no

longer respond to his will, and the book was eventually published posthumously without those final few sentences he so desperately wanted to write.

Contributing to his deteriorating condition was the fact that his relationship with Mary was also worsening. There were many angry, vitriolic confrontations growing in frequency and intensity during the final year of Ernest's life, and I myself witnessed several of these unfortunate exchanges, which more often than not got out of control. Looking back on them now, these altercations seem to blend into Ernest's final turbulent aberrations. As Mary later said, "he was just exactly, almost,

1. Ketchum, Idaho, 1 mile from Sun Valley at the foot of the Sawtooth Mountains.

2. Ernest, Pat DiCicco, Bud Purdy (with the glasses), and Gary Cooper on the Purdy Ranch near Sun Valley, Idaho, in the autumn of 1958.

3, 5. The house overlooking the Big Wood River in Ketchum, where Hemingway would make his permanent home during the last two years of his life.

4. Soon after he moved into the Ketchum house, Ernest began assembling a new family of cats. The magnificent view from the living room made up for the charmlessness of the house.

6. Hemingway presenting Fidel Castro with three cups at the end of the fishing tournament named in Ernest's honor. Castro had caught more swordfish than any other contestant, but there were some protests thathe had "fixed" his catches. Shortly thereafter, when the Castro regime began vilifying the United States, Ernest abandoned Cuba for life in the Far West.

the opposite of what he had been before—outgoing and exuberant and articulate and full of life—and this was all inward and quiet and inarticulate."

Ernest's agony finally reached the point where he made an attempt at suicide that was thwarted by his doctor, George Saviers, who happened to come in the door while Papa was loading his favorite shotgun to turn on himself. There was another suicide attempt before Dr. Saviers succeeded in convincing Ernest to go to the Mayo Clinic in Rochester, Minn. Although Papa was told he was being taken there to undergo tests relative to his high blood pressure, in actuality he was to be a patient in the psychiatric section of the hospital.

Ernest was flown to the Mayo Clinic in a private plane, but his condition had so deteriorated that during that flight he twice attempted suicide, once by trying to fling himself out the door of the plane (he was only restrained after a furious struggle), and again by almost walking into the moving propellers of the plane during a refueling stopover in Wyoming.

Ernest's period of treatment at the Mayo Clinic was ineffectual; in fact, his condition was worsened by the electric shock treatments he was given. Experts were of the opinion that he should have not been subjected to electric shock at all, and certainly not given only a portion of the full cycle required when shock was administered.

The Mayo doctors released Hemingway, assuring Mary that his compulsion to commit suicide had abated, but after a short stay at his home in Ketchum, Ernest again tried to take his life with a shotgun, and he was readmitted to the Mayo Clinic. This time the so-called "treatment" was even less effectual, but once more the Mayo doctors assured Mary that he was "cured" of his compulsion to commit suicide. Mary, as she later said, "knew that Ernest was not cured, that he entertained the same delusions and fears with which he had entered the clinic." In despair, she also "realized that he had charmed and deceived" his principal doctor.

7. Ernest writing on the edge of the Big Wood River below his house in Ketchum.

8. Papa and I had obviously enjoyed a bountiful day jump-shooting the canals around the base of the Sawtooth Mountains.

9. Papa on his veranda in Ketchum.

DEATH IN THE MORNING

Early in the morning of July 2, 1961—two days after he returned home from the Mayo Clinic, thirty-four years after his father had shot himself in the head in his own house, and two months after his old friend Gary Cooper, dying of cancer, had "made it to the barn" before he did—Ernest Hemingway left Mary sleeping upstairs, loaded a shotgun, crouched in the foyer of the Ketchum house, placed the twin barrels in his mouth, and pulled both triggers. In two and a half weeks he would have been sixty-two.

his wife

At first, Mary insisted to the press that it was not a suicide but, rather, an accident—that Ernest had been cleaning the gun not knowing that it was loaded—but eventually she was persuaded to tell the truth.

Papa was buried in a simple plot at a cemetery in Ketchum, with only his family and a few friends present, but the whole world grieved. Rising above his grave are the imposing Sawtooth Mountains where Ernest jump-shot mallards in the canals that ring its base. His gravesite is surrounded by the rolling hills and verdant pastures where over the years Ernest hunted pheasant and chukkers. "There are some things which cannot be learned quickly and time, which is all we have, must be paid heavily for their acquiring," Hemingway once wrote. "They are the very simplest things and because it takes a man's life to know them the little new that each man gets from life is very costly and the only heritage he has to leave."

Hemingway's heritage is considerable; almost three decades after his death his books—with their innovative style, technical virtuosity, and emotional intensity—are as widely read as when he lived. Moreover, the unique, vibrant, achieving person he was remains an enduring figure of mythic proportions in the eyes of the world.

Charles Poore, a former book editor for the *New York Times*, made this appraisal of Hemingway's place in the literary firmament: "I am most certain that he will stand with Yeats and Joyce as one of the three principal men of letters of our time. And since clocks and calendars move forward, not backward, from here on out he may be the strongest influence in literature that his age will give to posterity."

As far as I myself was concerned, Ernest's passing left a sad void in my life. The irreplaceable phone calls and letters describing his adventures or suggesting that I meet him in Paris or Venice or Havana. Not only that, but he was always there to listen and advise, to sympathize, to teach, to open my eyes to new wonders, to chastise when deserved.

And the world too has felt that void. "When nature removes a great man," Ralph Waldo Emerson observed, "people explore the horizon for a successor; but none comes, and none will. His class is extinguished with him."

It is true that there has been no successor but the remarkable thing is that Hemingway himself lives on—the man, his books, his exploits, the unique place he carved for himself in the imagination of those who read his books, saw the movies made from them, read about him in the world press.

He lives on, especially, in the minds and hearts of those of us who knew him well.

1. Nothing could stand in greater contrast to the Karsh portrait than this photograph made three years later, after the novelist had undergone shock treatments at the Mayo Clinic. The therapy damaged his total-recall memory and left him, at the age of sixty-one, looking frail, haunted, and elderly far beyond his actual years.

2. With his family and a few close friends present at a graveside ceremony on July 5, 1961, Hemingway was buried in a small cemetery near Ketchum, Idaho, in the valley below the magnificent Sawtooth Mountains close by some of his favorite hunting and fishing grounds.

3. Portrayed by Karsh in 1958, Hemingway was as handsome in his later years as he had been all his life, the famous countenance somehow conveying the same blend of masculine toughness and poetic delicacy that had distinguished his prose.

posterity has revealed that this heroic idea of a "real man" was merely a cloak of mythology and ~~his~~ fiction

that masked ignorance and labeled it "noble virtue." No doubt he was a good writer but as a man he was only a half-step above a baboon. —Zelda

BIBLIOGRAPHY

Arnold, Lloyd R. *High on the Wild with Hemingway.* Caldwell, Id., 1968.

Baker, Carlos. *Ernest Hemingway: A Life Story.* New York, 1969.

————. *Hemingway: The Writer as Artist,* 3rd ed. Princeton, 1968.

Beach, Sylvia. *Shakespeare and Company.* New York, 1959.

Berg, Scott. *Max Perkins: Editor of Genius.* New York, 1978.

Brian, Denis. *The True Gen: An Intimate Portrait of Hemingway by Those Who Knew Him.* New York, 1988.

Brinnin, J.M. *The Sway of the Grand Saloon.* New York, 1971.

Burgess, Anthony. *Ernest Hemingway and His World.* New York, 1978.

Callaghan, Morley. *That Summer in Paris.* New York, 1963.

Cowley, Malcolm. *Exile's Return,* rev. ed. New York, 1956.

Dietrich, Marlene. *Marlene by Marlene Dietrich,* trans. from German by Salvator Attanasio. New York, 1989.

————. "The Most Fascinating Man I Know," *This Week,* Feb. 13, 1955, pp. 8–9.

Donaldson, Scott. *By Force of Will.* New York, 1977.

Dos Passos, John. *The Best Times.* New York, 1966.

————. *The Fourteenth Chronicle: Letters and Diaries of John Dos Passos,* ed. by Townsend Ludington. Boston, 1973.

————. *Journeys Between the Wars.* New York, 1938.

Eastman, Max. "Bull in the Afternoon," *New Republic,* June 7, 1933, pp. 94–97.

Ellmann, Richard. *James Joyce.* New York, 1982.

Flanner, Janet. *Paris Was Yesterday.* New York, 1972.

Ford, Hugh. *Published in Paris.* New York, 1975.

Fuentes, Norberto. *Ernest Hemingway Rediscovered,* with photos by Robero Herrera Sotolongo. New York, 1988.

————. *Hemingway in Cuba.* Secaucus, N.J., 1984.

Gellhorn, Martha. *Travels with Myself and Another.* New York, 1978.

Greenfeld, Howard. *They Came to Paris.* New York, 1975.

Griffin, Peter. *Along with Youth.* New York, 1985.

Haight, Mary Ellen. *Walks in Gertrude Stein's Paris.* Salt Lake City, 1988.

Hemingway, Ernest. *Across the River and Into the Trees.* New York, 1950, 1978. First Scribner Classic/Collier Edition, 1987.

————. *By-Line: Ernest Hemingway: Selected Articles and Dispatches of Four Decades,* ed. by William White. New York, 1967.

————. *The Dangerous Summer,* with intro. by James Michener. New York, 1985.

————. *Death in the Afternoon.* New York, 1932, 1960.

————. *A Farewell to Arms,* New York, 1928, 1957. First Scribner Classic/Collier Edition, 1987.

————. *A Farewell to Arms,* with intro. by Ford Madox Ford. New York, 1932.

————. *The Fifth Column and the First Forty-nine Stories.* New York, 1938.

————. *For Whom the Bell Tolls.* New York, 1940, 1968. First Scribner Classic/Collier Edition, 1987.

————. *Green Hills of Africa.* New York, 1935, 1963. First Scribner Classic/Collier Edition, 1987.

————. "Homage to Ezra," *This Quarter,* May 1925, pp. 221–225.

————. *in our time.* Paris, 1924.

————. *In Our Time.* New York, 1925.

————. *A Moveable Feast.* New York, 1964.

————. *The Old Man and the Sea.* New York, 1952.

————. *The Short Stories of Ernest Hemingway (The First Forty-nine Stories,* with a brief preface by Ernest Hemingway). New York, 1966.

————. *The Spanish Earth,* with intro. by Jasper Wood. Cleveland, 1938.

————. *The Sun Also Rises.* New York, 1926, 1954.

————. *To Have and Have Not.* New York, 1937. First Scribner Classic/Collier Edition, 1987.

————. *The Torrents of Spring.* New York, 1926.

————. "Who Murdered the Vets?" *New Masses,* Sept. 17, 1935, pp. 9–10.

Hemingway, Gregory. *Papa.* Boston, 1976.

Hemingway, Jack. *Misadventures of a Fly Fisherman.* New York, 1986, 1987.

Hemingway, Leicester. *My Brother, Ernest Hemingway.* Cleveland and New York, 1962.

Hemingway, Mary Welsh. *How It Was.* New York, 1976.

Hotchner, A.E. *Papa Hemingway: The Ecstacy and Sorrow.* New York, 1955, 1983.

Ivancich, Adriana. *La Torre Bianca.* Milan, 1980.

Joost, Nicholas. *Ernest Hemingway and the Little Magazines.* Barre, Mass., 1968.

Kert, Bernice. *The Hemingway Women.* New York, 1983.

Kiley, Jed. *Hemingway: An Old Friend Remembers.* New York, 1965.

Laurence, Frank M. *Hemingway and the Movies.* Jackson, Miss., 1981.

Lewis, Wyndham, "The Dumb Ox: A Study of Ernest Hemingway," *Life and Letters,* April 1934, pp. 33–45.

Loeb, Harold. *The Way It Was.* New York, 1959.

Ludington, Townsend. *John Dos Passos: A Twentieth-Century Odyssey.* New York, 1980.

Lynn, Kenneth S. *Hemingway.* New York, 1987.

MacLeish, Archibald. *The Letters of Archibald MacLeish,* ed. by R.H. Winnick. Boston, 1983.

————. *Riders on the Earth: Essays and Recollections.* Boston, 1978.

Marshall, S.L.A. "How Papa Liberated Paris," *American Heritage,* April 1962, pp. 5–7, 92–101.

Matthews, Herbert. *Two Wars and More to Come.* New York, 1938.

————. *A World in Revolution.* New York, 1971.

McAlmon, Robert. *Being Geniuses Together,* rev. by Kay Boyle. Garden City, N.Y., 1968.

————. *McAlmon and the Lost Generation,* ed. by Robert E. Knoll. Lincoln, 1962.

Mellow, James R. *Charmed Circle: Gertrude Stein & Company.* New York, 1982.

Miller, Madelaine Hemingway. *Ernie.* New York, 1985.

Montgomery, Constance Cappel. *Hemingway in Michigan.* New York, 1966.

Myers, Jeffrey. *Hemingway: A Biography.* New York, 1986.

Nelson, Gerald B., and Glory Jones. *Hemingway: Life and Work.* New York, 1984.

Orwell, George. *Homage to Catalonia.* New York, 1980.

Painter, George D. *Marcel Proust: A Biography,* 2 vols. New York, 1950, 1978.

Parker, Dorothy. "The Artist's Reward," *The New Yorker,* Nov. 30, 1929, pp. 28–31.

Poli, Bernard J. *Ford Madox Ford and the "Transatlantic Review."* Syracuse, 1967.

Reynolds, Michael S., *The Young Hemingway.* Oxford, 1986.

Rochester, Stuart I. *American Liberal Disillusionment in the Wake of World War I.* University Park, Pa., 1977.

Roscoe, Burton, *We Were Interrupted.* Garden City, N.Y., n.d.

Ross, Lillian. *Portrait of Hemingway.* New York, 1961.

Sanford, Marcelline Hemingway. *At the Hemingways.* Boston, 1962.

Schleden, Ina Mae, and Marion Rawls Herzog, eds. *Ernest Hemingway as Recalled by His High School Contemporaries.* Oak Park, Ill., 1973.

Sokoloff, Alice Hunt. *Hadley: The First Mrs. Hemingway.* New York, 1973.

Stearns, Harold E. *Civilization in the United States.* Westport, Ct., 1971 (reprint of 1922 ed.).

Steffens, Lincoln. *The Autobiography of Lincoln Steffens.* New York, 1931.

Stein, Gertrude. *The Autobiography of Alice B. Toklas.* New York, 1933.

Stewart, Donald Ogden. *By a Stroke of Luck!* New York, 1975.

Tomkins, Calvin. *Living Well Is the Best Revenge.* New York, 1982.

Turnbull, Andrew. *Scott Fitzgerald.* New York, 1962.

Watts, Emily S. *Ernest Hemingway and the Arts.* Urbana, Ill. 1971.

Wiser, William. *The Crazy Years.* New York, 1980.

NOTES

Dr. Ed Hemingway
1. Ernest Hemingway, "Fathers and Sons," *The Short Stories of Ernest Hemingway* (New York, 1966), p. 496.
2. Ernest Hemingway, *For Whom the Bell Tolls* (New York, 1987), p. 338.

Walloon Lake
1. Hemingway, "Fathers and Sons," *op cit.*, pp. 492–493.

Hemingway in Paris
1. Carlos Baker, *Hemingway: The Writer as Artist* (Princeton, 1968), p. 18.
3. Alice Hunt Sokoloff, *Hadley: The First Mrs. Hemingway* (New York, 1973), p. 71.
4. Burton Roscoe, *We Were Interrupted* (Garden City, N.Y., n.d.), pp. 185–186.
5. Dorothy Parker, "The Artist's Reward," *The New Yorker* (Nov. 30, 1929), pp. 28–31.

Foreign Correspondent
1. Hemingway, *The Short Stories of Ernest Hemingway, op. cit.*, p. 96.

Ezra Pound
1. Sokoloff, *op. cit.*

More Literary Friends
3. Morley Callaghan, *That Summer in Paris* (New York, 1963), p. 81.

F. Scott Fitzgerald
1. Callaghan, *op cit.*, p. 232.
2. *Ibid.*, p. 208.

Spain and the Corrida
1. Calvin Tomkins, *Living Well Is the Best Revenge* (New York, 1982), pp. 99–100.
2. *Ibid.*, pp. 98–99.

The Sun Also Rises
1. Ernest Hemingway, *The Sun Also Rises* (New York, 1954), pp. 24–27.
2. *Ibid.*, pp. 160.
3. *Ibid.*, pp. 243–247.
4. Conrad Aiken, review in *The New York Herald Tribune Books* (Oct. 31, 1926), p. 4.

A Farewell to Arms
1. Ernest Hemingway, *A Farewell to Arms* (New York, 1987), p. 3.
2. Ernest Hemingway, "Introduction," *A Farewell to Arms* (New York, 1948), p. vii.
3. Hemingway, *A Farewell to Arms, op. cit.*, pp 184–185.

Death in the Afternoon
1. Ernest Hemingway, *Death in the Afternoon* (New York, 1960), pp. 206–207.
2. *Ibid.*, pp. 99–100.
3. *Ibid.*, pp. 270–271.

Green Hills of Africa
1. Actually, a holograph passage deleted from the final version of *Green Hills of Africa.* Quoted in Carlos Baker, *Ernest Hemingway: A Life Story* (New York, 1969), p. 609.
2. Ernest Hemingway, *Green Hills of Africa* (New York, 1963), p. 231.

Ocean Liners
1. Baker, *Ernest Hemingway: A Life Story, op. cit.*, p. 83.

2. J.M. Brinnin, *The Sway of the Grand Saloon* (New York, 1971).

The Pilar
1. Denis Brian, *The True Gen: An Intimate Portrait of Hemingway by Those Who Knew Him* (New York, 1988), p. 96.

To Have and Have Not
1. Jack Hemingway, *Misadventures of a Fly Fisherman* (New York, 1987), p. 13.
2. Ernest Hemingway, "Who Murdered the Vets?" *New Masses* (Sept. 17, 1935), p. 9.
3. Ernest Hemingway, *To Have and Have Not* (New York, 1987), pp. 245–246.

The Spanish Civil War
1. Herbert Matthews, *A World in Revolution* (New York, 1971), pp. 24–25.
2. *Ibid.*, pp. 369–370.

For Whom the Bell Tolls
1. Hemingway, *For Whom the Bell Tolls, op cit.*, pp. 125–127.

World War II and Wife IV
1. Air Marshal Sir Peter Wykeham, "Hair Raising," *Times* (London, Aug. 5, 1969), p. 8. Quoted in Jeffrey Meyers, *Hemingway: A Biography* (New York, 1986), pp. 397–398.
2. Letter from David Bruce to a war correspondent (1947–48) in the Hemingway Archives at the John F. Kennedy Library, Boston, Mass. Quoted in Myers, *op cit.*, pp. 406–407.

Liberating the Ritz
1. George D. Painter, *Marcel Proust: A Biography*, vol. 2 (New York, 1978), p. 361.

INDEX

207

ACKNOWLEDGMENTS

Many people helped in the preparation of *Hemingway and His World,* and all have our warmest thanks. However, a very special acknowledgment must go to Alan Goodrich at the Audiovisual Division of the John F. Kennedy Library in Boston. Without his limitless patience, cooperation, and good cheer, the present endeavor would not have been possible. Also at the John F. Kennedy Library, we wish to thank Megan Desnoyers, curator of the Hemingway Collection. In Oak park, Ill., we gratefully received assistance from Carol Kelm at the Oak Park Historical Society, Phil Jerousek at the Oak Park Public Library, Meg Klinkow at the Frank Lloyd Wright Memorial Foundation, and Jeannete Fields at the Ernest Hemingway Foundation. Especially generous towards us were Patricia Hemingway of Silver Springs, Md., Mr. and Mrs. Anthony Mason of Tuxedo Park, N.Y., and Mrs. William Donnelly of Palm Beach, Fla. The following university librarians gave unstinting aid: Jean Preston and Charles Greene at the Princeton University Library; Carley Robison, archivist at the Seymour Library, Knox College, Galesburg, Ill., Kenneth Lohf of the Butler Library, Columbia University; and Particia Middleton of the Beinecke Rare Book Library, Yale University. For information and materials about the painter Waldo Peirce, we are indebted to Patience Anne Link of the Colby College Library and Hugh Goulery of the Colby College Museum of Art, Waterville, Me. In regard to Hemingway's portrait by Henry Strater, we must thank Michael Culver of the Ogunquit Museum of Art, Me. For help with movies derived from Hemingway's novels and stories, we express our appreciation to Mark Wanamaker of Bison Archives in Los Angeles, Ned Comstock of the University of Southern California Cinema–Television Library, and Scott Busby of the Academy of Motion Picture Arts and Sciences in Beverly Hills. Without the help of Tillie Arnold in Hailey, Id., we would not have such interesting pictures of Hemingway's three sons. In Paris, we were fortunate in being able to rely on the research skills of Kate Lewin.

For excerpts that we have been permitted to reprint from copyrighted sources, we make the following grateful acknowledgments:

Carlos Baker, *Ernest Hemingway: A Life Story.* Reprinted with permission of Charles Scribner's Sons, an imprint of Macmillan Publishing Company. Copyright © 1969 by Carlos Baker and Mary Hemingway.

Ernest Hemingway, *Death in the Afternoon.* Reprinted with permission of Charles Scribner's Sons, an imprint of Macmillan Publishing Company. Copyright 1932 by Charles Scribner's Sons; copyright renewed © 1960 by Ernest Hemingway.

Ernest Hemingway, *A Farewell to Arms.* Reprinted with permission of Charles Scribner's Sons, an imprint of Macmillan Publishing Company. Copyright 1929 by Charles Scribner's Sons; copyright renewed © 1957 by Ernest Hemingway.

Ernest Hemingway, "Fathers and Sons," *Winner Take Nothing.* Reprinted with permission of Charles Scribner's Sons, an imprint of Macmillan Publishing Company. Copyright 1933 by Ernest Hemingway; copyright renewed 1961 © by Mary Hemingway.

Ernest Hemingway, *For Whom the Bell Tolls.* Reprinted with permission of Charles Scribner's Sons, an imprint of Macmillan Publishing Company. Copyright 1940 by Charles Scribner's Sons; copyright renewed © 1968 by Mary Hemingway.

Ernest Hemingway, "minerets," *In Our Time.* Reprinted with permission of Charles Scribner's Sons, an imprint of Macmillan Publishing Company. Copyright 1925 by Charles Scribner's Sons; copyright renewed © 1953 by Ernest Hemingway.

Ernest Hemingway, *The Sun Also Rises.* Reprinted with permission of Charles Scribner's Sons, an imprint of Macmillan Publishing Company. Copyright 1926 by Charles Scribner's Sons; copyright renewed 1954 by Ernest Hemingway.

Ernest Hemingway, *To Have and Have Not.* Reprinted with permission of Charles Scribner's Sons, an imprint of Macmillan Publishing Company. Copyright 1937 by Ernest Hemingway; copyright renewed © 1965 by Mary Hemingway.

Calvin Tomkins, *Living Well Is The Best Revenge.* Copyright © 1962, 1971, 1982 by Calvin Tomkins. Reprinted by permission of Lescher and Lescher.

William Wiser, *The Crazy Years.* Copyright © 1983. Published by and reprinted with the permission of Thames and Hudson.